IMAGES
of America

SWANNANOA

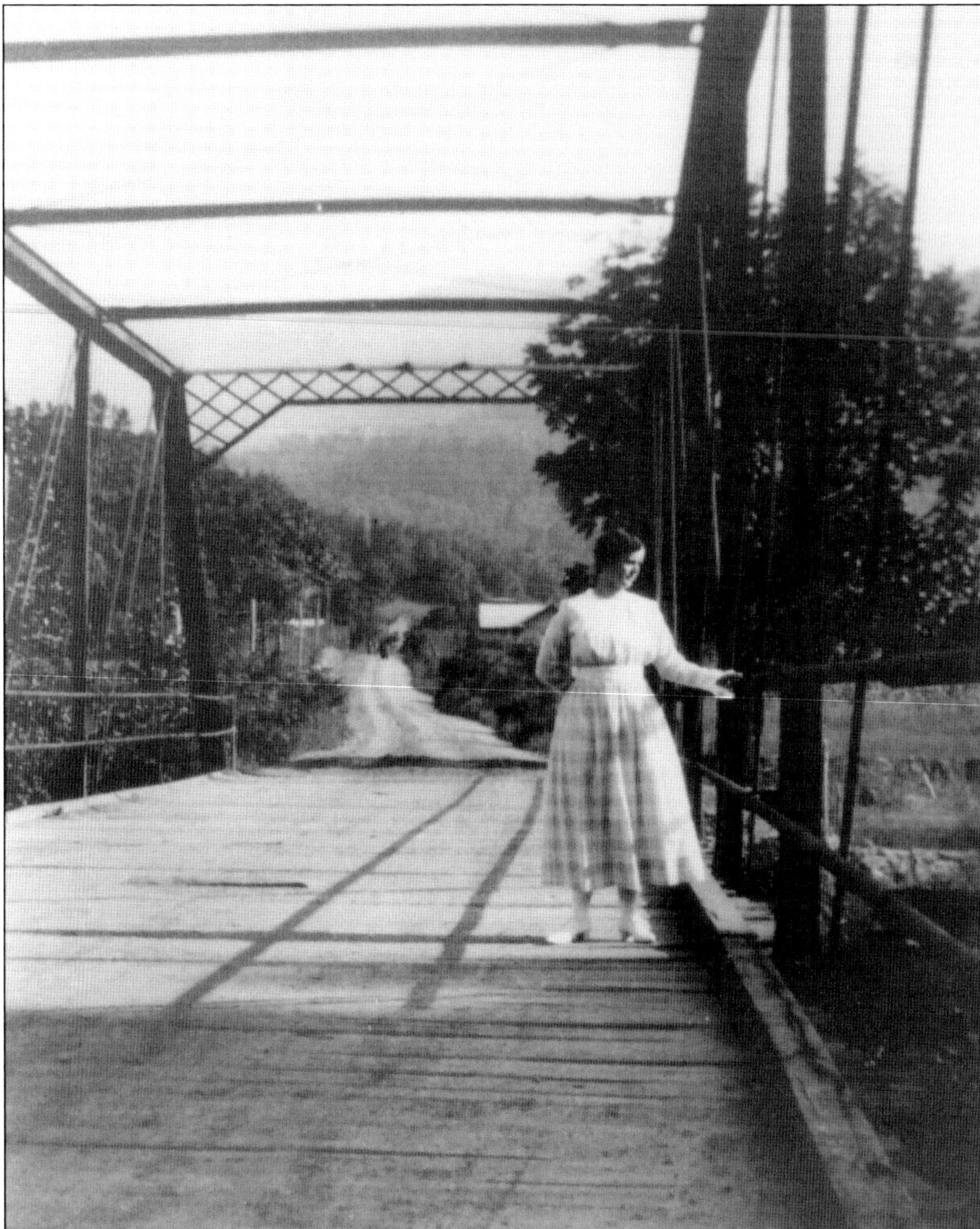

Swannanoa resident Ula Isreal stands on the bridge that crossed over the Swannanoa River and led south into the center of town. (Courtesy of the Swannanoa Valley Museum.)

On the Cover: In this photograph, taken on September 30, 1945, by well-known photographer W.B. Gragg of Black Mountain, native preacher Rev. James Caswell Coggins baptizes a young man in Bee Tree Creek, a tributary of the Swannanoa River. Reverend Coggins baptized more than 150 people into the Christian faith in the waters of Bee Tree Creek. (Courtesy of the Swannanoa Valley Museum, Robert Brunk collection.)

IMAGES
of America

SWANNANOA

Anne E. Chesky Smith
for the Swannanoa Valley Museum

ARCADIA
PUBLISHING

ISBN 978-0-7385-9940-3

Published by Arcadia Publishing
Charleston, South Carolina

Printed in the United States of America

Library of Congress Control Number: 2012955777

For all general information, please contact Arcadia Publishing:
Telephone 843-853-2070
Fax 843-853-0044
E-mail sales@arcadiapublishing.com
For customer service and orders:
Toll-Free 1-888-313-2665

Visit us on the Internet at www.arcadiapublishing.com

To all who call Swannanoa home—past, present, and future

Contents

Acknowledgments

Since the Swannanoa Valley Museum was founded in 1989 as Buncombe County's primary museum of general local history, hundreds of volunteers have contributed tens of thousands of hours to the preserve the history of the Swannanoa Valley. It is impossible to thank all of those volunteers individually, but without their hard work and their love of the valley, this book would not have been possible.

I also wish to thank Bill Alexander for introducing me to many of the people, places, and "facts" that make Swannanoa such a special place.

And, finally, thanks go to my husband, Ryan, whose patience and burgeoning cooking skills allowed this book to come together.

INTRODUCTION

Tens of thousands of years before white settlers traveled across the Blue Ridge Mountains to make their homesteads in the Swannanoa Valley, Native Americans used the area as a hunting ground. The name Swannanoa originally referred to the broad river that ran through the valley, and it was derived, most likely, from a Cherokee Indian word meaning "beautiful river." The abundance of wildlife, plentiful water, and fertile land made Swannanoa attractive to settlers from many cultures.

In 1776, Gen. Griffith Rutherford and his troops ravaged their way west through the valley, which at that time belonged to Indian tribes, razing villages and destroying crops to keep the Indians from joining forces with the British during the Revolutionary War. After the war ended, the US government declared the Indian territory open to settlement, and many soldiers journeyed back to the valley they had ridden through with General Rutherford, remembering its beauty.

In the early 1780s, Samuel Davidson, his family, and one female slave were some of the first settlers to make the long journey up the mountain from Old Fort to Swannanoa by following the buffalo trails. Not long after they settled, a group of disgruntled Native Americans lured Davidson into a trap and shot and killed him on Jones Mountain in Swannanoa.

A few years after Davidson's ill-fated attempt to settle, several of his relatives became the first families to arrive and form a settlement west of the Blue Ridge Mountains. The Davidson and Alexander families established the Swannanoa Settlement in 1787 at the confluence of Bee Tree Creek and the Swannanoa River. These first families set up homesteads, gristmills, mica mines, and farms, and the area began to attract more settlers.

Religion was and continues to be extremely important to members of the Swannanoa community. One of the earliest public buildings was Robert Patton's meetinghouse, a church founded in 1794 that eventually became the First Presbyterian Church of Swannanoa.

By the 1830s, tourists, known locally as "summer people," began to arrive in Swannanoa to escape the sweltering summer heat and insects of towns to the east and south. During this time, they arrived by stagecoach, wagon, or on horseback at the many inns and boardinghouses that opened to accommodate them.

Even with the burgeoning tourist industry in Swannanoa, the area remained primarily a rural, farming community until the late 1870s. When the railroad was finally completed in 1879, after being stalled by the Civil War and by the difficulty of laying track up the steep grade from Old Fort to Black Mountain, it connected the western part of North Carolina with the eastern part, and new businesses began to spring up near railroad stations. The route traversed by the train had been an important passage from east to west after Samuel Davidson came to the valley. Today, Interstate 40, which follows a similar path, is the busiest roadway connecting western North Carolina to the Piedmont.

Just after 1900, Edwin Wiley "E.W." Grove, who was in the Asheville area building his famed Grove Park Inn, saw a flat piece of land near the Swannanoa quarry, Grove Stone & Sand Company, which he had built to supply rock for his building projects. Over the next 20 years, Grove purchased a nearby flat tract from the Alexander family and began developing his dream town, Grovemont-on-Swannanoa. Grovemont was billed as America's first planned community, designed to mimic Grove's grandparents' town in England. Though Grove died in 1927 before his dream could be fully realized, he was also able to develop a summer resort at Lake Eden, which later became the famous Black Mountain College.

Not long after Grove began developing Grovemont, Charles D. Owen II, the son of a blanket manufacturer from Massachusetts, saw a 160-acre farm beside Swannanoa's railroad tracks that was well suited for a new southern branch of the Beacon Blankets Manufacturing Company. Between 1924 and 1933, the entire New Bedford, Massachusetts, plant was moved via freight train to Swannanoa. Once the plant began operations, the Owen family provided housing in mill villages, paved roadways, water lines, sanitation services, and fire and police protection to their employees. Beacon also more fully developed the downtown Swannanoa business district, and a grocery and general merchandise store, a drugstore, clothing stores, a movie theater, and a bank were all opened in the early years of the mill.

In the 1940s, Beacon sent more men and women to the armed forces percentagewise than any other industry in the country. It also began exclusively manufacturing blankets for use by the military.

Also during this era, 200 acres were purchased from the Mountain Agricultural Research Center in Swannanoa to build Moore General Hospital, a 1,520-bed facility for wounded soldiers. German prisoners of war were quartered at the hospital as well. Over the years, the center has transitioned from a veterans' hospital to a youth detention center to a women's prison.

In 1957, the land that was once home to A.N. Alexander's farm in Bee Tree was purchased by an industrial plant that manufactured weapons for use during the Cold War. The plant changed hands several times before being bought by Chemtronics in the 1980s to be used to manufacture hallucinogenic chemical weapons. The area is now identified by the Environmental Protection Agency as a Superfund site.

The many small one-room schoolhouses in the valley were first consolidated in the 1920s and then again in 1955, when Swannanoa High School students and Black Mountain High School students began attending Charles D. Owen High School in Swannanoa. Owen High School has produced many famous athletes, including Brad Daugherty, who played basketball professionally for the Cleveland Cavaliers, and Brad Johnson, the quarterback of the Super Bowl champion Tampa Bay Buccaneers. Roy Williams coached basketball at Owen before going on to coach at the University of North Carolina. Well-known author Patricia Cornwell also graduated from Owen High School.

By the 1970s, the textile industry in Swannanoa began to decline, and Beacon laid off workers. With improved transportation, more people began shopping at chain stores in Asheville rather than at Swannanoa's independent businesses. At the same time, the Owen family sold all of its stock in Beacon to a company called National Distillery. The company changed hands again in the 1980s and the 1990s. Changes in ownership brought more layoffs, as more of the business was moved offshore. By 2000, Beacon only employed a couple hundred people, far less than the 2,200 employed there in the 1940s. After years of losses, the Beacon plant closed its doors for good in the spring of 2002.

On September 4, 2003, an arsonist set the vacant Beacon Manufacturing Company plant on fire and it burned to the ground. The blaze, which made national headlines, brought out more than 500 personnel from 32 different fire departments. Today, the lot that was once home to America's largest blanket manufacturer—and in many ways the lifeblood of Swannanoa—lies vacant. As Wade Martin, a former Beacon employee, said in a 2002 interview after the plant closed, "My name for Beacon was the big red heart of Swannanoa and when that heart was beating good, the community thrived, and when there were times when it was suffering a little, some people didn't do so well."

Still, the Swannanoa community carries on. A number of new businesses have opened in Swannanoa since the plant closed. The grocery store chain Ingles expanded its warehouse on the edge of Swannanoa, thus becoming the largest employer in the Swannanoa Valley. High-end developments, although stalled by the 2008 recession, have also been drawn to Swannanoa's beauty and climate. And in June 2013, plans to redevelop the vacant Beacon site as a "mixed-use, green, sustainable community" were officially announced. According to local, long-term residents Harriet Styles and Bill Alexander, old and new residents alike continue to be active forces in Swannanoa, daily working "to rebuild the economic base of the community, and explore avenues for the growth and rebirth of the town."

One

Settling Swannanoa

The Founding Families

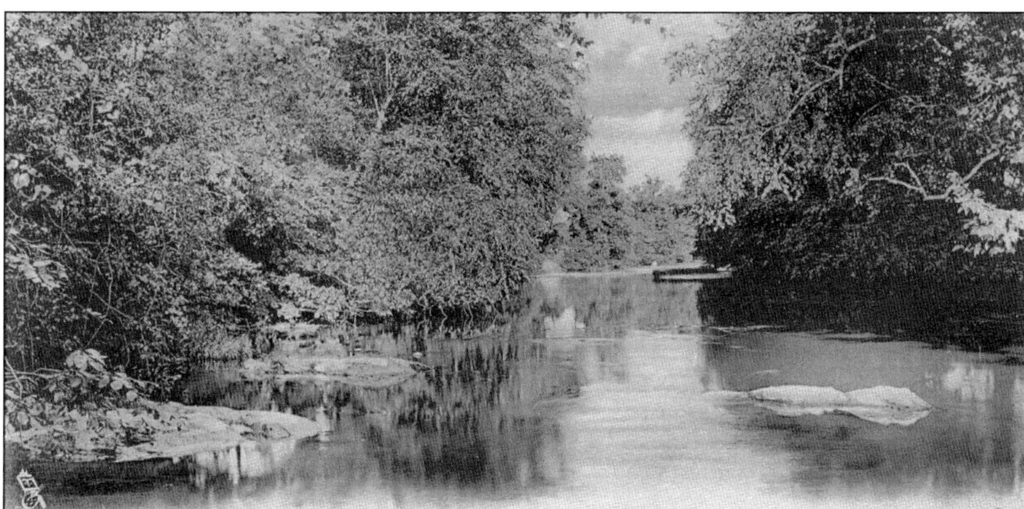

The name Swannanoa most likely derives from a Cherokee word meaning "beautiful river." The ample water from the river fed the fertile soil, attracting abundant wildlife. Native Americans used the area as a hunting ground for thousands of years until Gen. Griffith Rutherford and his troops raided the valley in 1776 to keep Cherokee Indians from joining forces with the British during the Revolutionary War. After the war ended, soldiers who remembered the beauty and abundance of the valley returned to settle on the banks of the river. (Courtesy of the Swannanoa Valley Museum.)

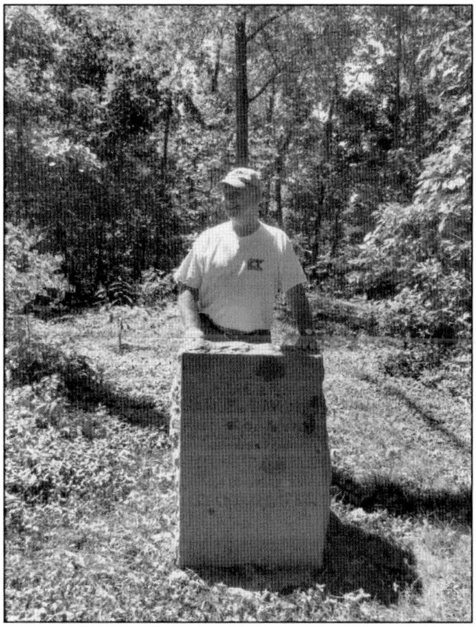

Once the US government opened Indian Territory for settlement, the first settler to make the trek up the Blue Ridge Mountains was Samuel Davidson. In the early 1780s, Davidson brought his wife, his female slave, and possibly his daughter to settle on Christian Creek in Swannanoa. Not long after settling, Native Americans that used the land lured Davidson into a trap, shooting and killing him. His family buried him on the spot where he fell. In 1913, his descendants placed a grave marker on the top of Jones Mountain in Swannanoa to commemorate his death. Here, William "Bill" C. Alexander, a descendent of Davidson, stands with the marker. (Courtesy of the Swannanoa Valley Museum.)

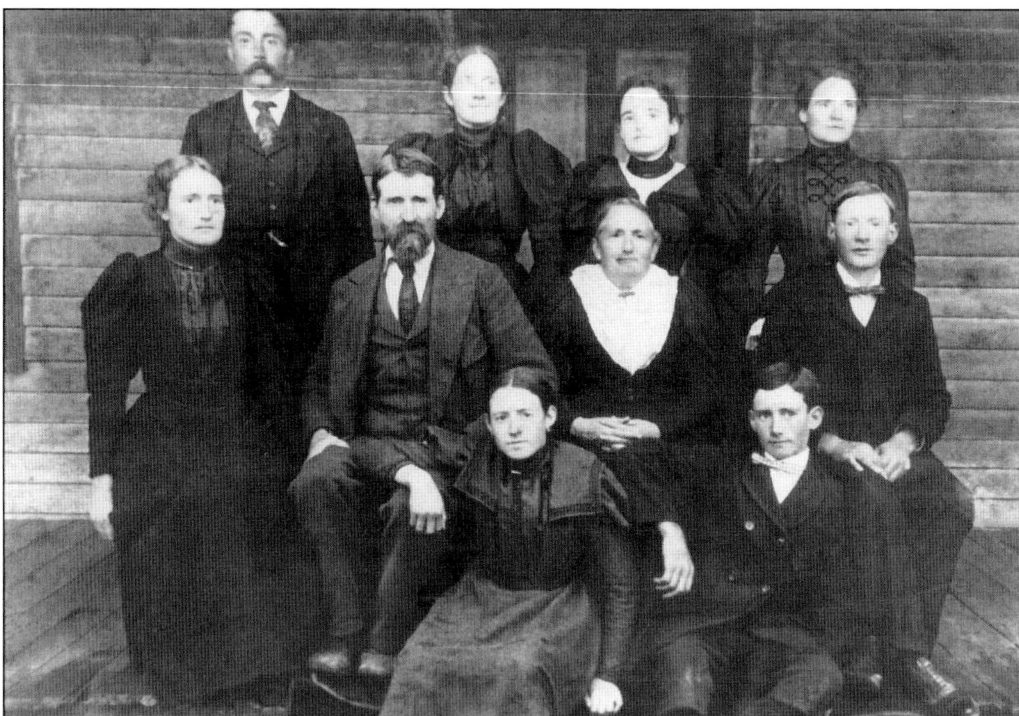

After Samuel Davidson's death, his twin brother, Maj. William Davidson, his sister Rachel, and their families ventured back up the mountain to form the first pioneer village west of the Blue Ridge, the Swannanoa Settlement, located at the confluence of Bee Tree Creek and the Swannanoa River. These descendants of William C. Davidson, seen here in 1897, are, from left to right, (first row) Alice and Don; (second row) Mary, Samuel Winslow, Nannie Sherrill, and Jack; (third row) Robert, Emma, Carrie, and Sally. (Courtesy of the Swannanoa Valley Museum.)

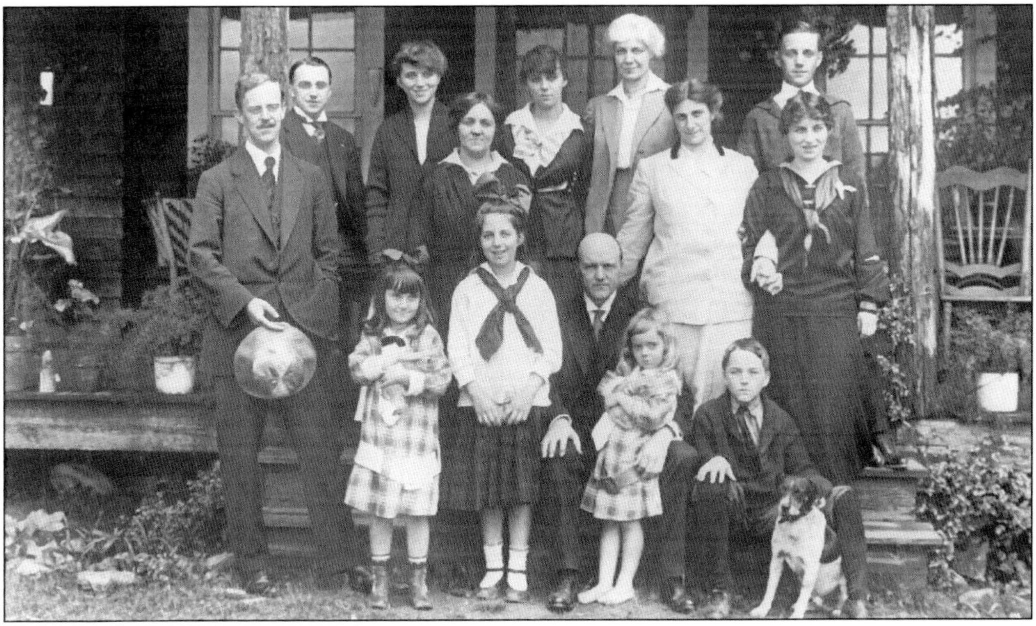

The Davidsons were not the only early family to settle in Swannanoa. Samuel Davidson's sister Rachel and her husband, John Alexander, also settled on Bee Tree Creek in 1787, with their son James and his wife's family, the Cunninghams. The Alexander family is seen here in 1915 at Alexander Hill in Swannanoa. (Courtesy of the Swannanoa Valley Museum.)

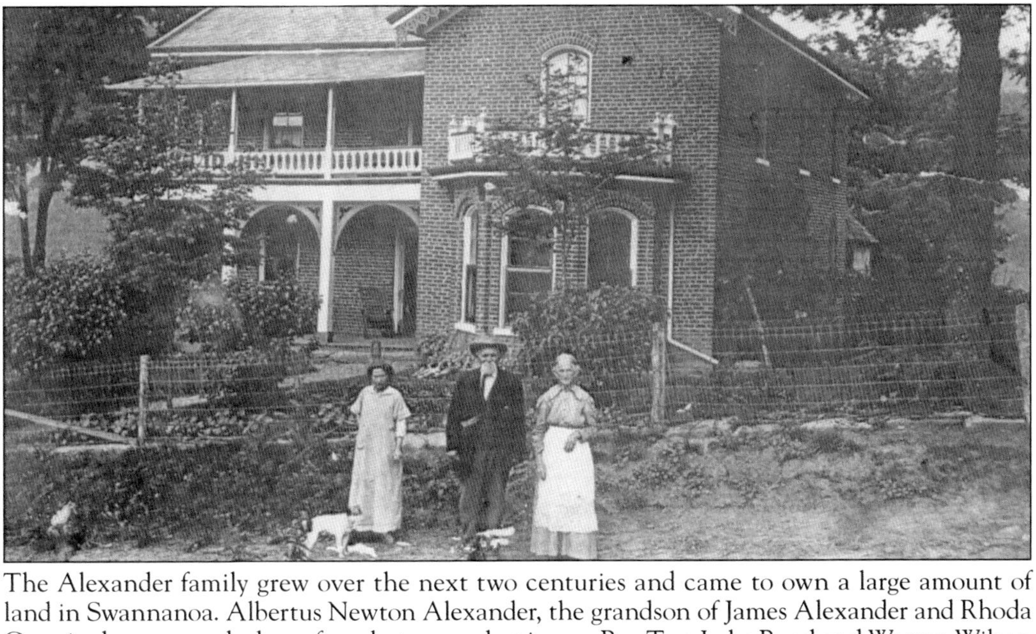

The Alexander family grew over the next two centuries and came to own a large amount of land in Swannanoa. Albertus Newton Alexander, the grandson of James Alexander and Rhoda Cunningham, owned a large farm between what is now Bee Tree Lake Road and Warren Wilson College Road. He is seen here standing with his daughter (left) and his wife, Mary Adaline Davidson Alexander, in front of their home, which was built around 1880. Their farm was part of the Alexander family's original 685-acre tract on Bee Tree Creek, which Albertus inherited from his father. In 1957, this land was sold to Oerlikon Tool and Arms Corporation. (Courtesy of the Swannanoa Valley Museum, Bill Alexander collection.)

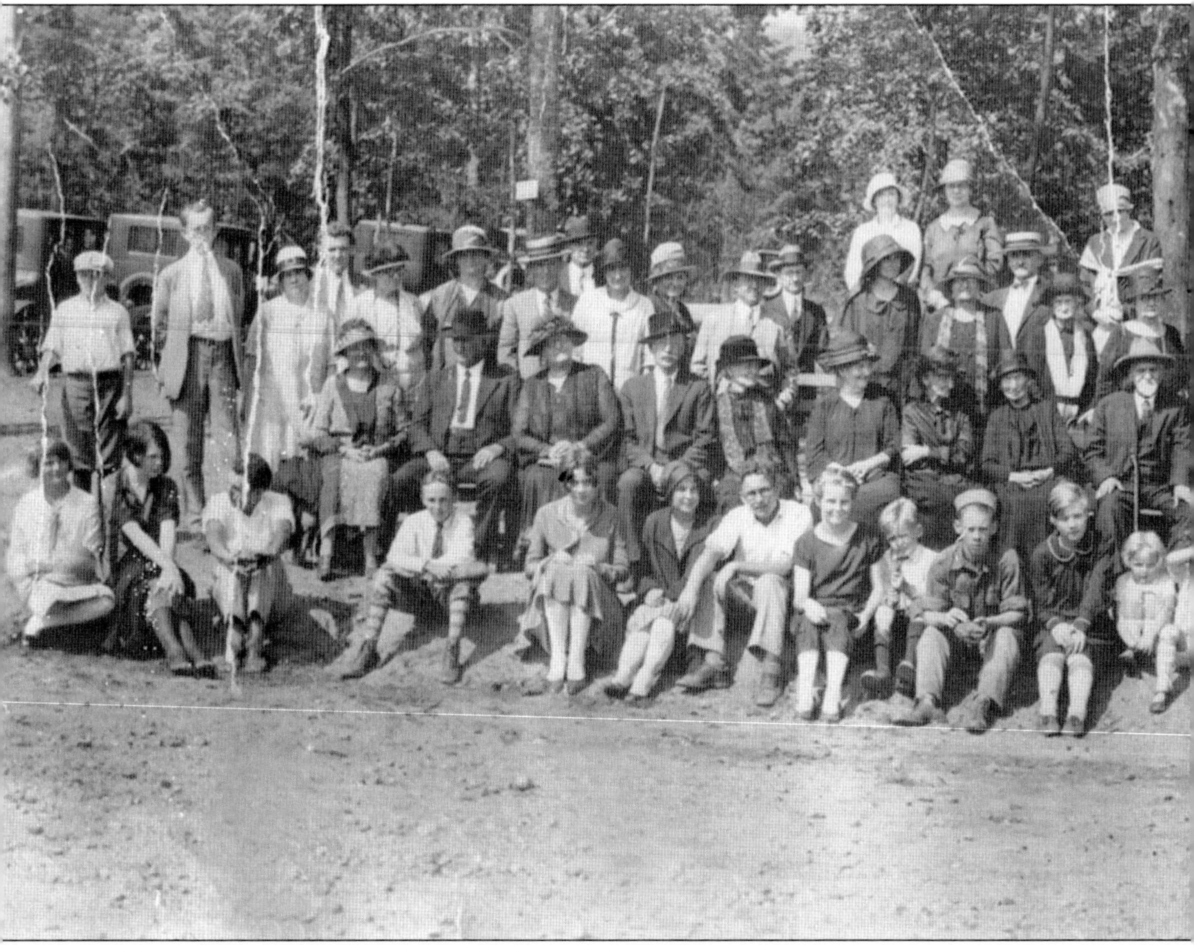

This photograph of a Davidson-Alexander family reunion around 1925 shows the interconnectedness

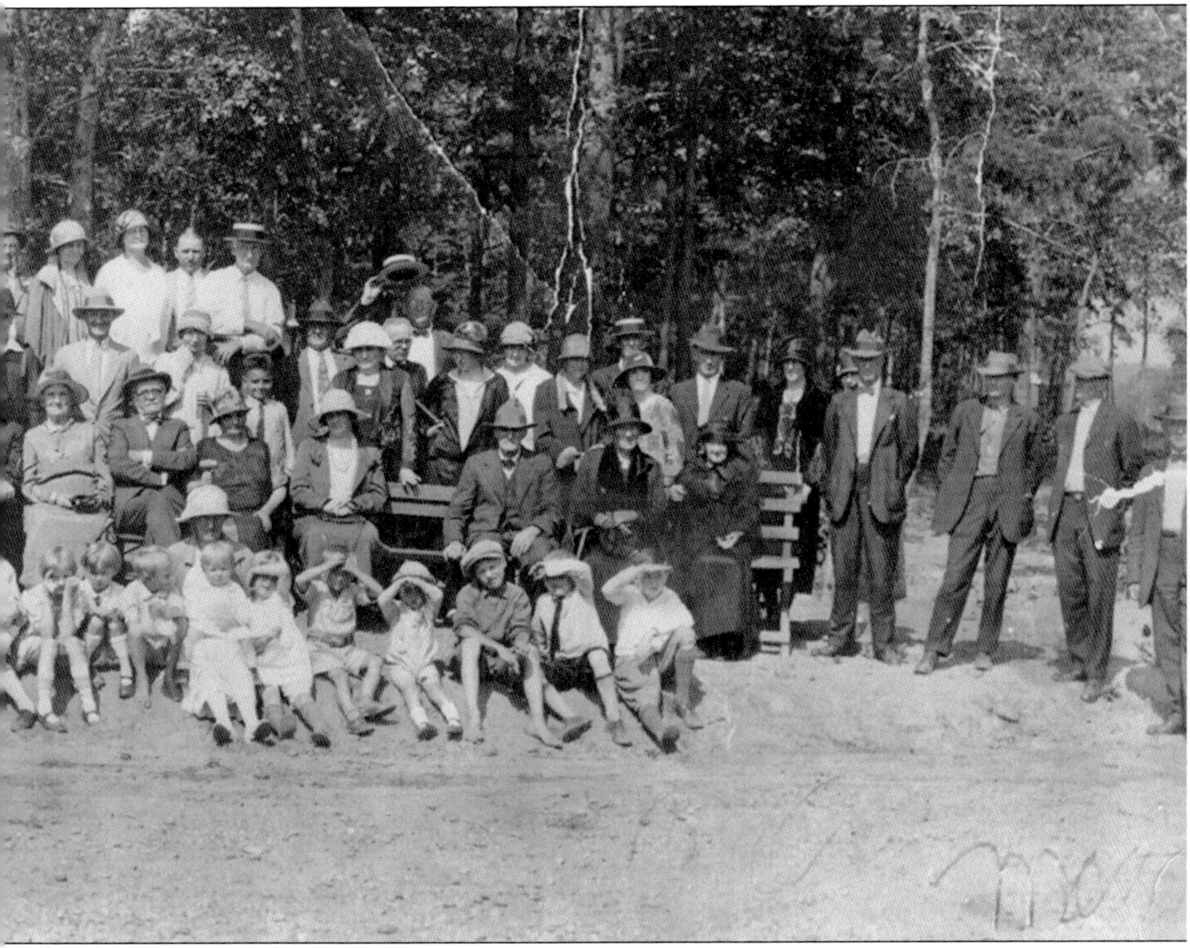

of Swannanoa's two founding families. (Courtesy of the Swannanoa Valley Museum.)

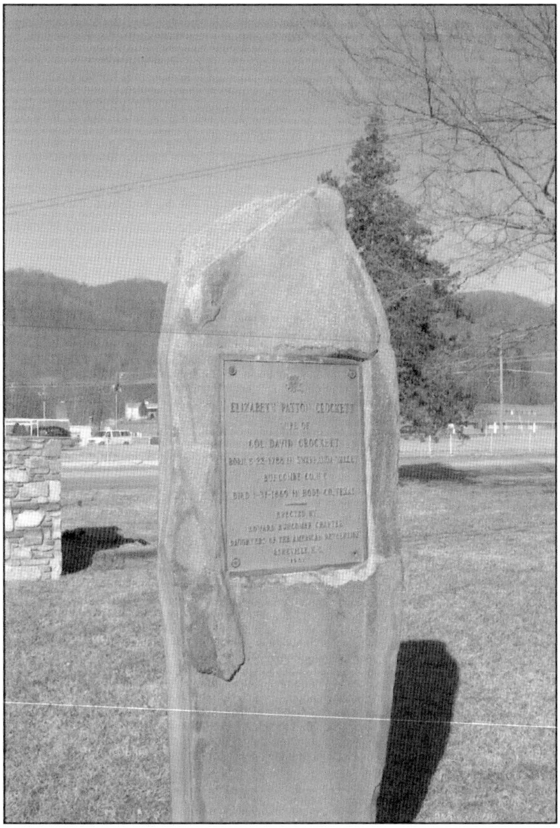

The Pattons also settled in Swannanoa during the first years of its development. Robert Patton bought a tract of land to the east of the Davidsons and Alexanders, near what is now Patton Hill Road. He donated some of this land for an early Presbyterian meetinghouse and cemetery. The Patton meetinghouse was built in 1794. In 1839, Col. Samuel Davidson donated two acres for a new church building, known now as Piney Grove Presbyterian Church. Patton Cemetery is still an active burial ground. Near the cemetery is a memorial marker for Elizabeth Patton Crockett, Robert Patton's daughter. Elizabeth married folk hero Davy Crockett after he brought the personal effects of her deceased husband, James Patton, to her in Swannanoa. (Courtesy of the Swannanoa Valley Museum.)

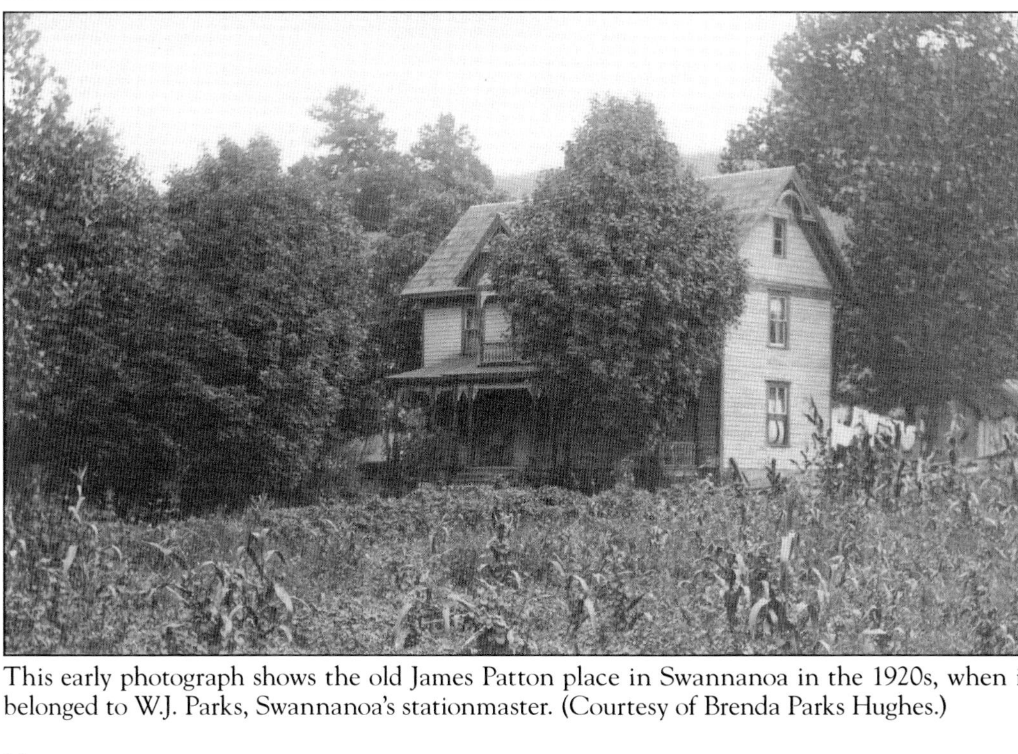

This early photograph shows the old James Patton place in Swannanoa in the 1920s, when it belonged to W.J. Parks, Swannanoa's stationmaster. (Courtesy of Brenda Parks Hughes.)

As Swannanoa grew, more families began to call the area home. Early family names also included Bartlett, Burgin, Burnett, Fox, Penland, and Pressley. The Burgins settled in Swannanoa in the early 1800s. Here, a member of the Burgin family feeds his pets. (Courtesy of the Swannanoa Valley Museum, Penland Burgin collection.)

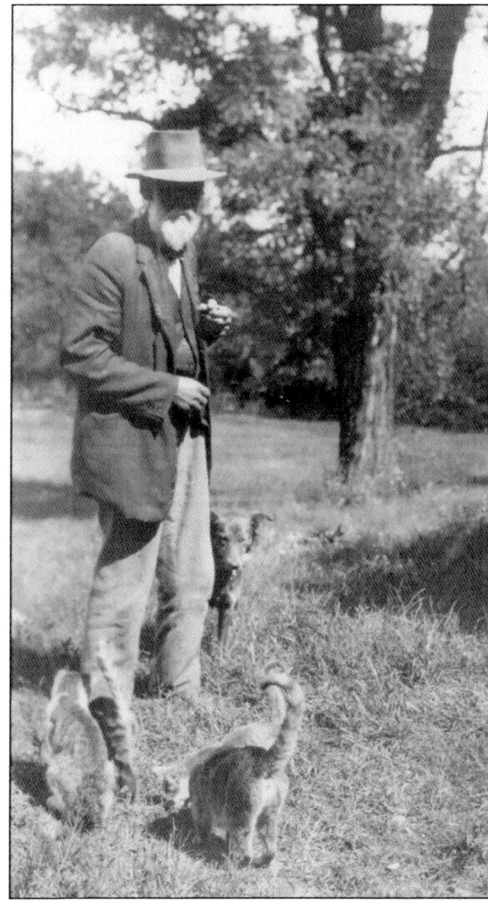

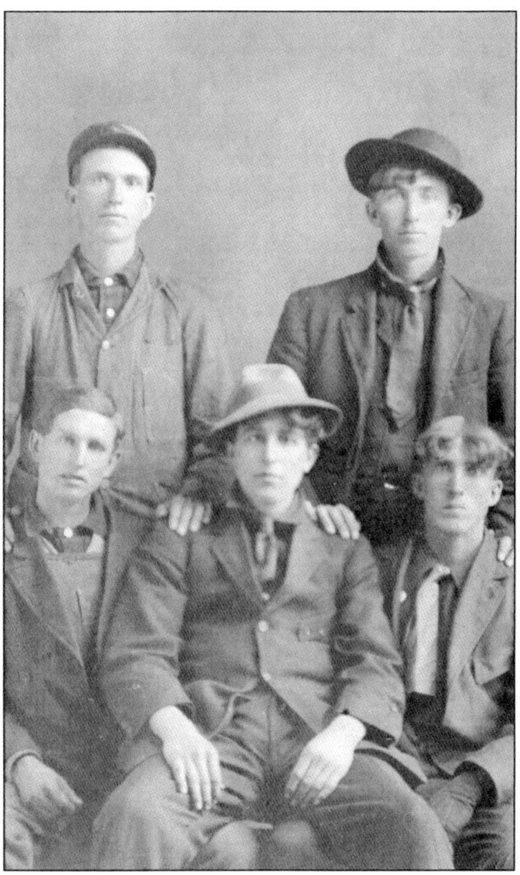

This photograph, taken around 1890, shows early residents, from left to right, (first row) Will Burnett, George Bartlett, and George Pressley; (second row) Jess and Walt Pressley. (Courtesy of the Swannanoa Valley Museum, Dan Pressley collection.)

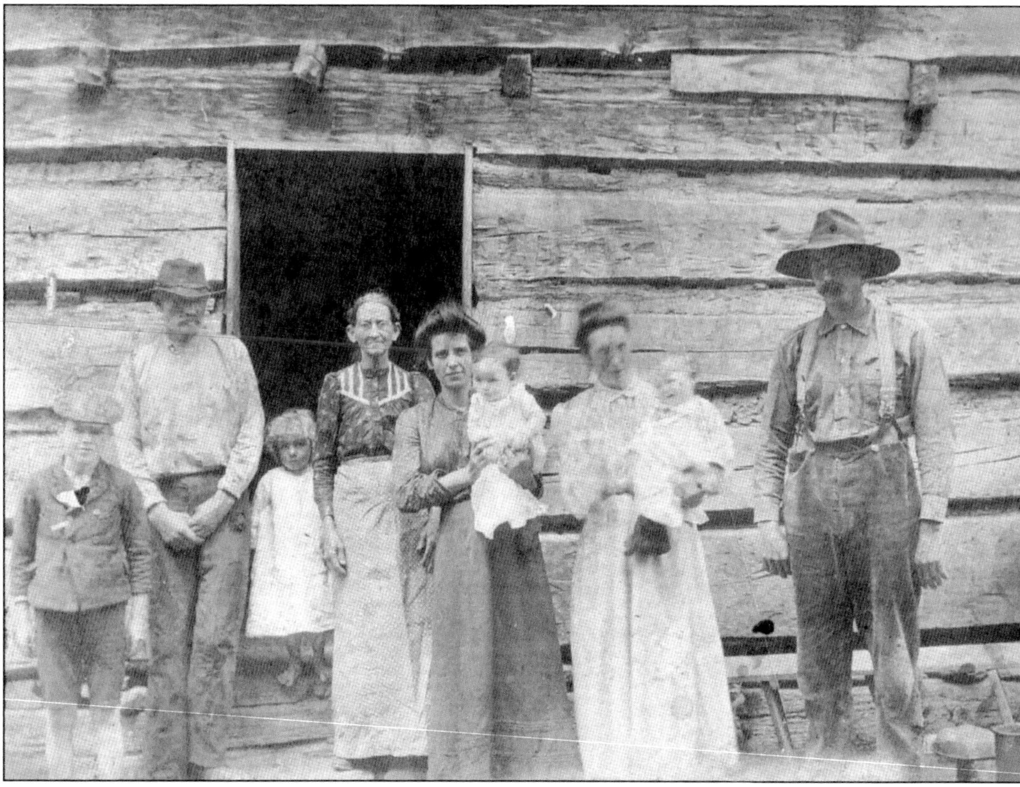

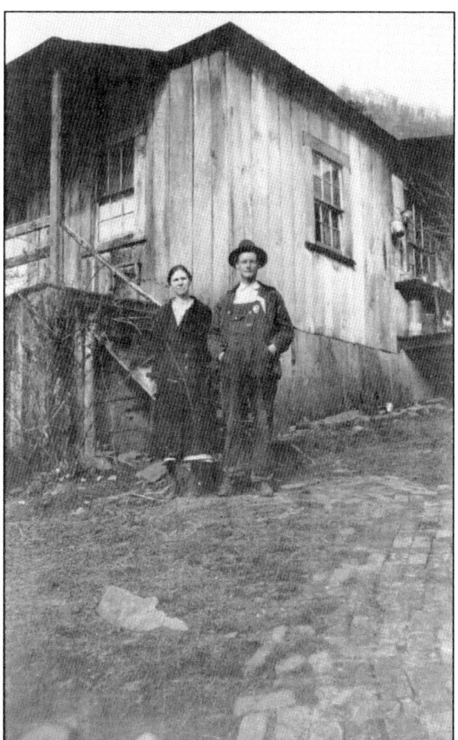

The first pioneers built their homes mainly from hand-hewn logs. Construction methods changed, however, once sawmills were introduced, and most homes were then built using frame construction methods and timber from local sawmills. Thus, early homes in Swannanoa ranged from small log cabins to large sprawling farmhouses. Above, members of the Fox and Bartlett families stand in front of their log cabin along Bee Tree Creek. At left, Elmore and Grace Burnett pose in front of their home in Bee Tree around 1935. (Both, courtesy of Sybil Fox.)

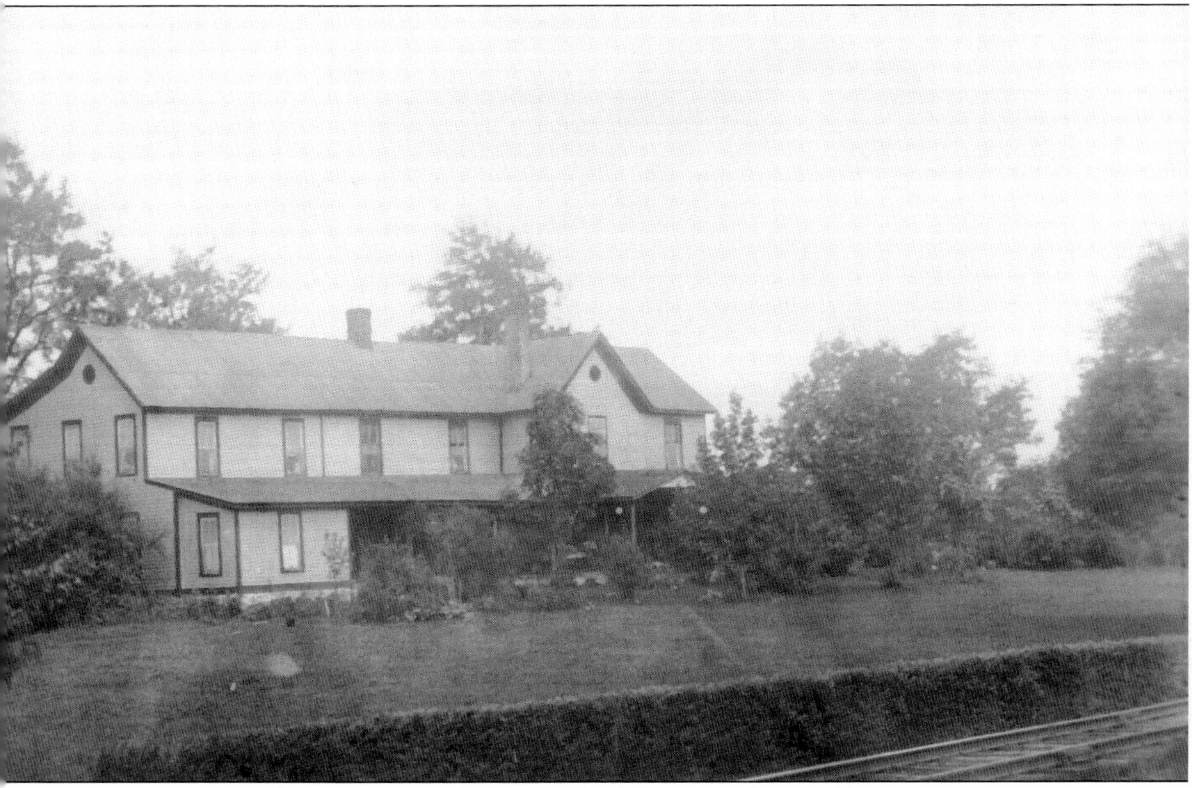

Bricks were rarely used in construction before the Civil War, though several houses in Swannanoa were built with bricks made from clay found on the property. This farmhouse, owned by the Penland family, is a good example of early wood-frame construction. (Courtesy of the Swannanoa Valley Museum, Penland Burgin collection.)

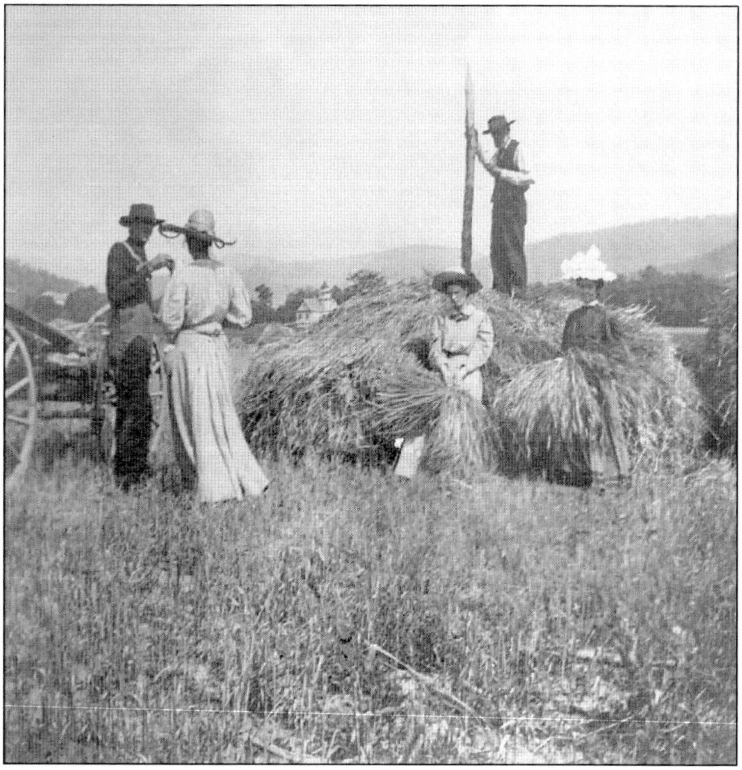

Farming was the main livelihood for the residents of Swannanoa in the 1800s, and most food consumed by the family was grown at home. In this photograph, members of the Penland and Burgin families spend time together in their hayfields near Swannanoa School (in the distance). (Courtesy of the Swannanoa Valley Museum, Penland Burgin collection.)

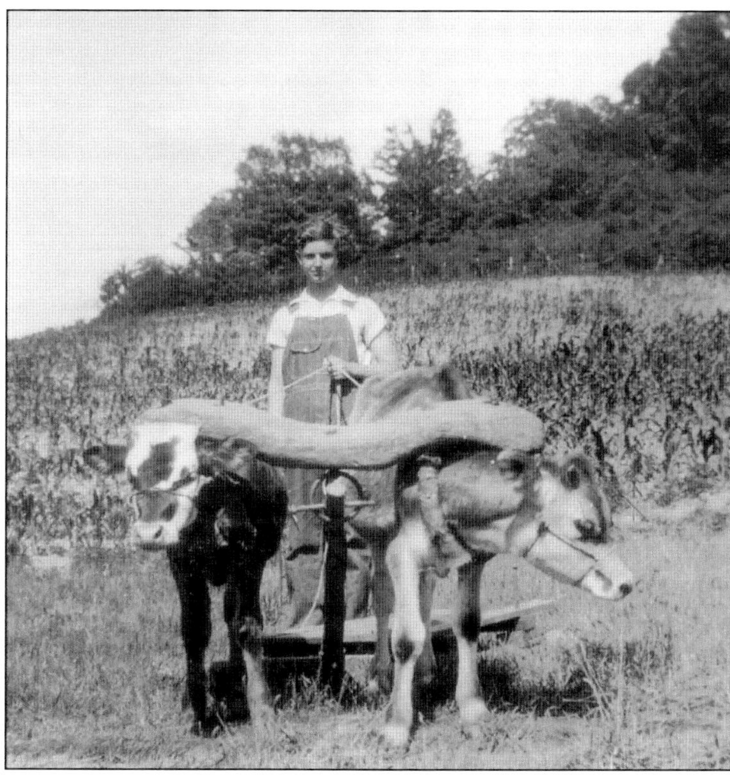

Corn was a common crop in Swannanoa. Here, Martin Lynnville Carr, the son of Francis Burgin Carr, uses cattle to plow his fields, as was typical of the time. (Courtesy of the Swannanoa Valley Museum, Penland Burgin collection.)

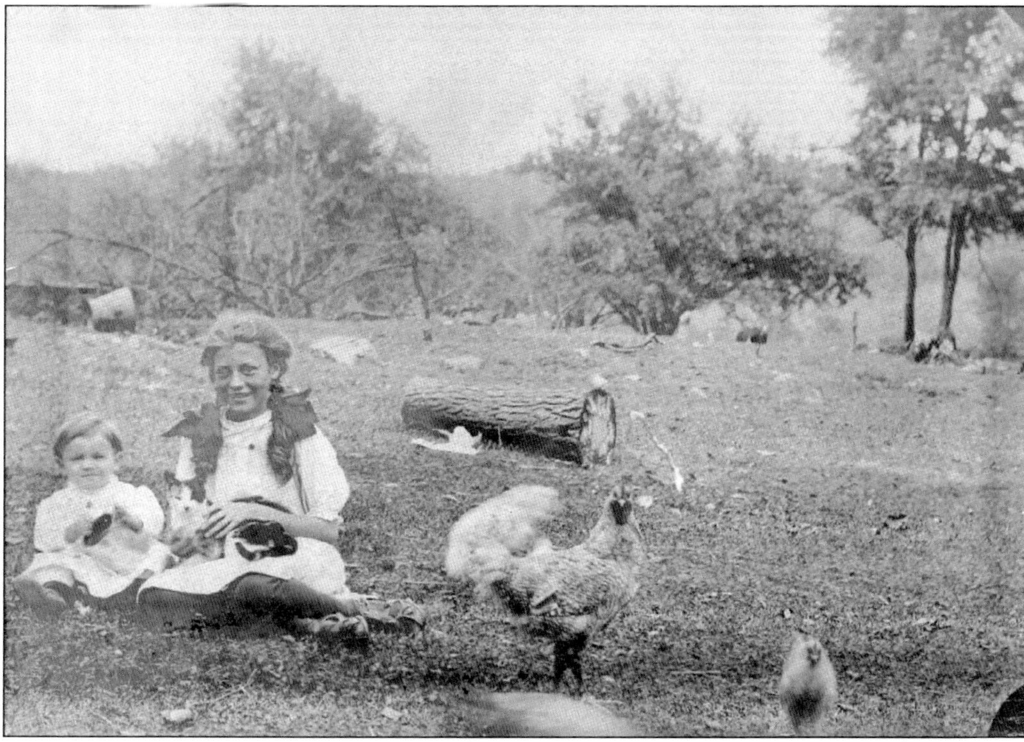

Children also had responsibilities on their family's farm, from collecting eggs and carrying water to helping seed and plow the fields. In these photographs, children from the Penland and Burgin families spend their free time playing with their pets and hiking through the surrounding woods. (Both, courtesy of the Swannanoa Valley Museum, Penland Burgin collection.)

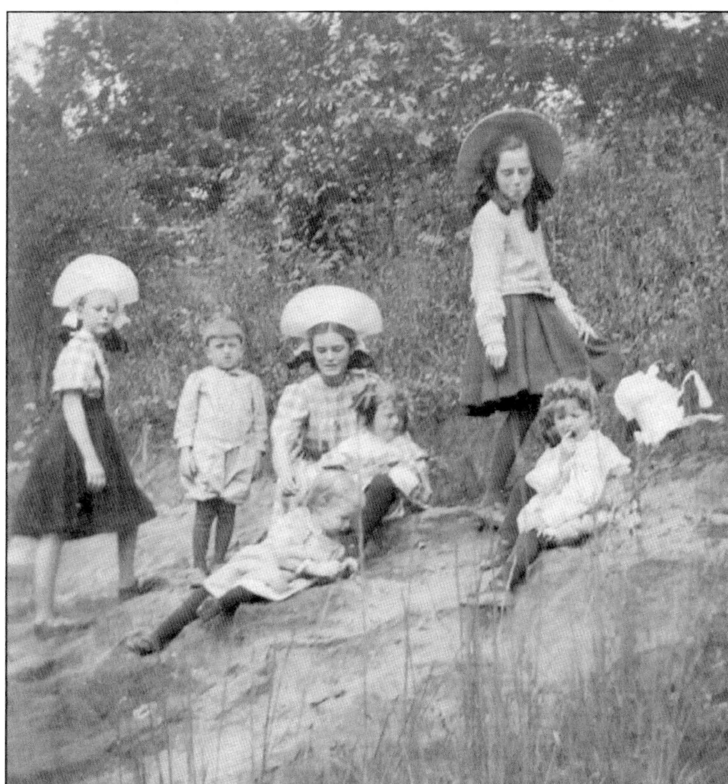

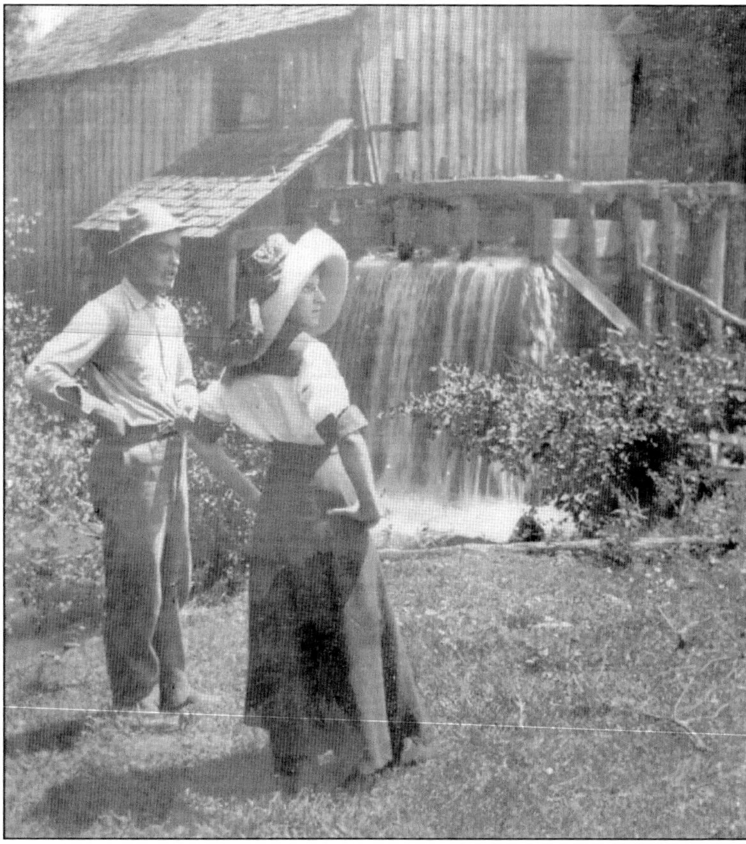

Soon after the area was settled by these early families, gristmills, sawmills, mica mines, and blacksmith shops began to open, and a village center developed. Residents built mills on nearly every creek in the Swannanoa Valley to grind their corn into meal. (Courtesy of the Swannanoa Valley Museum, Penland Burgin collection.)

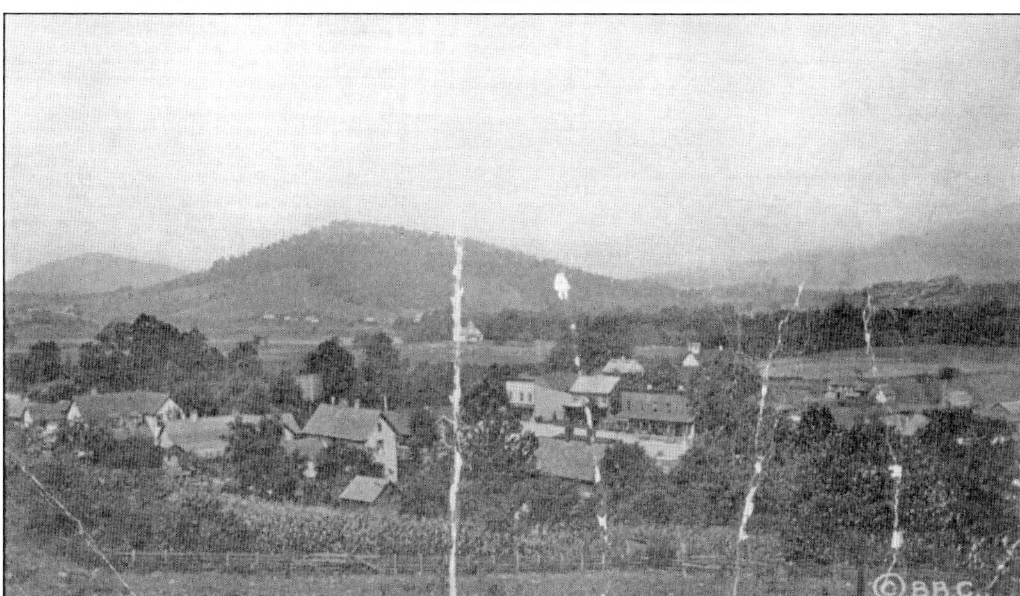

As Swannanoa became a community, its need for social services grew. Churches and one-room schoolhouses were built beginning in the late 1700s. This photograph shows downtown Swannanoa soon after 1900. (Courtesy of the Swannanoa Valley Museum, Penland Burgin collection.)

Two

Community Foundations

Education and Religion

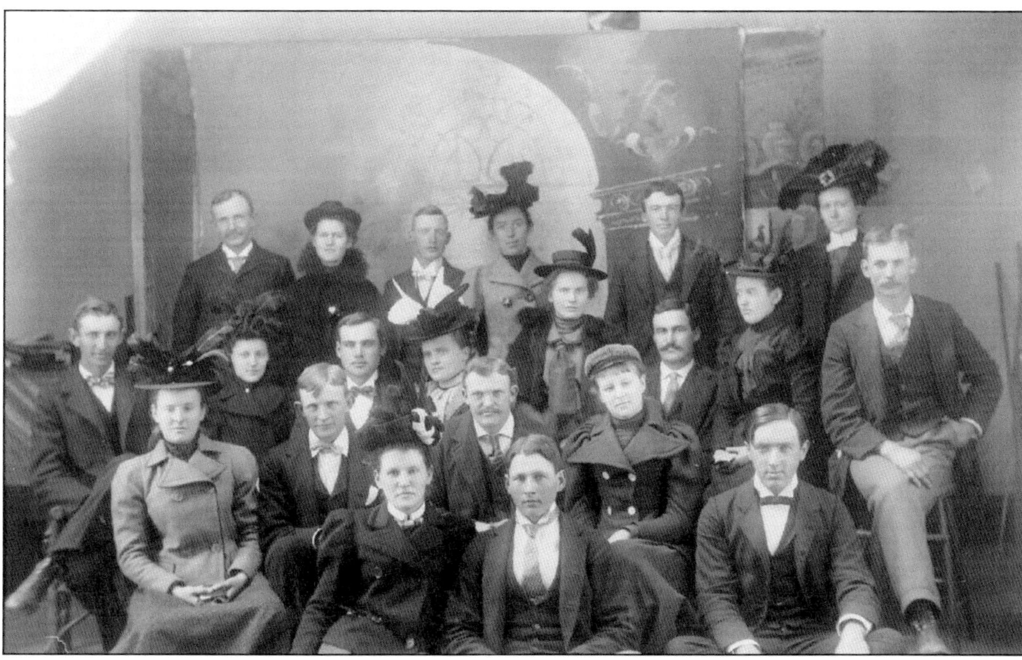

A burgeoning community required active planning from its residents. The Swannanoa Community Group is seen here at a social in Asheville around 1900. The group includes, from left to right, (first row) Jean French Patton, Josh Burgin, and McFarland Young; (second row) Kitty Sue Patton Parish, George Watkins, Arthur Watkins, and Patricia McRee Patton Croyle; (third row) Benjamin F. Patton, Irene Burgin Fortune, Robert Patton, Hester Alexander Echols, Dolly Alexander Haun, George White, unidentified, and Sam Alexander; (fourth row) Charles Watkins, Addie Dewey Hall, Jack Davidson, Sue Davidson Gudger, James White, and Minnie Davison White. (Courtesy of the Swannanoa Valley Museum.)

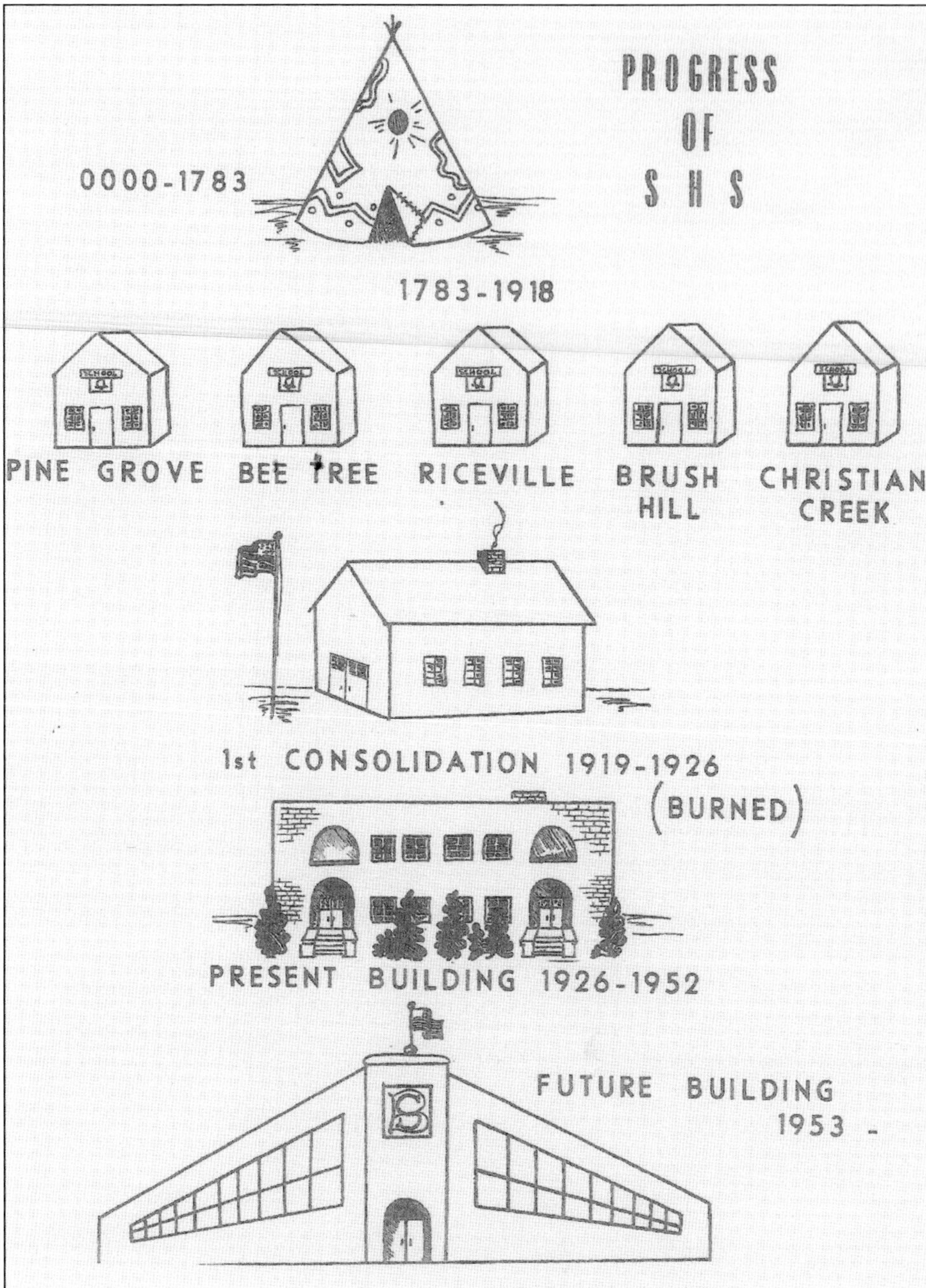

Many of the first formal schools in the Swannanoa Valley were founded by the Presbyterian Board of Home Missions in the mid- to late 1800s. Until the schools were consolidated in 1919, children who were able to attend school generally walked to the one- or two-room schoolhouses. This graphic from the 1952 Swannanoa High School yearbook shows the progression of Swannanoa's schools. In 1955, students from Swannanoa High School and Black Mountain High School began attending Charles D. Owen High School. Their mascot, the Warhorse, was created by combining Black Mountain's mascot, the Dark Horses, with Swannanoa's, the Warriors. (Courtesy of Nancy Wrenn.)

This 1862 advertisement for the little-known, short-lived Swannanoa Male and Female Academy notes, "In the present excited condition of the country [the Civil War], its geographical position renders it a great and safe retreat." True to the advertisement, there were no battles in the Swannanoa Valley during the Civil War. (Courtesy of the Swannanoa Valley Museum.)

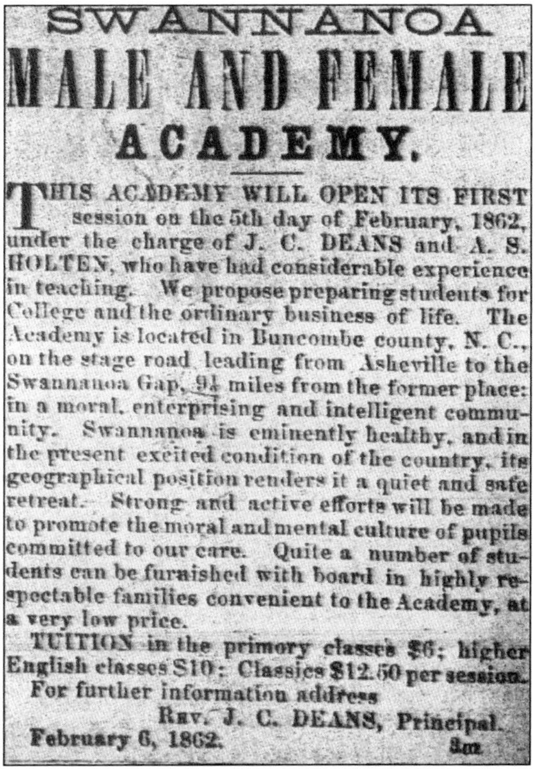

SWANNANOA

MALE AND FEMALE

ACADEMY.

THIS ACADEMY WILL OPEN ITS FIRST session on the 5th day of February, 1862, under the charge of J. C. DEANS and A. S. HOLTEN, who have had considerable experience in teaching. We propose preparing students for College and the ordinary business of life. The Academy is located in Buncombe county, N. C., on the stage road leading from Asheville to the Swannanoa Gap, 9½ miles from the former place: in a moral, enterprising and intelligent community. Swannanoa is eminently healthy, and in the present excited condition of the country, its geographical position renders it a quiet and safe retreat. Strong and active efforts will be made to promote the moral and mental culture of pupils committed to our care. Quite a number of students can be furnished with board in highly respectable families convenient to the Academy, at a very low price.

TUITION in the primory classes $6; higher English classes $10; Classics $12.50 per session.

For further information address

Rev. J. C. DEANS, Principal.

February 6, 1862. 3m

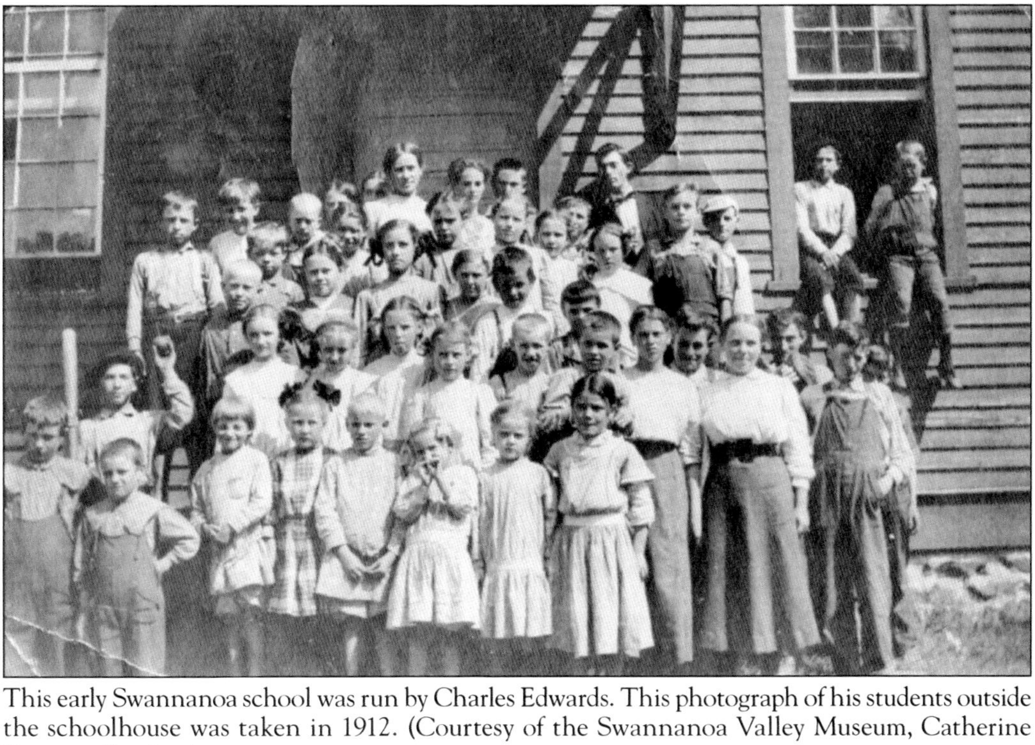

This early Swannanoa school was run by Charles Edwards. This photograph of his students outside the schoolhouse was taken in 1912. (Courtesy of the Swannanoa Valley Museum, Catherine Pruett collection.)

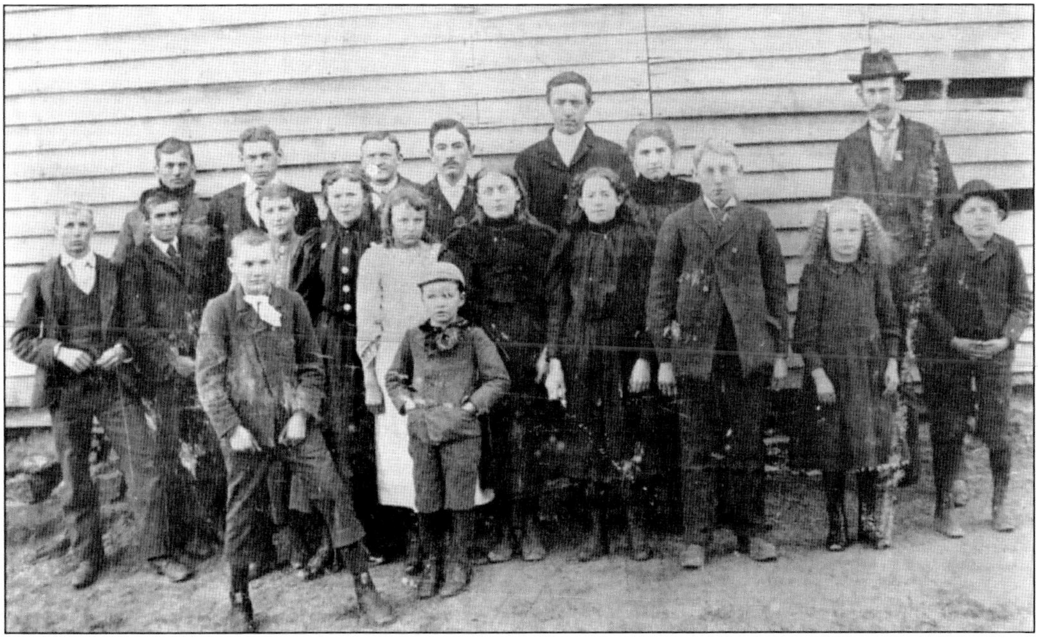

Students pose for a photograph outside their school in Swannanoa in 1890. Their teacher (far right, in hat) also played the fiddle in the Swannanoa String Band. (Courtesy of the Swannanoa Valley Museum.)

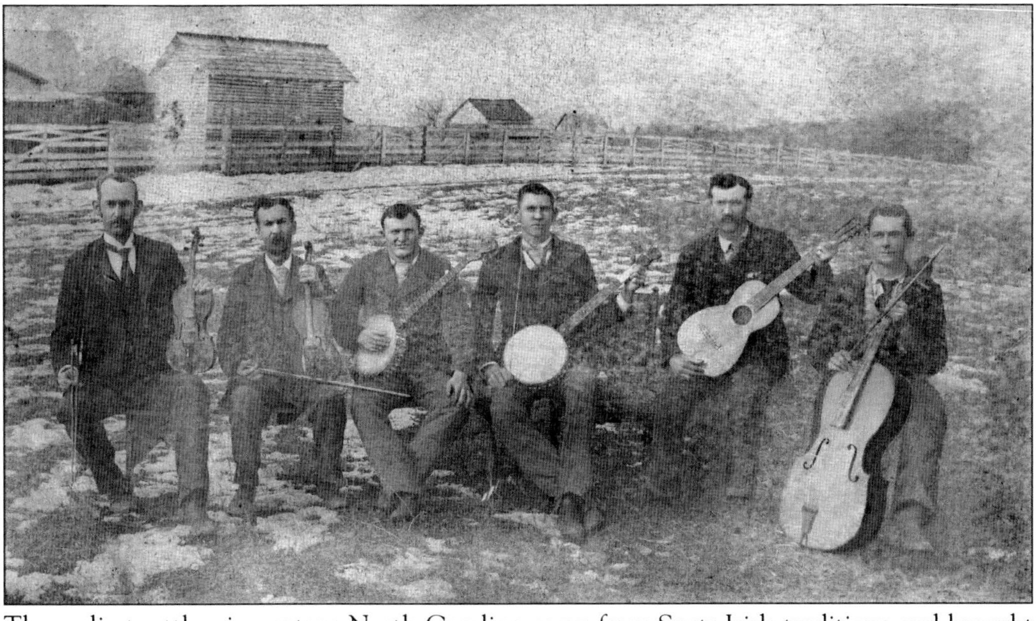

The earliest settlers in western North Carolina came from Scots-Irish traditions and brought with them a variety of traditional vocal and instrumental music. Women were generally the ballad carriers, while men played instruments. A fiddle, in particular, was often one of the few possessions families brought with them to America. Because of their ability to provide entertainment, musicians were highly regarded in rural communities like Swannanoa. The men in the Swannanoa String Band are seen in this 1895 photograph. (Courtesy of the Swannanoa Valley Museum, Don Talley collection.)

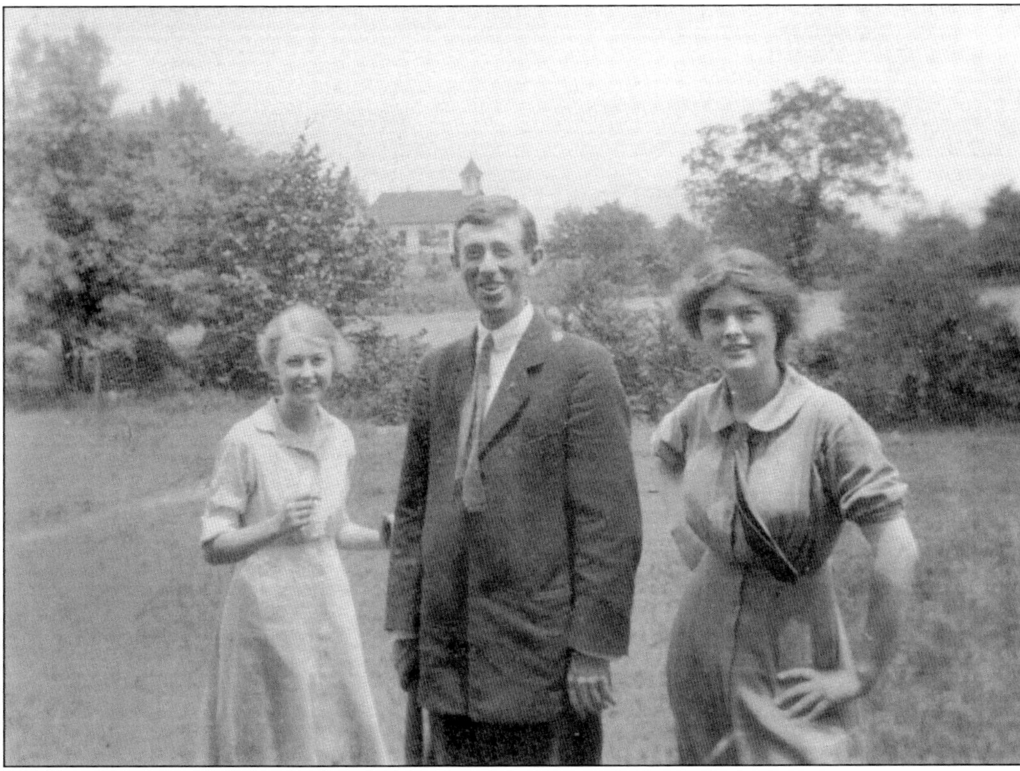

The Swannanoa School educated girls and boys from across the community and was significantly larger than the previous one-room schoolhouses that dotted the valley. The school was located between present-day US Route 70 and Interstate 40, near where the Swannanoa post office is today. (Above, courtesy of the Swannanoa Valley Museum, Penland Burgin collection; below, courtesy of the Swannanoa Valley Museum, Charles Whitson collection.)

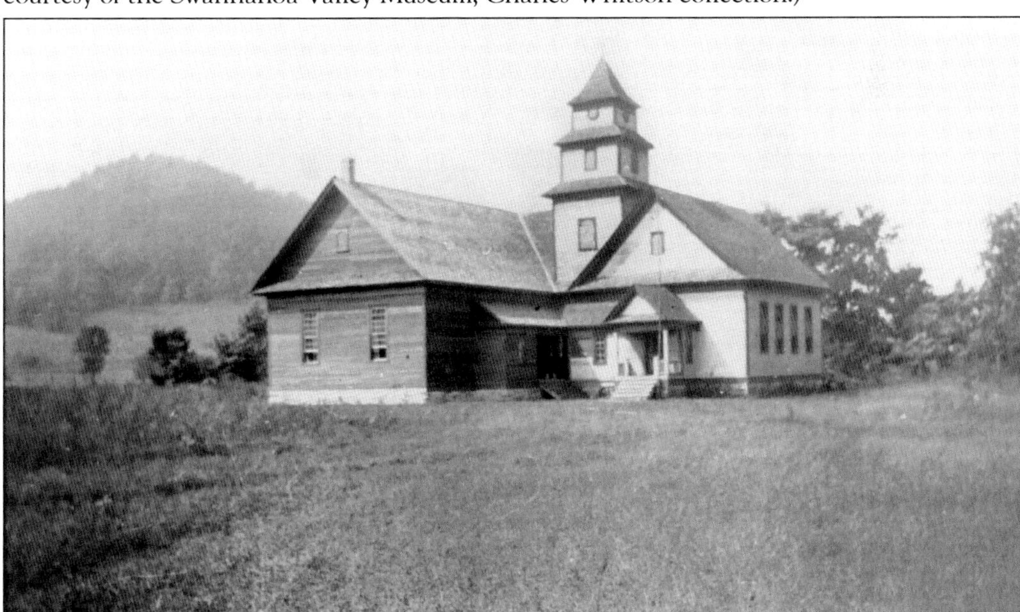

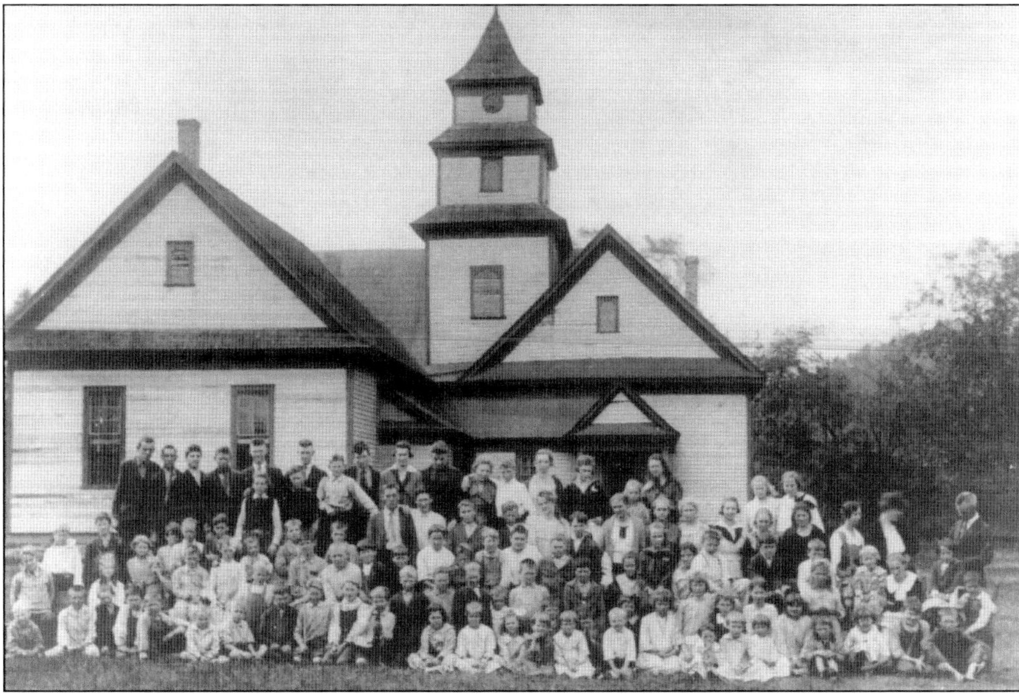

Around 100 students attended Swannanoa School when the photograph above was taken, around 1920. Below, students line up for a class photograph in 1919. Their teacher was Candler native Circo Owenby (in front of doorway in back). The students below are, from left to right, (first row) Howard Burrell, Floyd E. Patton, Mark Bass, Paul Fore, James Solerbee, and Tom Bass; (second row) Lester Connelly, Elbert Byas, Adjor Spivey, Emma Goldsmith, Nan Davidson Tanner, Virginia Harrison Huggins, Beatrice Buchanan Pace, Emma Reed, Nina Jones, Clarence G. "Doc" Taylor, Clarence "Brother" Fore, Lynn E. Reighard Jr., and Sam Alexander; (third row) Rankin Patton, Carl Martin, Richard Moser, Jess Harper, James Watkins, Horace Stephenson Sr., George Edney, Callie Edney, Carrie Byas, Gussie Stephenson, Verie Mann, Sam Davidson, and George King. (Above, courtesy of the Swannanoa Valley Museum; below, courtesy of the Swannanoa Valley Museum, Harold Patton collection.)

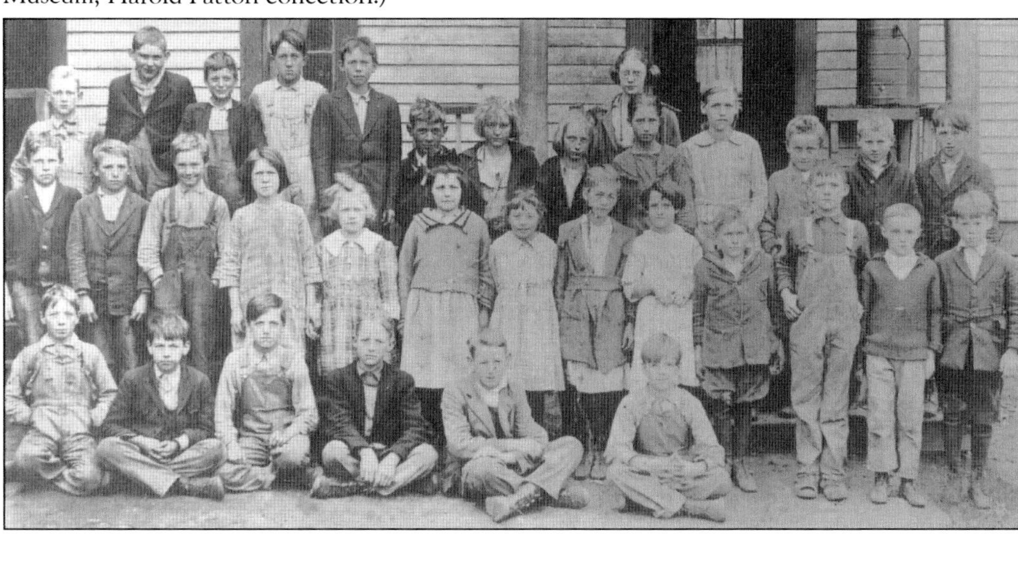

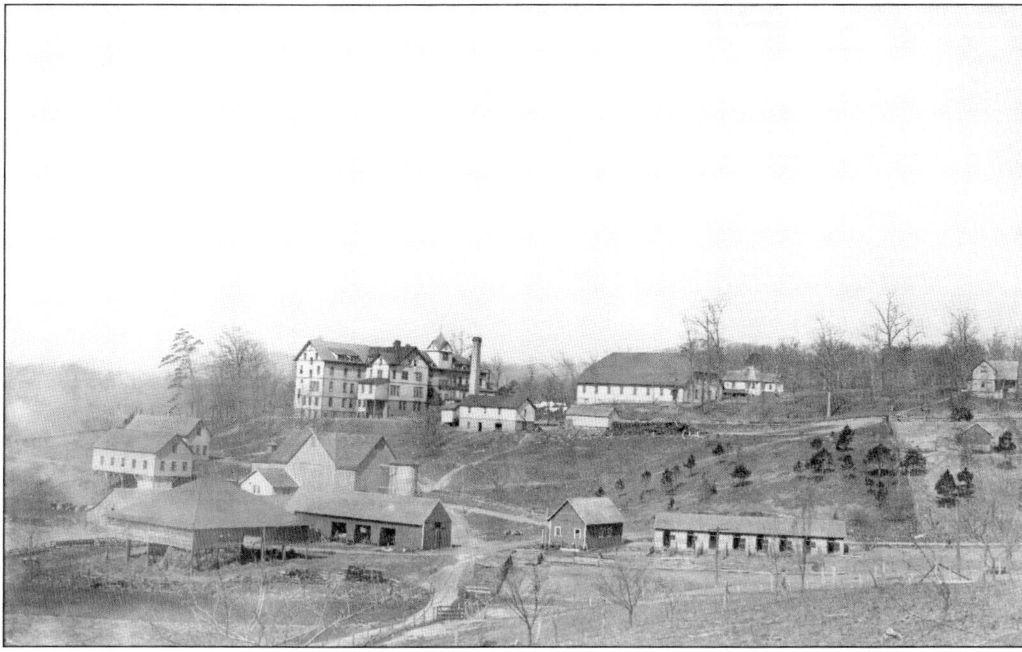

In 1894, the mission school of the North Presbyterian Church opened the Asheville Farm School on the westernmost side of Swannanoa to educate boys in the agricultural sciences. In 1942, the farm school merged with the Dorland-Bell residential school, near Hot Springs, to become Warren Wilson College. The photograph above shows the original Asheville Farm School campus and buildings around 1900. The photograph below shows a typical classroom on the Asheville Farm School campus. (Both, courtesy of the Warren Wilson College Archives.)

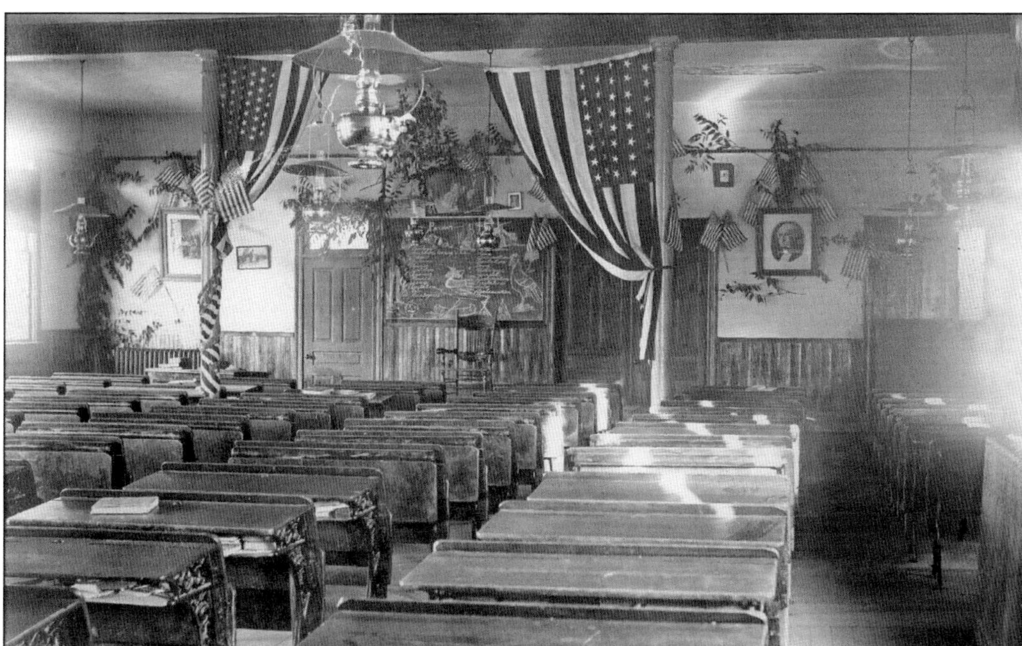

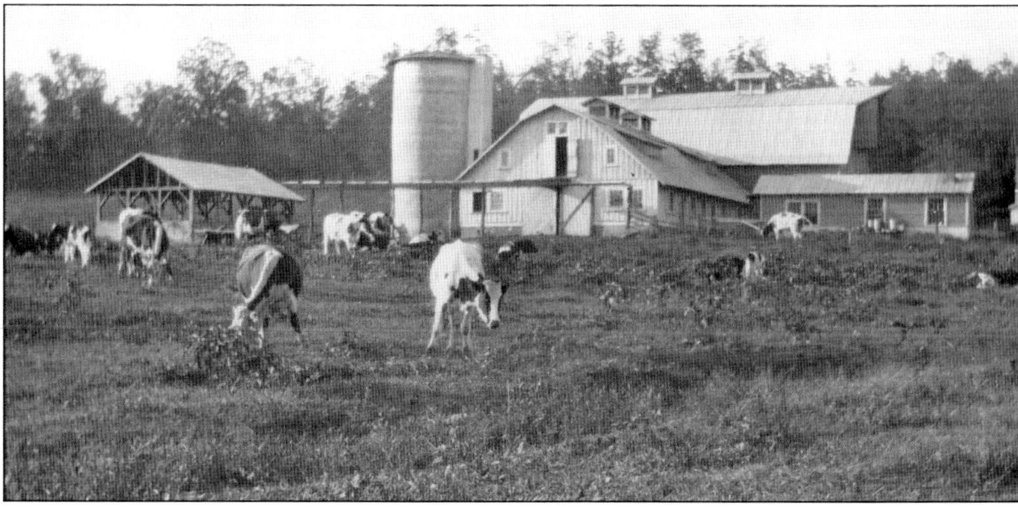

The Asheville Farm School's farm and barn, seen in this early-1900s promotional photograph, are still active today. This photograph is captioned, "All of the boys receive training in agriculture on the 700 acres of land. They also become farmers, dairymen, poultry raisers, pig experts, orchard workers, and truck gardeners as they assume in turn their share of the work. Between 30 and 40 of the boys remain at the school during the summer to care for the crops and livestock. This gives those who have little or no money the chance to work out their tuition." (Courtesy of the Warren Wilson College Archives.)

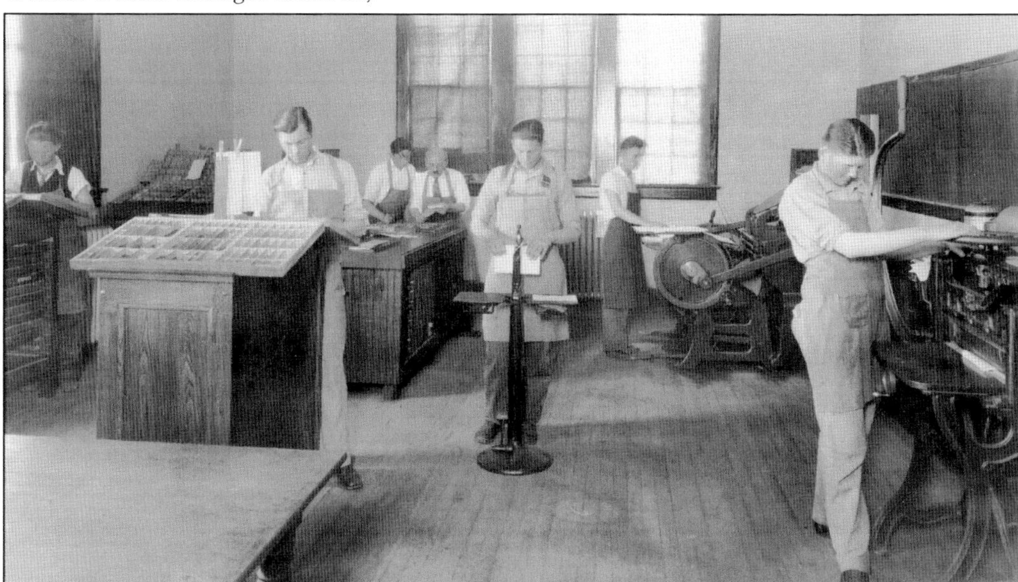

Boys at the Asheville Farm School were also taught other trades besides farming. This photograph, also from a promotional brochure, shows the school's print shop. This caption reads, "From sections where it is difficult to earn a living because the soil is unproductive and hard to farm and where there is often no chance to go to school, the boys come as eagerly as the girls. Outside interests have already opened many industries in the mountains, but the mountaineer has not been trained to meet the new industrial situation. Farm School prepares boys for Christian citizenship and industrial leadership in the Southern Highlands." (Courtesy of the Warren Wilson College Archives.)

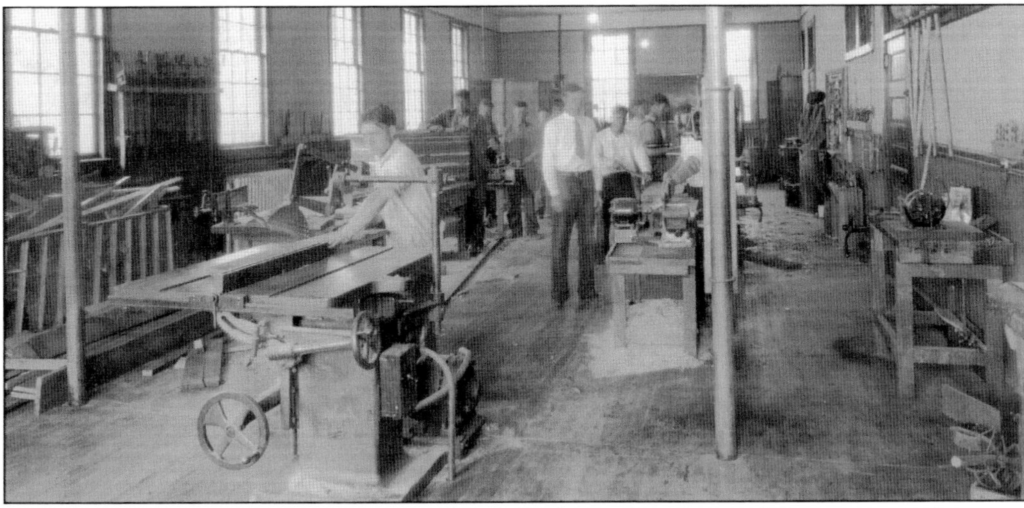

Many of the boys at the Asheville Farm School also learned carpentry skills, as seen in this image from a promotional brochure, which reads, "Some of these boys return to their home communities to farm, but many go into industries and trades in other sections. Training in mechanics, printing, construction and cabinet work gives them the education necessary to earn an adequate living. One boy, who came to Farm School from a backward community, supervised the construction of the National Mission dispensary at Sunset Gap, Tennessee, during one of his vacations." (Courtesy of the Warren Wilson College Archives.)

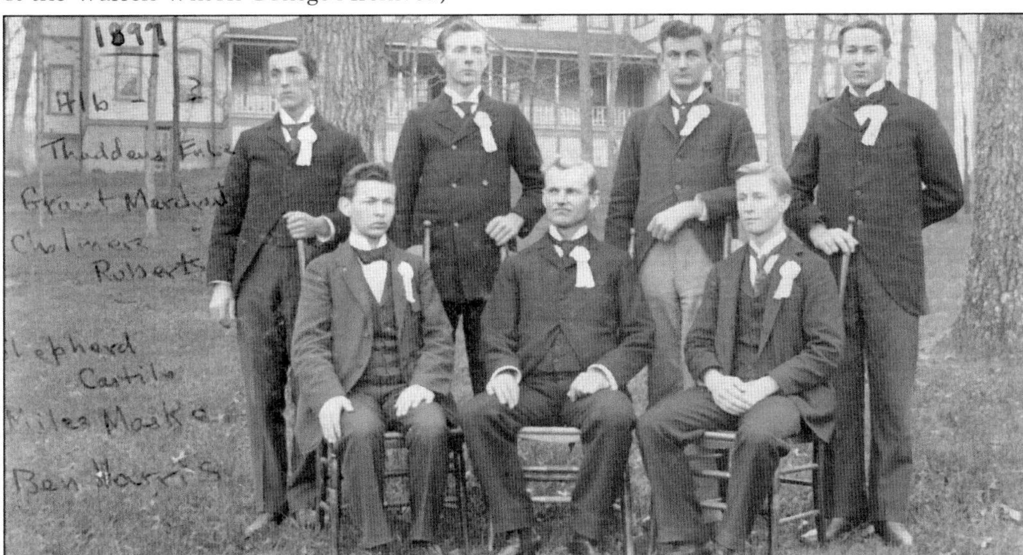

The first graduating class at the Asheville Farm School is seen here in 1897. These boys, who were graduating eighth grade, are, from left to right, (first row) Sherpherd Castile, Mile Maske, and Ben Harris; (second row) unidentified, Thaddeus Enloe, Grant Merchant, and Chalmers Roberts. A school brochure produced in the early 1900s notes the accomplishments of boys who had graduated from the school: "Former Farm School boys are now social, political, industrial and agricultural leaders in all parts of the United States. Among the graduates are nine ministers, four missionary workers, four Y.M.C.A. secretaries, and twenty-one educators. Others are doctors, contractors, county farm agents, mill officials, and business men. Still others are farmers, carpenters, and merchants through the South." (Courtesy of the Warren Wilson College Archives.)

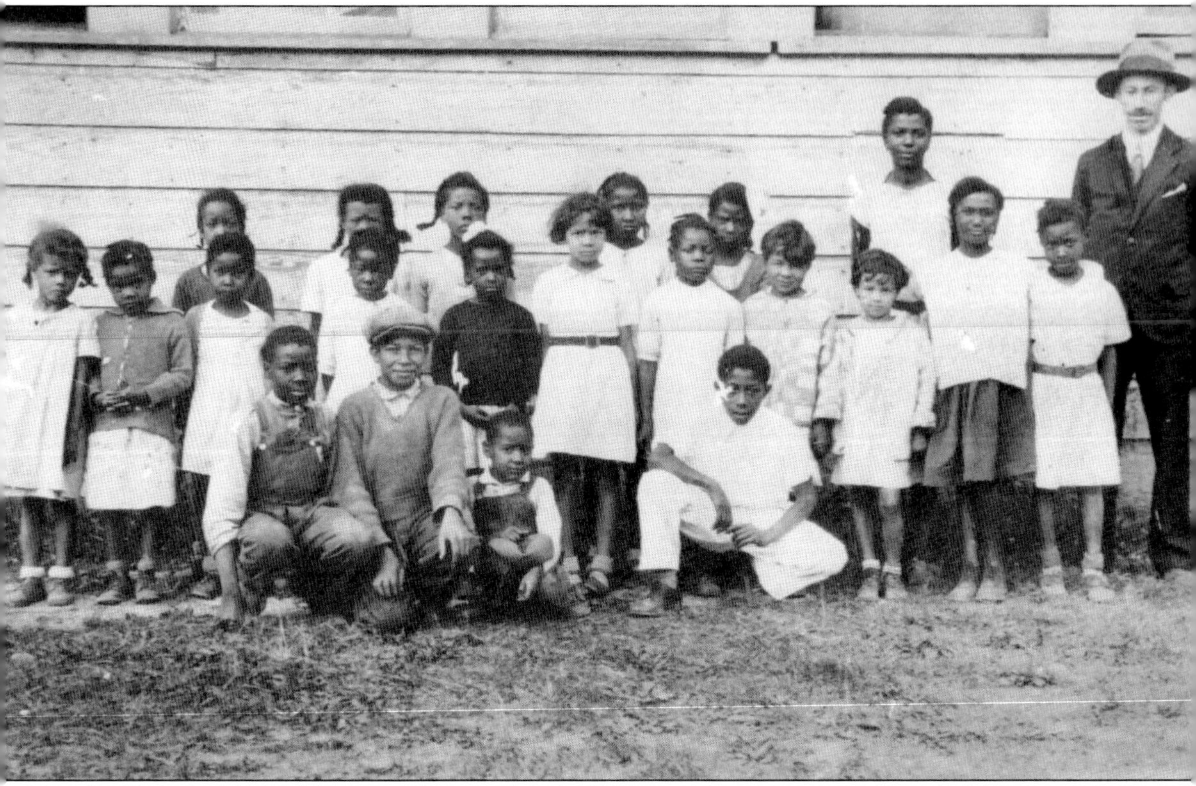

Swannanoa Valley schools were segregated well into the 1960s. Julius Rosenwald, the son of a German-Jewish immigrant and a part owner of Sears, Roebuck & Co., contributed matching donations through the Rosenwald Fund to more than 5,000 schools nationwide for the education of African American students. One of these Rosenwald Schools was in Swannanoa. This photograph shows the school and some of its students in the 1930s. James Thaddis Sapp (far right) was the principal. (Courtesy of the Swannanoa Valley Museum.)

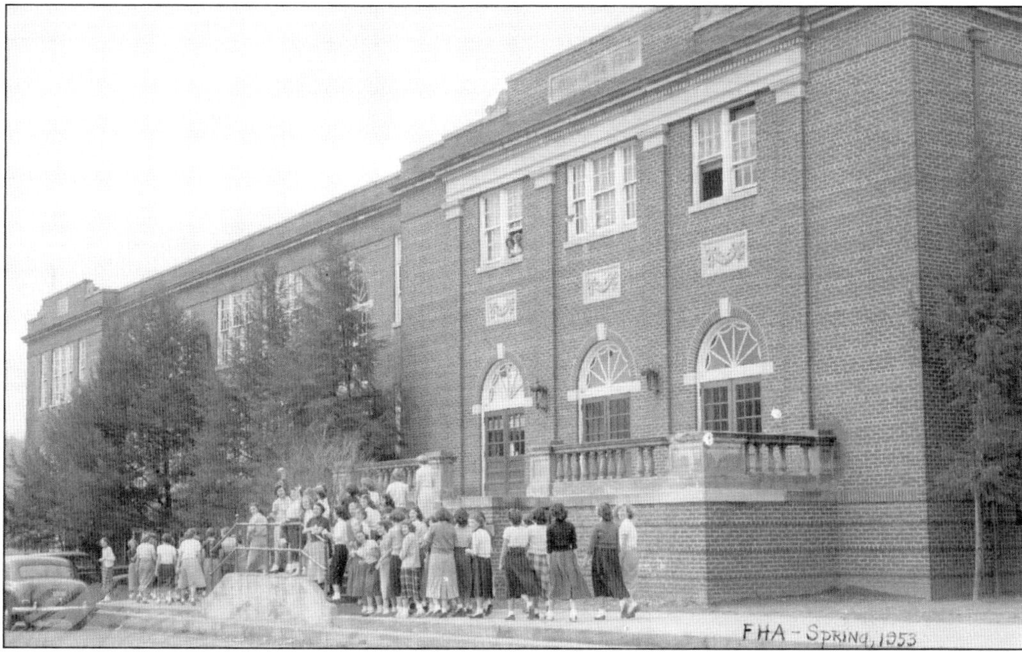

After its first building burned, Swannanoa High School relocated to this building in 1926. Seen here in the spring of 1953 during a meeting of the Future Homemakers of America, the high school served white students in grades 8–12 until Swannanoa's and Black Mountain's high schools were consolidated. In 1953, Charles D. Owen High School was built. It opened to students in 1955 and still educates the valley's teenagers. The former Swannanoa High School building is now home to Buncombe County Community High School. (Courtesy of the Swannanoa Valley Museum.)

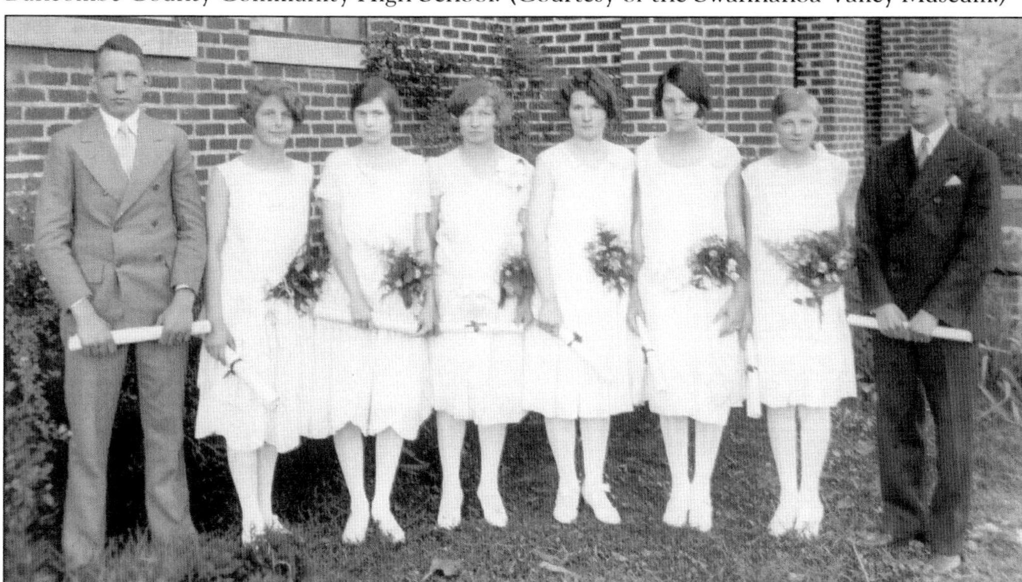

Swannanoa High School's 1927 graduating class poses for a photograph in front of the school building. The graduates are, from left to right, Sidney Wilfong, Helen Reighard, Mary Grace Baldwin, Ada Morgan, Eva Padgett, Ruth Johnson, Mary Coggins, and Wayne Stephenson. (Courtesy of the Swannanoa Valley Museum.)

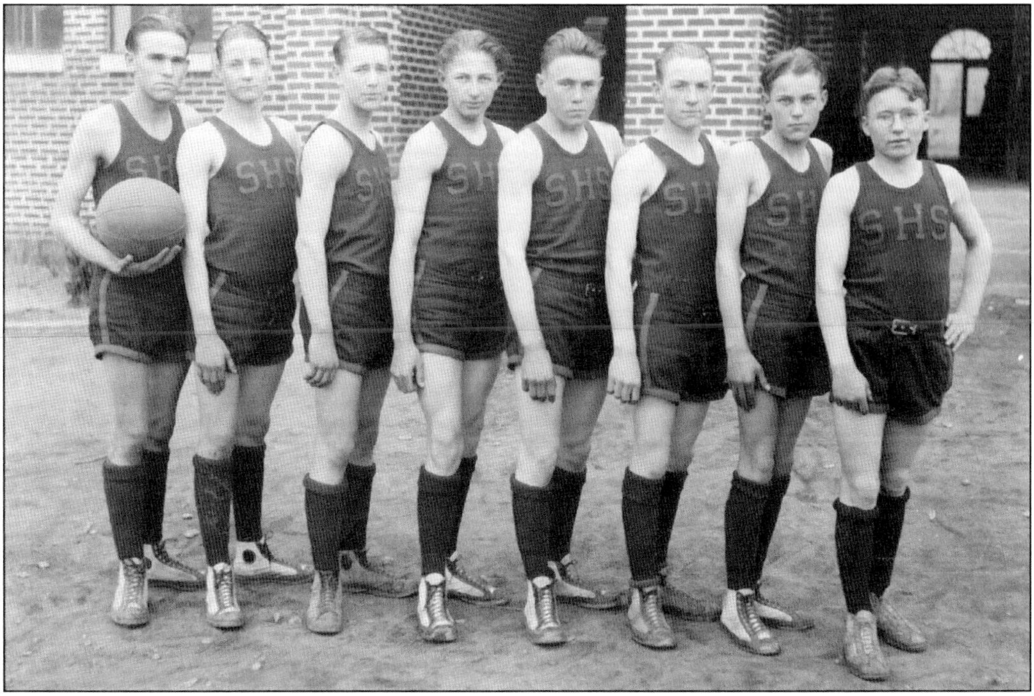

Though football and baseball were typically the most popular sports in the Swannanoa community, Swannanoa High School had a variety of sports teams for both men and women. The 1925 men's basketball team is seen above. The 1926 ladies' basketball team photograph includes, from left to right (first row) Beatrice Buchanan, substitute; and Mary Virginia Cox, forward; (second row) Katherine Shope, guard; Belle Wilfong, guard; Mae Gibson, center; Lona Belle Moffitt, guard; Ruth Johnson, substitute; W.W. Morgan, coach; and Helen Reighard, forward. (Both, courtesy of the Swannanoa Valley Museum.)

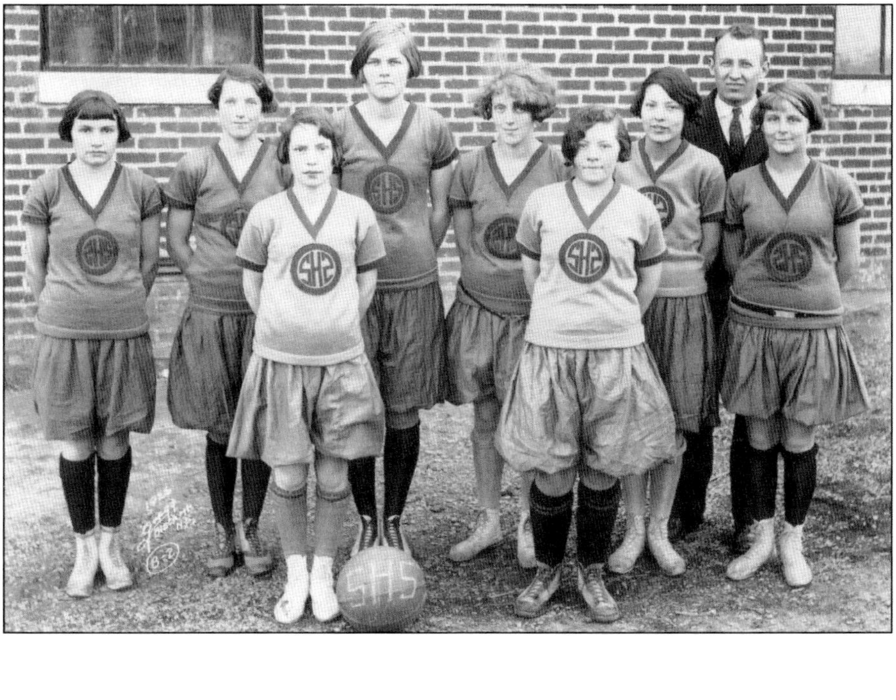

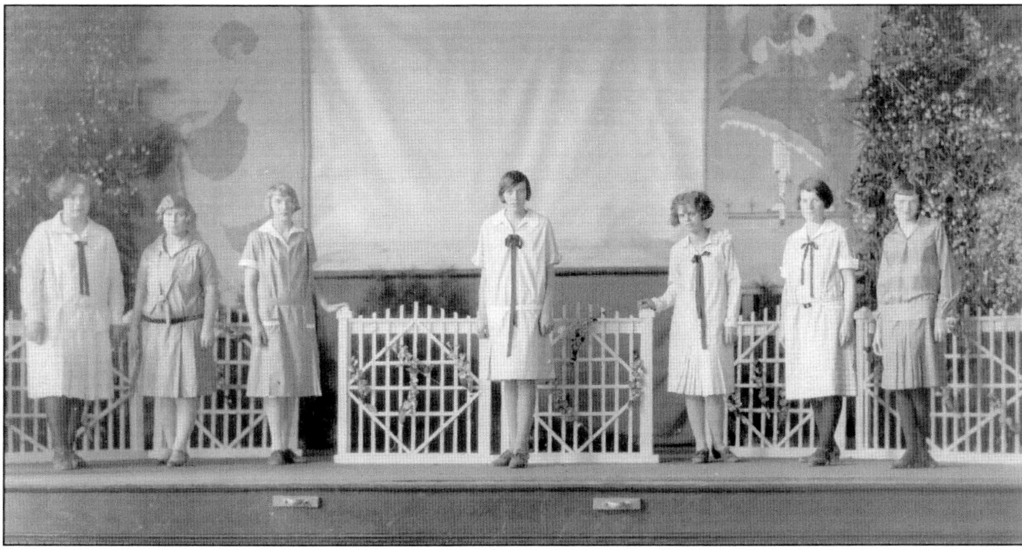

Swannanoa High School home economics teacher Ruth E. Merrick sponsored an annual dress competition for her students. In the 1926–1927 school year, Beaulah Stephenson's dress placed first overall for all the dresses made in the department; Dorothy Burnette was second overall; Eva Padgett was best from the 11th grade; Edith Stroup was best from the 10th grade; Bonnie Dolen was best from the 9th grade; Nedra Shope was best from the 8th grade's section A, and Elsie Redmond was best from the 8th grade's section B. The second place entries were Sis Reighard, from the 11th grade; Mary Stroupe, from the 10th grade; Helen Morgan, from the 9th grade; Helen Stroupe, from the 8th grade's section A; and Fay West, from the 8th grade's section B. (Courtesy of the Swannanoa Valley Museum.)

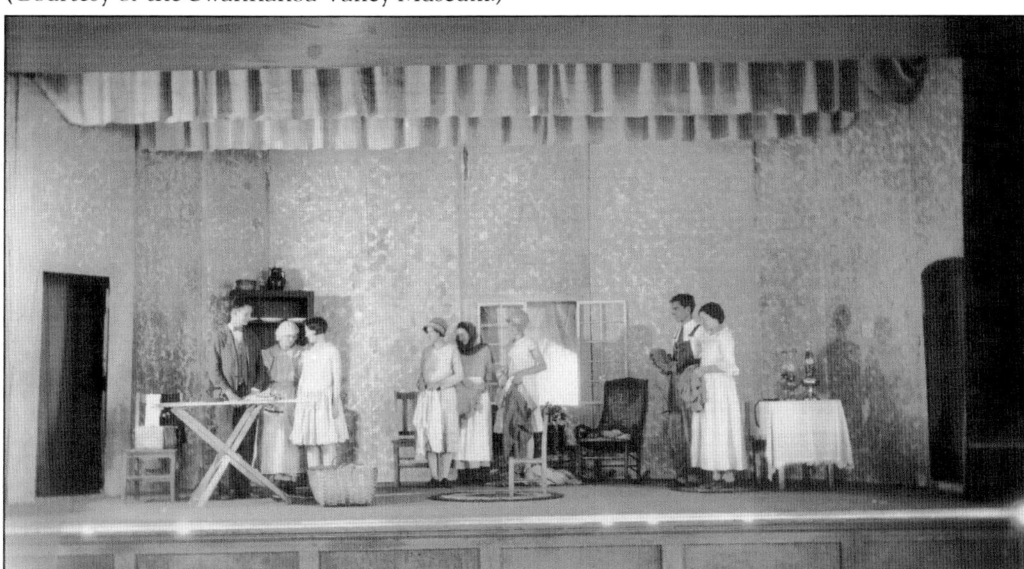

Seen here is a scene from the one-act play *The Neighbors*, performed at Swannanoa High School on Friday, November 9, 1928, by the Creative English Class. Reading, from left to right, are William Shope, as Peter; Margaret Rice, as Grandma; Sallie Owenby, as Inez; Marjorie Connelly, as Mrs. Ellsworth; Oletta Robinson, as Mrs. Moran; Dorothy Burnette, as Mrs. Able; Frank Williams, as Ezra; and Mae Harbin, as Mrs. Trot. (Courtesy of the Swannanoa Valley Museum.)

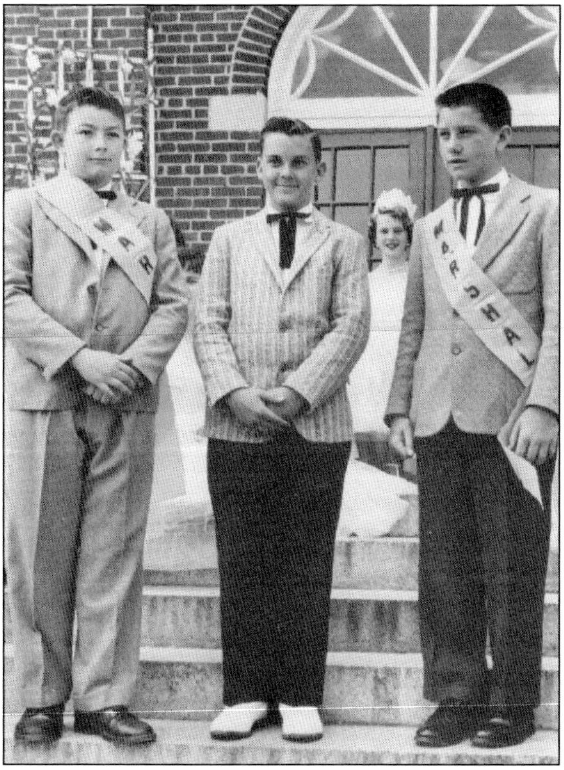

Swannanoa High School's May Day marshals stand on the front steps of their school awaiting the senior May queen. This image most likely dates from the 1940s. (Courtesy of the Swannanoa Valley Museum.)

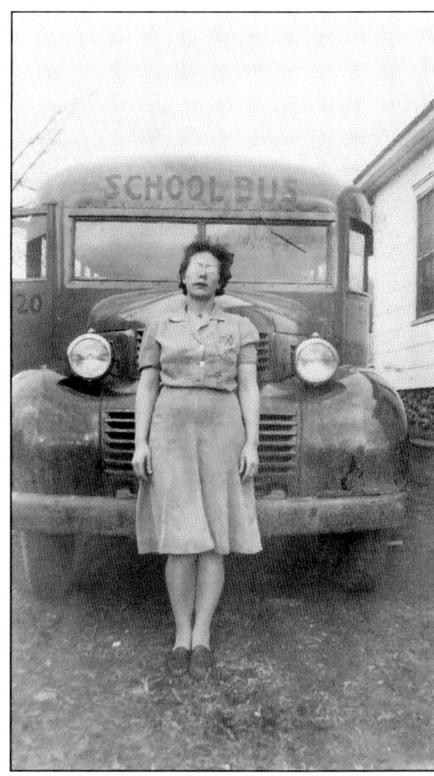

Louise Davidson drove the Swannanoa High School bus for many years. She is seen here with her bus in 1946. (Courtesy of the Swannanoa Valley Museum.)

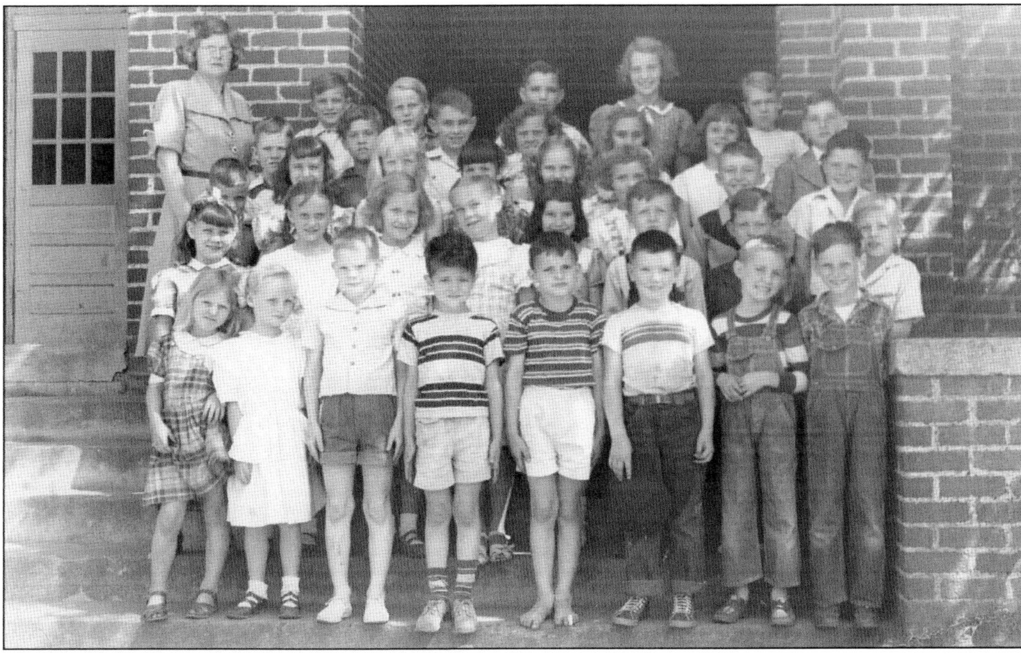

The Swannanoa Elementary School students seen here in 1951 are, from left to right, (first row) Helen Pegg, Nancy Kelly, Malcolm Burnette, Tony Cavoll, Robert Jarvis, Charles Rector, Donald Bradley, and David Craig; (second row) Brenda Bridges, Rita Putman, Glenda Andrews, Carolyn Bryant, Olivia Penland, Sammie Cole, unidentified, and Freddie Robinson; (third row) Joe Hensley, Brenda Faye Plemmons, Frances Robinson, Betty Jean Banks, Peggy Jo Banks, Janice Burch, Jerry Cline, and Johnny Rhymer; (fourth row) Bobby Watkins, Coy McIntosh, Joe Penley, Sarah Bell, Betty Pressley, Martha Ferguson, and Wayne Burleson; (fifth row) Billy Ogle, George Banks, Harrell Banks, Emogene Norman, and Ronnie Brown. The teacher is unidentified. (Courtesy of the Swannanoa Valley Museum.)

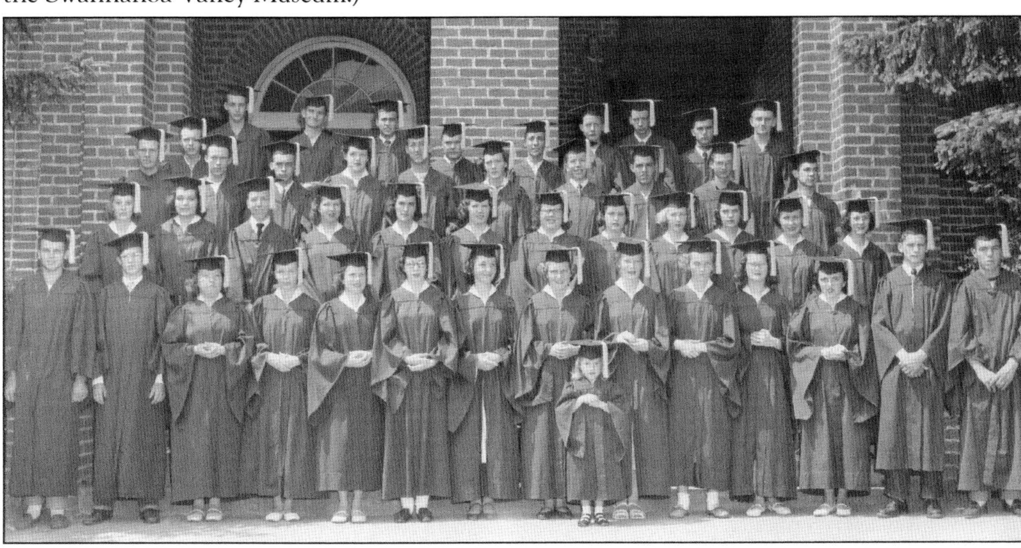

Swannanoa High School's 1952 graduating class, seen here, was one of the high school's final classes before all students began attending Charles D. Owen High School, in Black Mountain, in 1955. (Courtesy of the Swannanoa Valley Museum.)

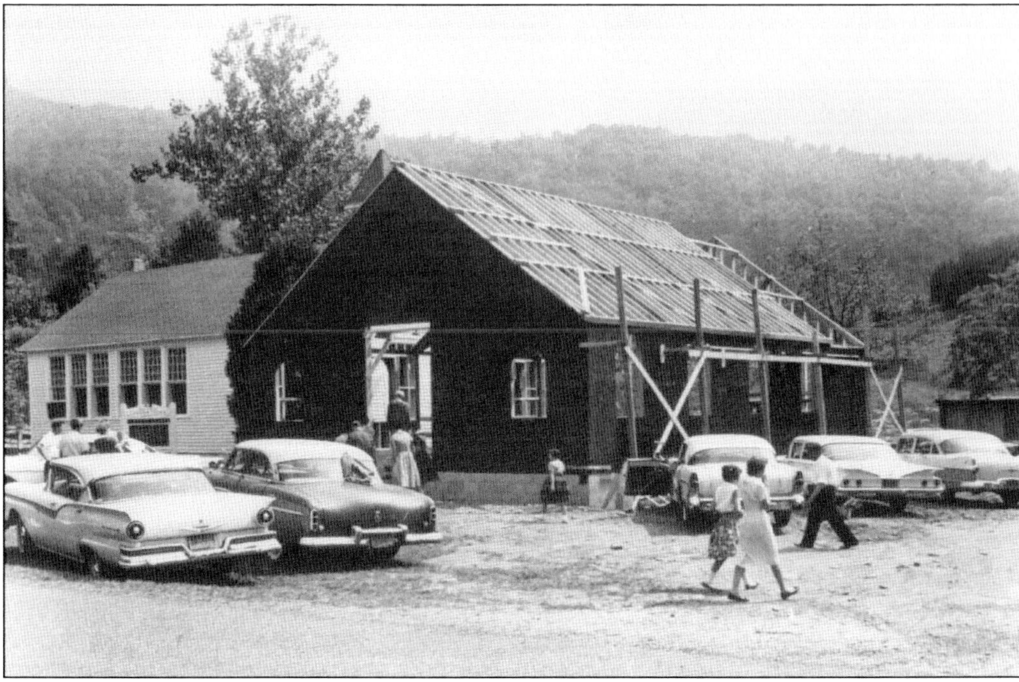

The Christian religion has been a part of Swannanoa's community life since the first white settlers made their way to the valley in the 1780s. Religious meetinghouses were some of the first public structures built after settlers made their homesteads. Often, these structures served the community as schools during the week and houses of worship on Sundays. The Bee Tree Church was built in 1903 and was primarily used as a school until the schools consolidated in the 1920s. After consolidation, the building was purchased for use by the Bee Tree Christian Church. This photograph of the church was taken during the construction of the present-day sanctuary. (Courtesy of the Swannanoa Valley Museum, Jan McGlohon collection.)

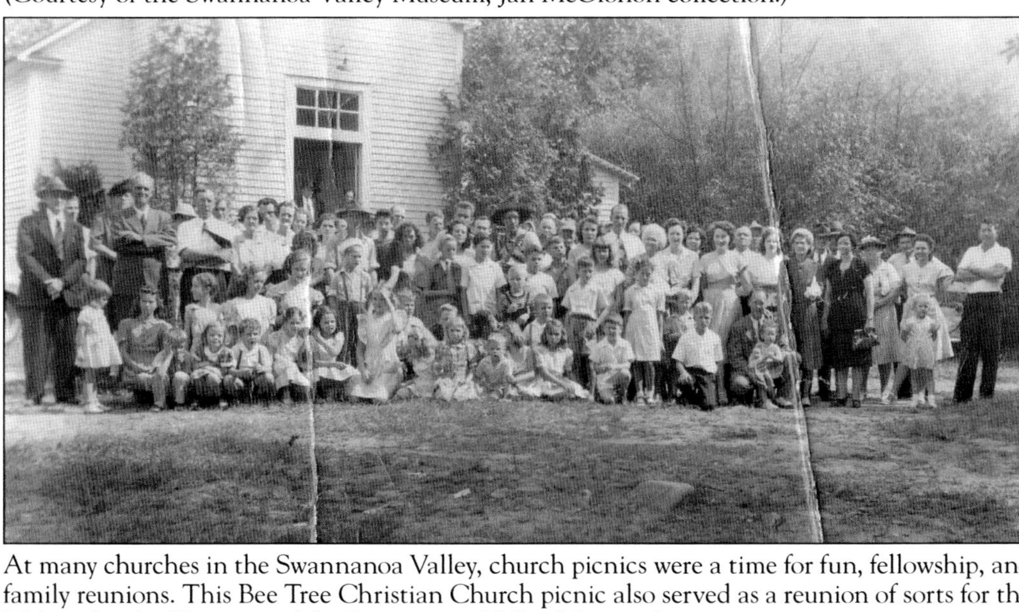

At many churches in the Swannanoa Valley, church picnics were a time for fun, fellowship, and family reunions. This Bee Tree Christian Church picnic also served as a reunion of sorts for the Melton family. (Courtesy of the Swannanoa Valley Museum.)

Piney Grove Presbyterian Church, also known as the First Presbyterian Church of Swannanoa, was founded in 1794. The first official church building stood on land donated by the Patton family and was known as the Patton meetinghouse. This still-active church is the oldest established congregation west of the Blue Ridge Mountains. Though the original church was retired in 1839, Piney Grove Cemetery, which surrounds it, is still the final resting place for many of the valley's earliest settlers. The photograph at right shows the church's third house of worship in 1908. The bricks used to make the church, which was dedicated in 1883, were made by hand at the Winnie Patton farm, one mile north of the church, and hauled to the site by mules and oxen. This building was in use until a new sanctuary was built in 1964. Below, students attending Piney Grove Presbyterian's 1918 summer Bible school pose with their teachers in front of the church. (Both, courtesy of the Swannanoa Valley Museum.)

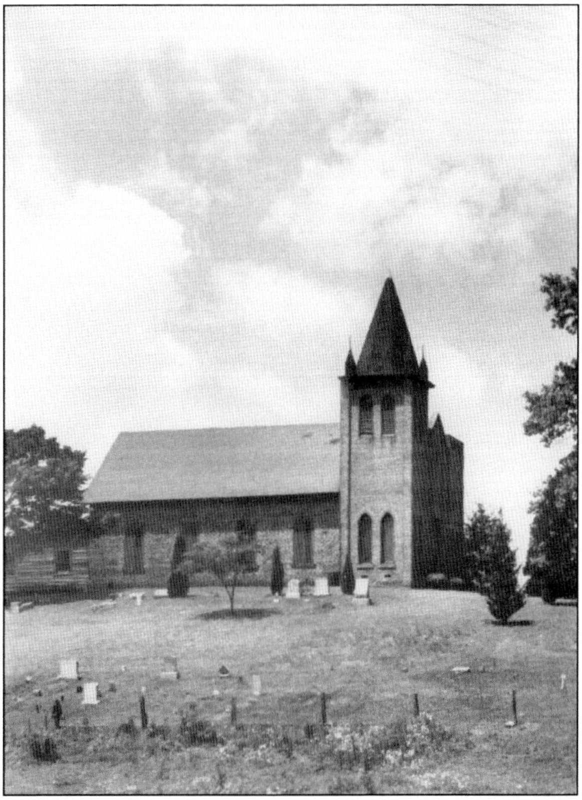

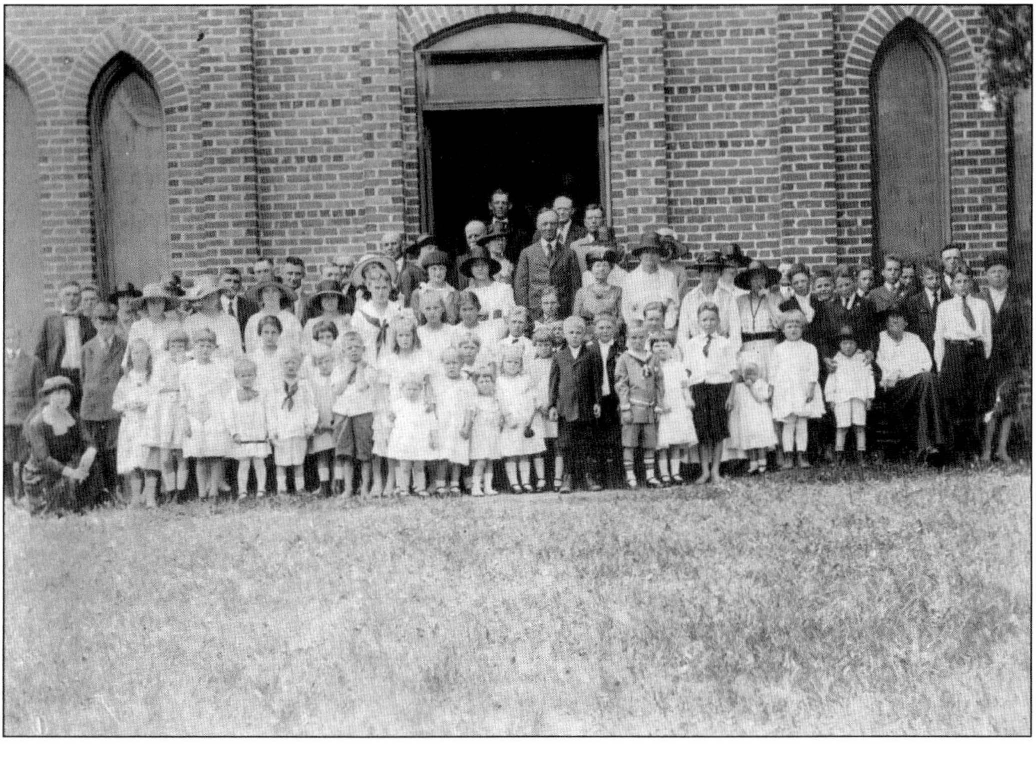

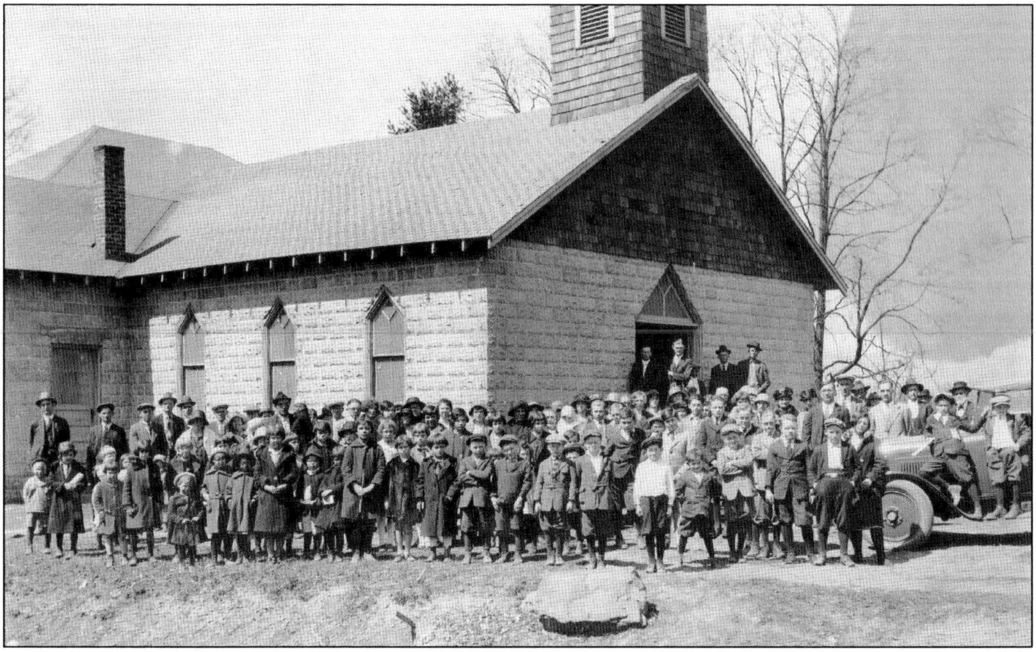

In 1883, the Polk family deeded a tract of land at Cooper's Station, on the banks of the Swannanoa River, to the Swannanoa Baptist Church, and a one-room frame building was built. The church was founded by 13 former members of Berea Baptist Church, on Riceville Road: Rev. W.S. Mitchell, T.S. Mitchell, Colon Mitchell, Elizabeth Mitchell, J.E. Morris, E.F. Morris, John Smith, Murray Smith, Robert Smith, Nancy Smith, James Denny, M.A. Denny, and Wally Medlin. In 1922, the wooden building was replaced by a one-room concrete-block building. This photograph, taken by Gragg Studios of Black Mountain, shows the congregation in front of the second building on March 21, 1926. (Courtesy of the Swannanoa Valley Museum.)

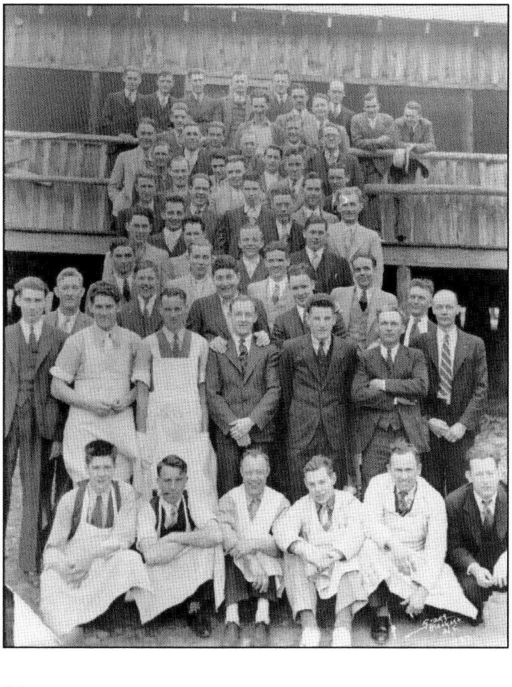

In 1935, Swannanoa Baptist Church added an auditorium on the back of the building. Then, in 1939, the church purchased more property to the west of the original structure. This property is now home to the church's educational building. In this 1937 photograph, members from the church's Baraca Sunday school class pose on the steps of Swannanoa 4-H camp during their class picnic. In 1951, the church changed its name to the First Baptist Church of Swannanoa. (Courtesy of the Swannanoa Valley Museum.)

Three

Escaping the Heat

The Tourists Arrive

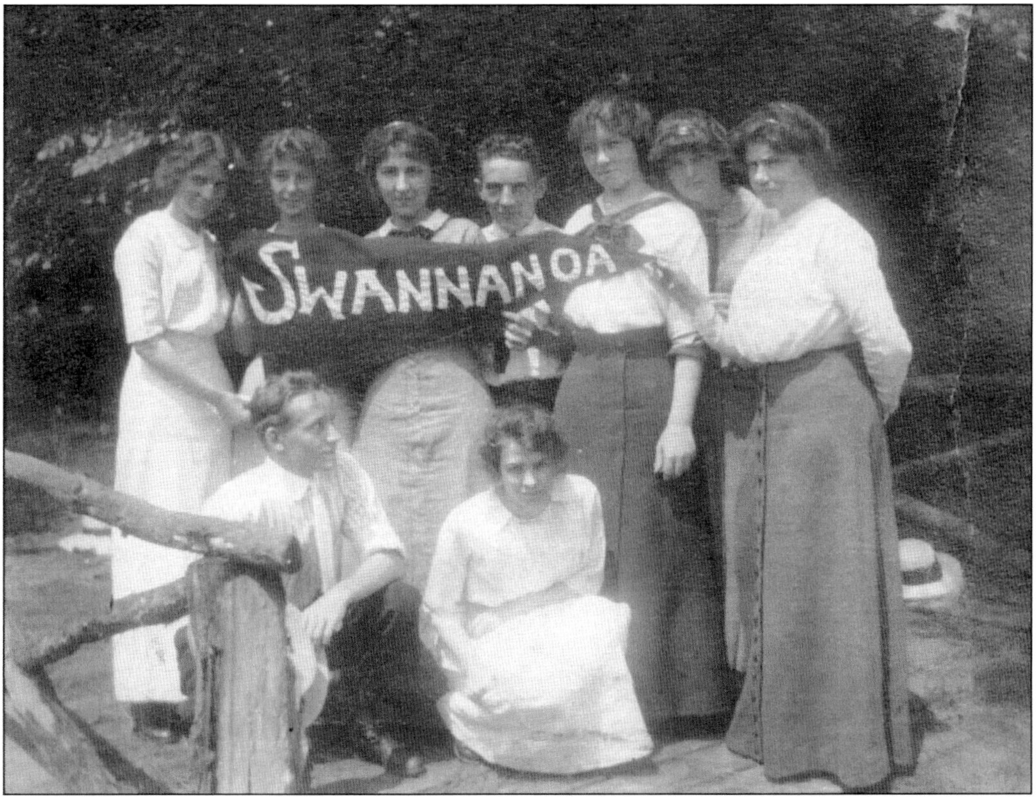

By the late 1830s, the beauty and climate of the Swannanoa Valley had begun attracting "summer people." These tourists came by stagecoach and wagon to escape the heat and the pests of the coastal regions. Here, a group of tourists staying at a nearby boardinghouse shows its pride for Swannanoa. (Courtesy of the Swannanoa Valley Museum, Penland Burgin collection.)

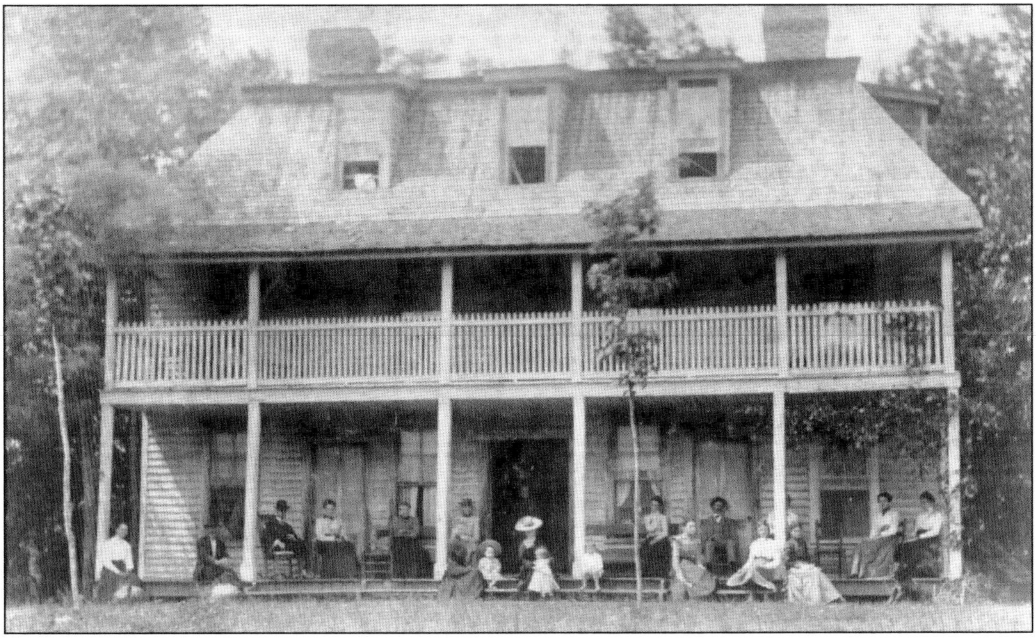

In the early years of valley tourism, many residents opened their homes to visitors. Some large boardinghouses were also built, like Squire Patton's, seen here around 1890. (Courtesy of the Swannanoa Valley Museum.)

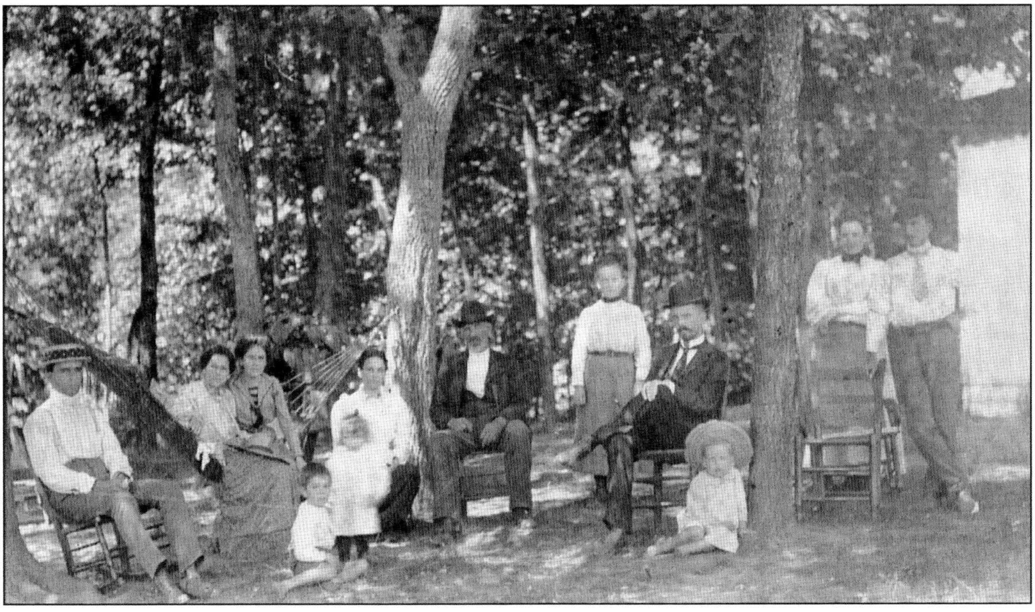

Many boarders stayed in the valley for the entire summer, and they often came back to the same home year after year, becoming like family to the staff and the other boarders. Here, around 1900, a few of the summer boarders at Squire Patton's pose for the camera with the inn's proprietor. They are, from left to right, an unidentified boarder, Mary Dwelle Tickner, Hattie E. MacMillian (Kirkpatrick), C. Wright MacMillain, Elsie MacMillan (Whitson), Mrs. Walter Jones, Squire Patton, Emma Alexander, Mr. Church, Dibbrelle Jones, Laura Patton, and Landen Wilkins. (Courtesy of the Swannanoa Valley Museum.)

Many hotels also established themselves in the Swannanoa Valley as more tourists made their way to the area. Hotels and boardinghouses often hosted parties and other events for their guests. This invitation for a "wit party," dated Saturday, September 15, 1900, is an example of the types of functions that attracted both new and returning guests. (Courtesy of the Swannanoa Valley Museum.)

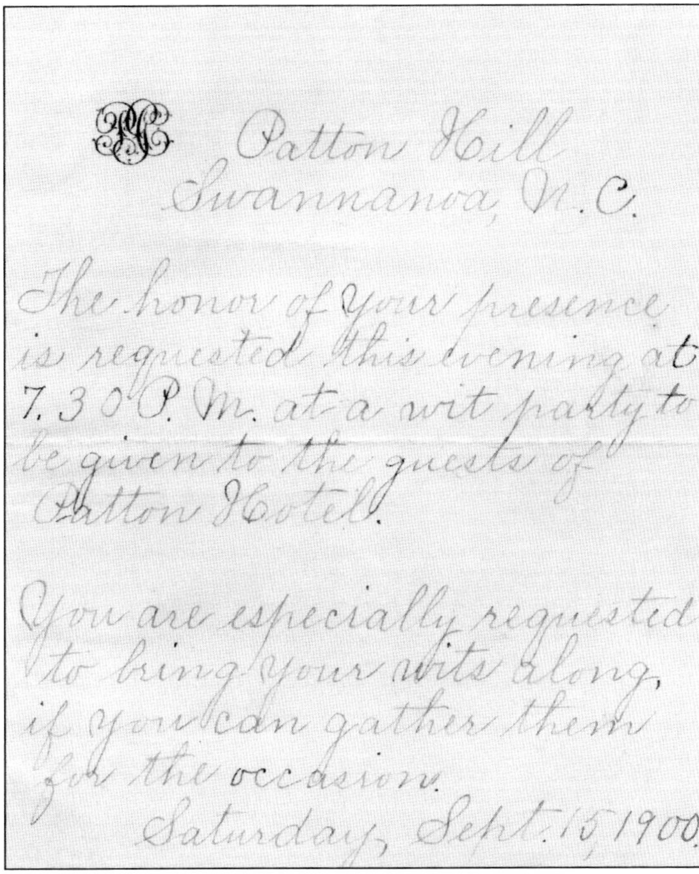
Patton Hill
Swannanoa, N.C.

The honor of your presence is requested this evening at 7.30 P.M. at a wit party to be given to the guests of Patton Hotell.

You are especially requested to bring your wits along, if you can gather them for the occasion.

Saturday, Sept. 15, 1900.

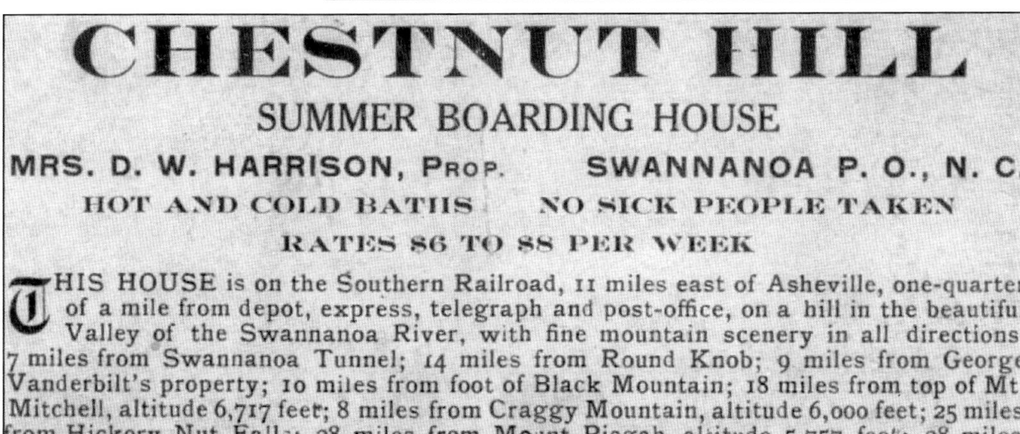
CHESTNUT HILL

SUMMER BOARDING HOUSE

MRS. D. W. HARRISON, Prop. SWANNANOA P. O., N. C.

HOT AND COLD BATHS NO SICK PEOPLE TAKEN

RATES $6 TO $8 PER WEEK

THIS HOUSE is on the Southern Railroad, 11 miles east of Asheville, one-quarter of a mile from depot, express, telegraph and post-office, on a hill in the beautiful Valley of the Swannanoa River, with fine mountain scenery in all directions; 7 miles from Swannanoa Tunnel; 14 miles from Round Knob; 9 miles from George Vanderbilt's property; 10 miles from foot of Black Mountain; 18 miles from top of Mt. Mitchell, altitude 6,717 feet; 8 miles from Craggy Mountain, altitude 6,000 feet; 25 miles from Hickory Nut Falls; 28 miles from Mount Pisgah, altitude 5,757 feet; 28 miles from Chimney Rock; 28 miles from the Cave of the Wind Pools; 54 miles from Cezar's Head; 42 miles from Waynesville White Sulphur Springs; 23 miles from Blackwell's White Sulphur Springs; 48 miles from Hot Springs on French Broad River. Altitude of House 2,800 feet. Average winter temp. 38.1. Average summer temp. 71.9.

Telephone connections with Southern Bell Telephone and Telegraph Company.

This advertisement for Chestnut Hill, which Mrs. D.W. Harrison ran as a summer boardinghouse, lists the many tourist attractions in and around the Swannanoa Valley. (Courtesy of the Swannanoa Valley Museum.)

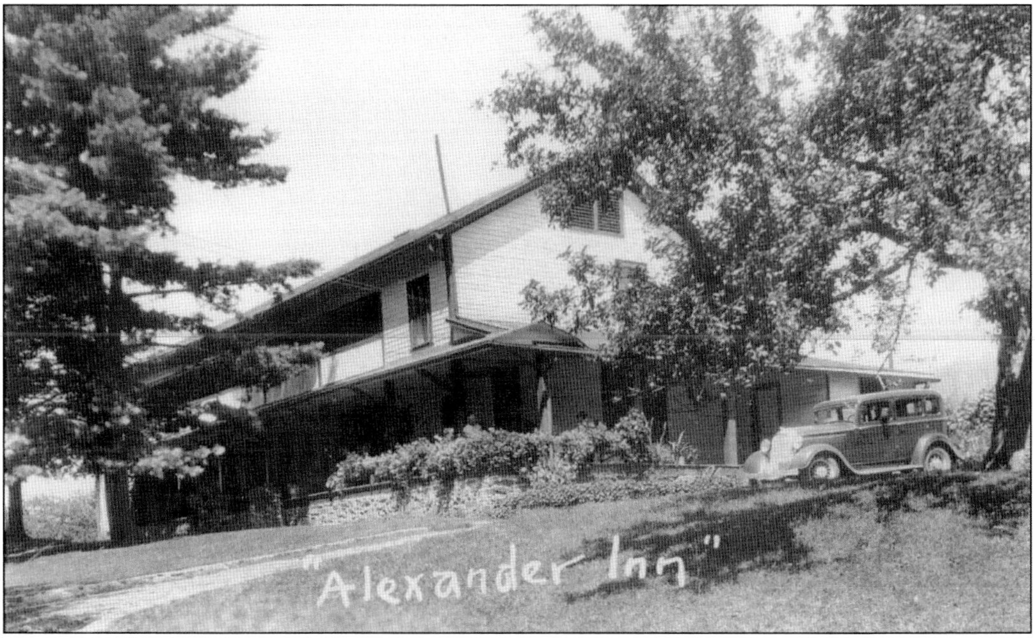

One of Swannanoa's first boardinghouses was the Alexander Inn (above). In 1819, George Couples Alexander, the son of James Alexander and Rhoda Cunningham, decided to build an inn on the stagecoach road—approximately where Old Route 70 runs today—that was bringing travelers through Swannanoa. Keeping up his land occupied his daylight hours, so he spent his nights building his inn, lit only by the burning of pine knots collected by his wife and children. He soon finished constructing the two-story log house, and the family opened the Alexander Inn to visitors by 1820. The Alexander Inn springhouse (below) is seen during the inn's heyday. (Both, courtesy of the Swannanoa Valley Museum, Bill Alexander collection.)

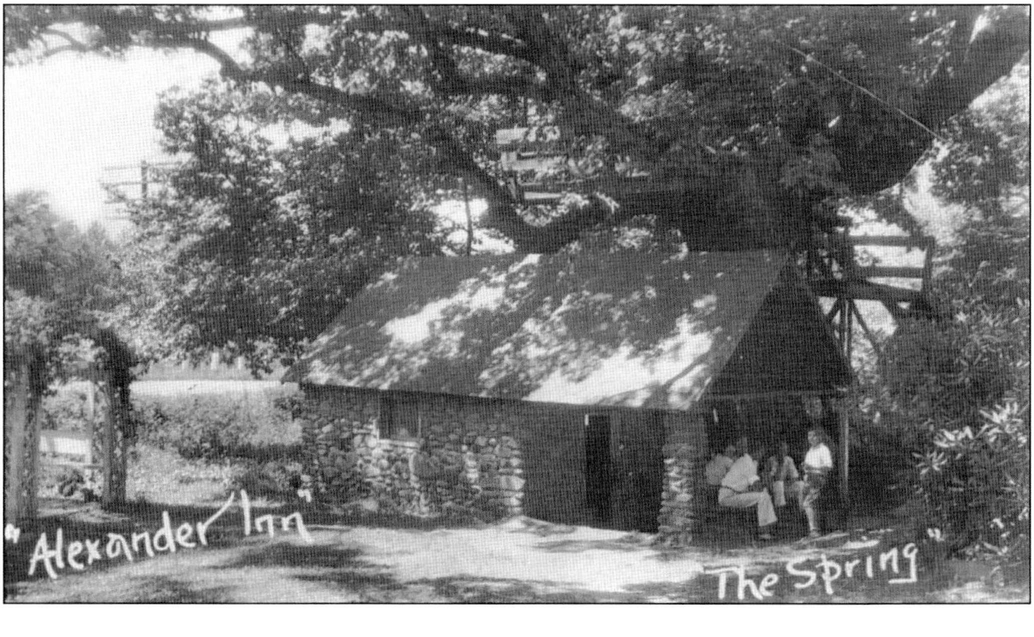

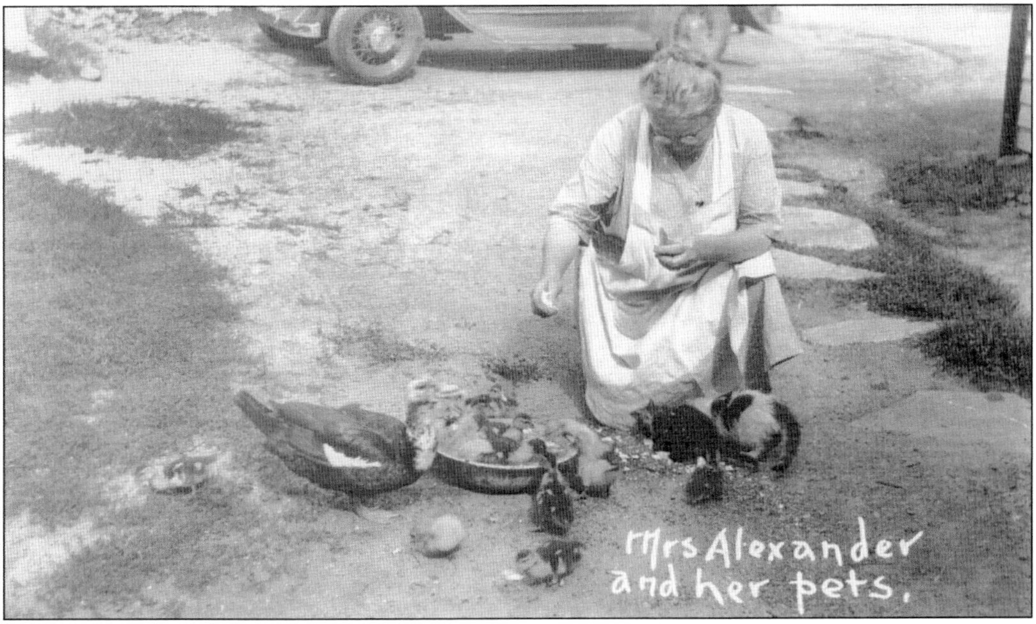

George C. Alexander transferred ownership of the Alexander Inn to his son George N. Alexander in 1869. Around this time, the inn doubled in size to keep up with the increased number of travelers to the Swannanoa Valley after the Civil War. George N. Alexander's nephew Rufus Davidson Alexander ran the inn with his wife, Carrie Cornelius Davidson, until his death in 1918, when Carrie took over care of the establishment. Though short in stature, Carrie Davidson Alexander, seen here with her pets, was a shrewd businesswoman determined to send her children to college. When Dr. E.W. Grove (see chapter five) came to Swannanoa looking for a tract of land, Carrie haggled with him for months until she got the price she wanted for the 275 acres of Alexander property that eventually became Grovemont-on-Swannanoa. (Courtesy of the Swannanoa Valley Museum, Bill Alexander collection.)

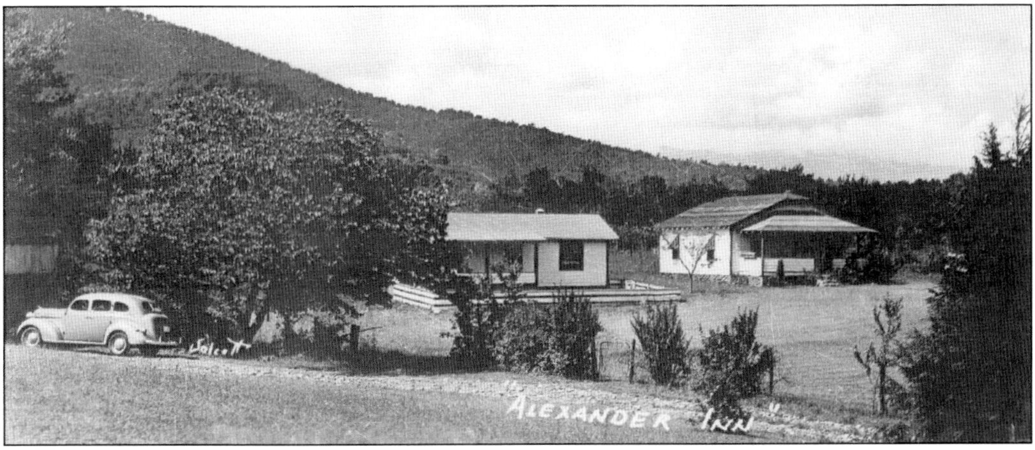

Because it was a stagecoach inn at Cooper's Station, the Alexander Inn housed coaches and horses in a long barn behind the inn. At this stop, horses were exchanged so travelers could continue the journey. The inn was about a day's ride from Asheville. Seen here are two of the guest cottages that were built in the early 1930s west of the big house. The cottage with a fenced-in yard is a two-bedroom, one-bathroom house with a porch but no kitchen. People staying at the cottage took their meals at the inn. (Courtesy of the Swannanoa Valley Museum, Bill Alexander collection.)

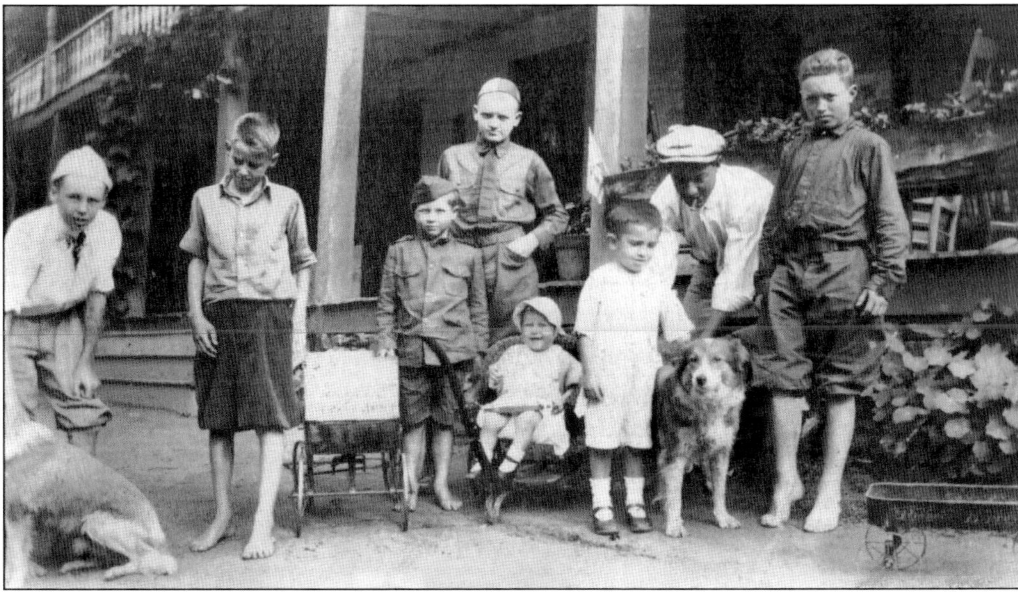

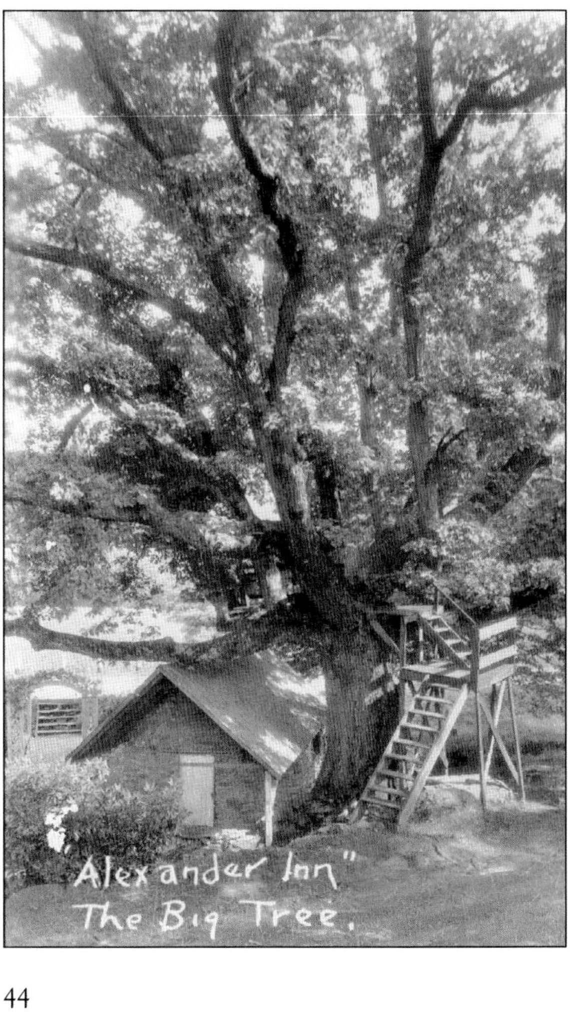

The Alexander Inn continued to host guests without interruption until 1949, when Carrie Davidson Alexander passed away. The inn then passed to Elizabeth Alexander Deal, Carrie's only daughter, who lived there until her death in 1982. Elizabeth passed the inn to her daughter Mary Deal Garner, who, upon her death in 2012, passed the inn to her granddaughter Carrie Garner Poteat. The Alexander children and the children of the inn's guests spent much of their time playing outdoors. Above, children gather outside the inn with some toys and their dogs. Seen at left is the big tree that stood beside the inn's springhouse and proved to be an ideal location for a tree house. (Above, courtesy of the Western Regional Archives, State Archives of North Carolina; left, courtesy of the Swannanoa Valley Museum, Bill Alexander collection.)

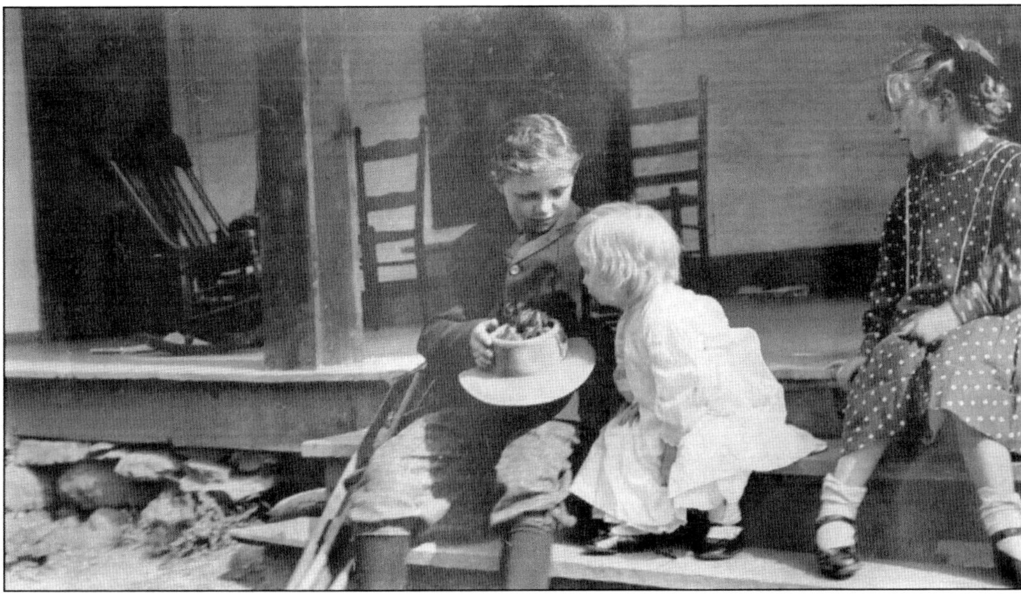

The original Alexander Inn, which is listed in the National Register of Historic Places, still stands on Old Route 70. It is the oldest structure lived in continuously by the same family in Buncombe County. While the inn was primarily operated by the Alexander family, the cooking and cleaning associated with a mid-sized inn, especially during the summer season, was done with the help of African American servants, including the Whitener family, who are seen below. Two African American families lived and worked at the inn. One family, who performed most of the domestic chores at the inn, lived in a small three-room house beside the barn. The other lived across the stagecoach road and worked the land as sharecroppers. (Both, courtesy of the Western Regional Archives, State Archives of North Carolina.)

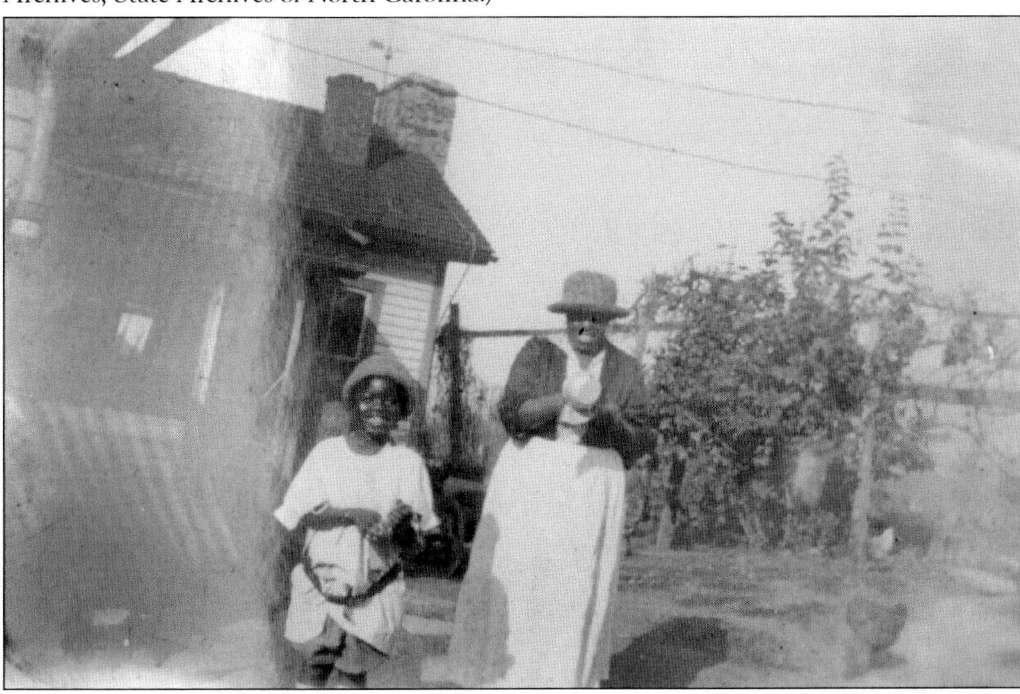

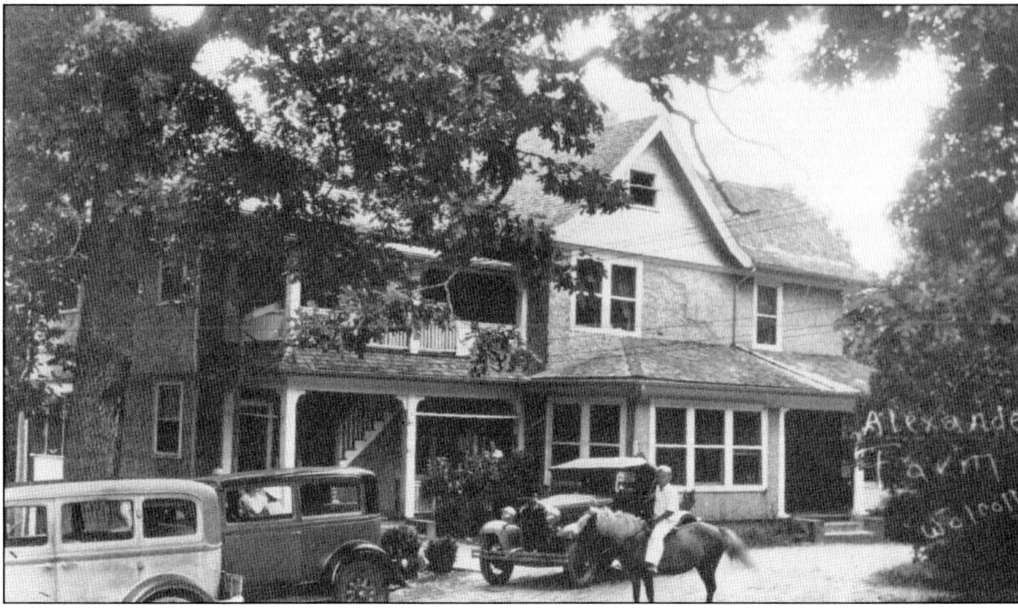

The Alexanders also owned and operated another boardinghouse in Swannanoa, known as Alexander Farm. The farm, near where Samuel Davidson first settled on Christian Creek, was operated by Charles Alexander. These 1930s photographs show Alexander Farm in its heyday. Below, guests play shuffleboard outside the inn. The inn was deconstructed by Warren Wilson College when they bought the property in 1956. Hikers on the college's trails can still see the stairs and the foundation of the house. (Both, courtesy of the Swannanoa Valley Museum.)

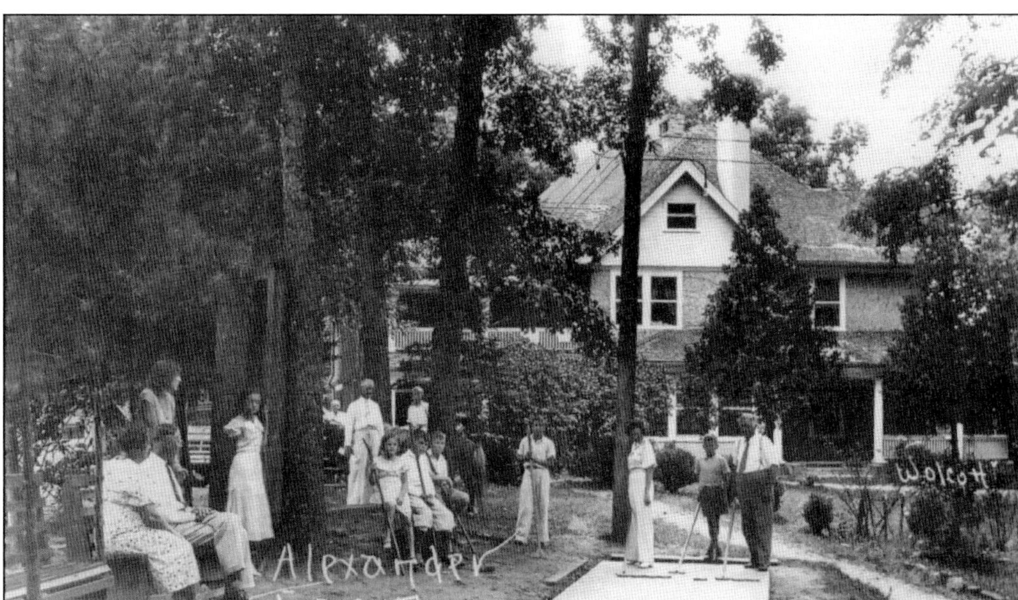

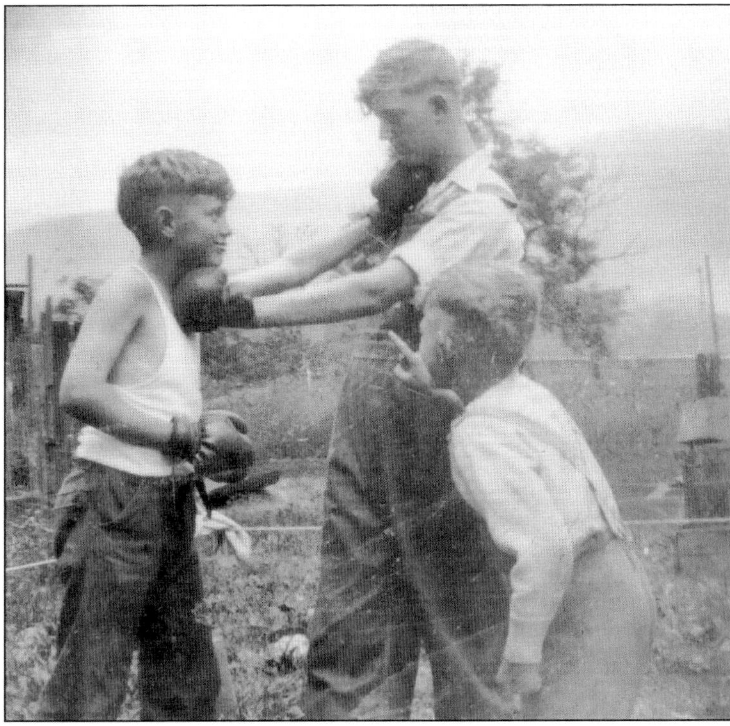

Swannanoa had ample opportunities for outdoor recreation for tourists and natives alike. Here, some local boys practice their boxing skills. (Courtesy of the Swannanoa Valley Museum, Penland Burgin collection.)

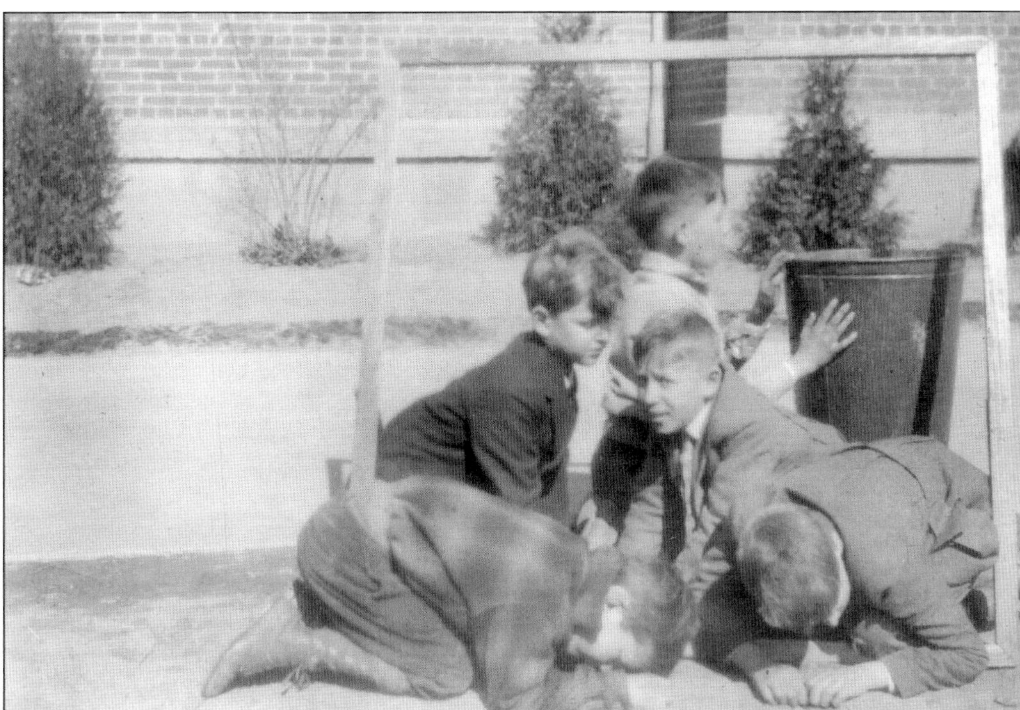

Without television, or even electricity in some places, children made their own fun. These friends plays outside their school. (Courtesy of the Swannanoa Valley Museum, Penland Burgin collection.)

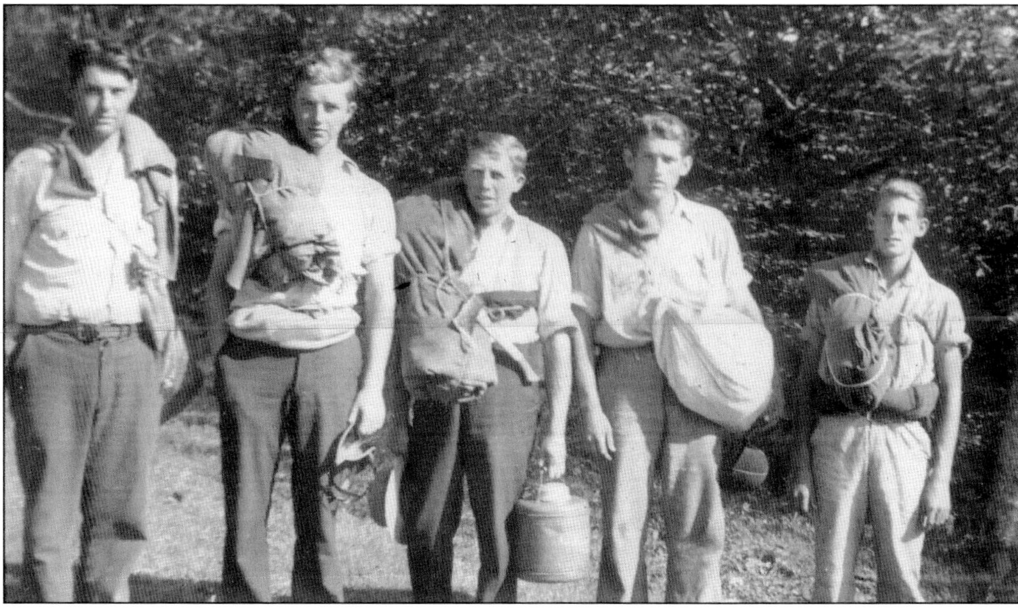

Camping was a popular pastime for tourists from the coast, who came for the beauty and climate of the Blue Ridge Mountains. This group of men prepares for a hiking trip to Mount Mitchell, which, at 6,684 feet above sea level, is the highest peak east of the Mississippi River and one of the main tourists attractions in the Swannanoa Valley area. (Courtesy of the Swannanoa Valley Museum, Penland Burgin collection.)

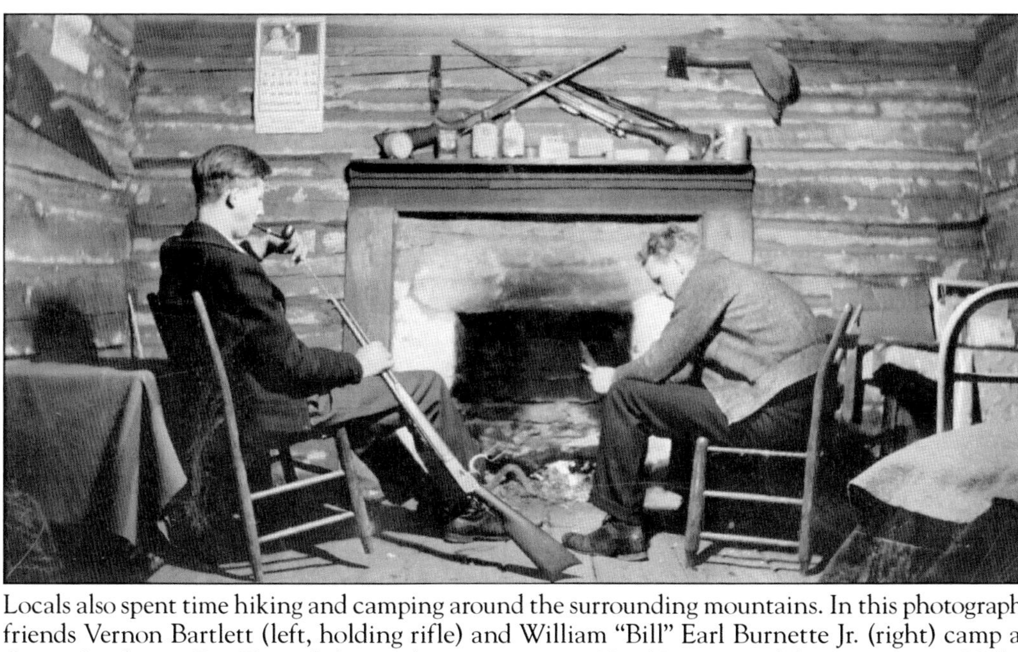

Locals also spent time hiking and camping around the surrounding mountains. In this photograph, friends Vernon Bartlett (left, holding rifle) and William "Bill" Earl Burnette Jr. (right) camp at Coggin's cabin in Bee Tree while on a hunting trip in 1934. (Courtesy of the Swannanoa Valley Museum, Cindy Medlock collection.)

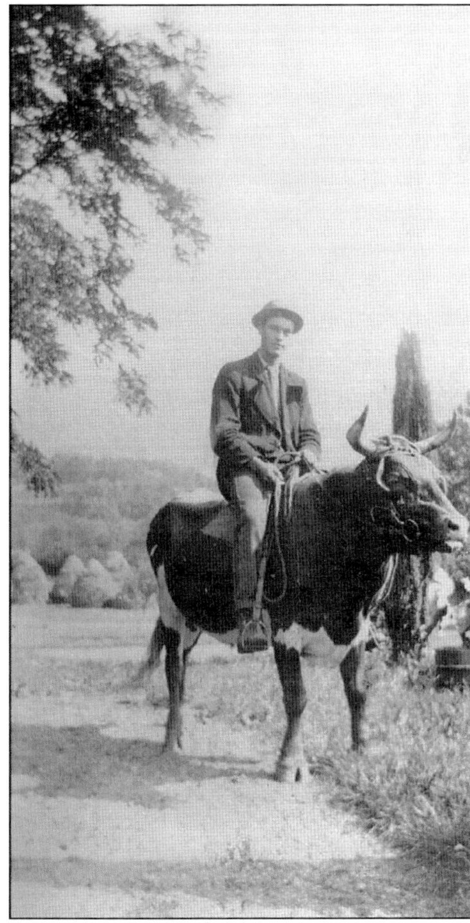

Before the coming of the railroad, tourists mainly arrived in Swannanoa via stagecoach, horseback, or wagon on the dirt road that ran up the mountain from Old Fort and continued into Asheville. Once they arrived, however, many tourists would get around in whatever way they could, whether by foot, mule, or bull. The visitors in these photographs make use of a bull (right) and a mule (below). (Both, courtesy of Swannanoa Valley Museum, the Penland Burgin collection.)

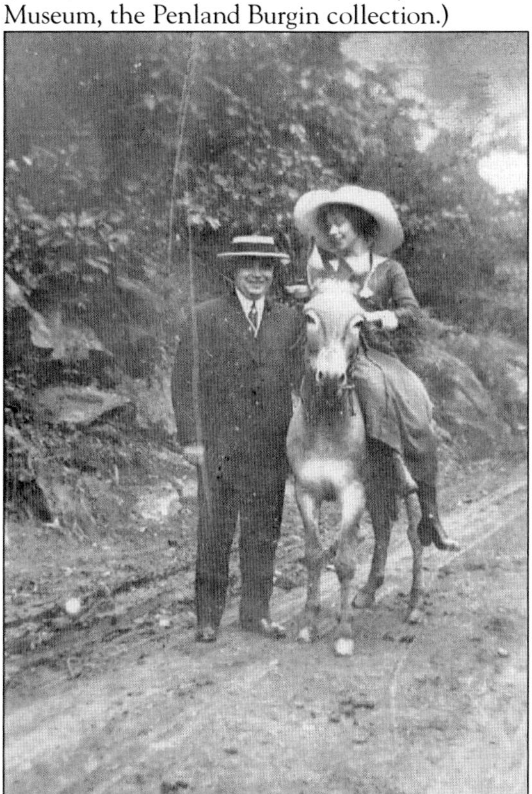

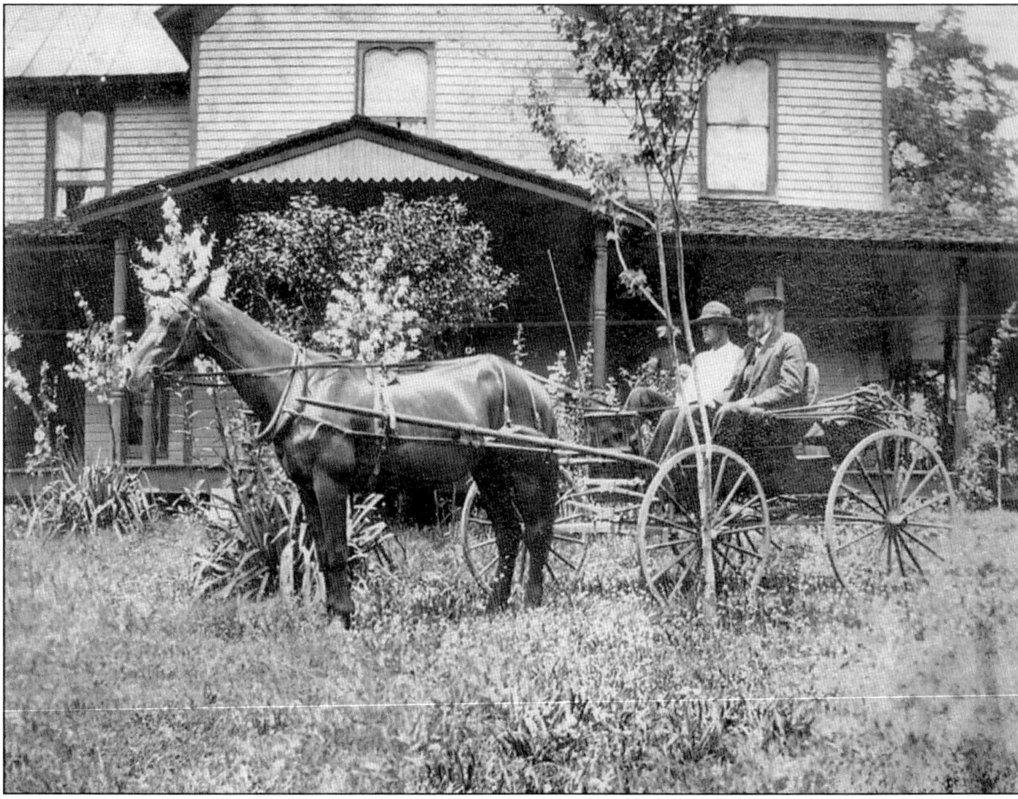

Most natives traveled around the community by wagon or on horseback. Here, Dr. Burgin (with beard) drives his carriage in front of his home, Penwood Farm. (Courtesy of the Swannanoa Valley Museum, Penland Burgin collection.)

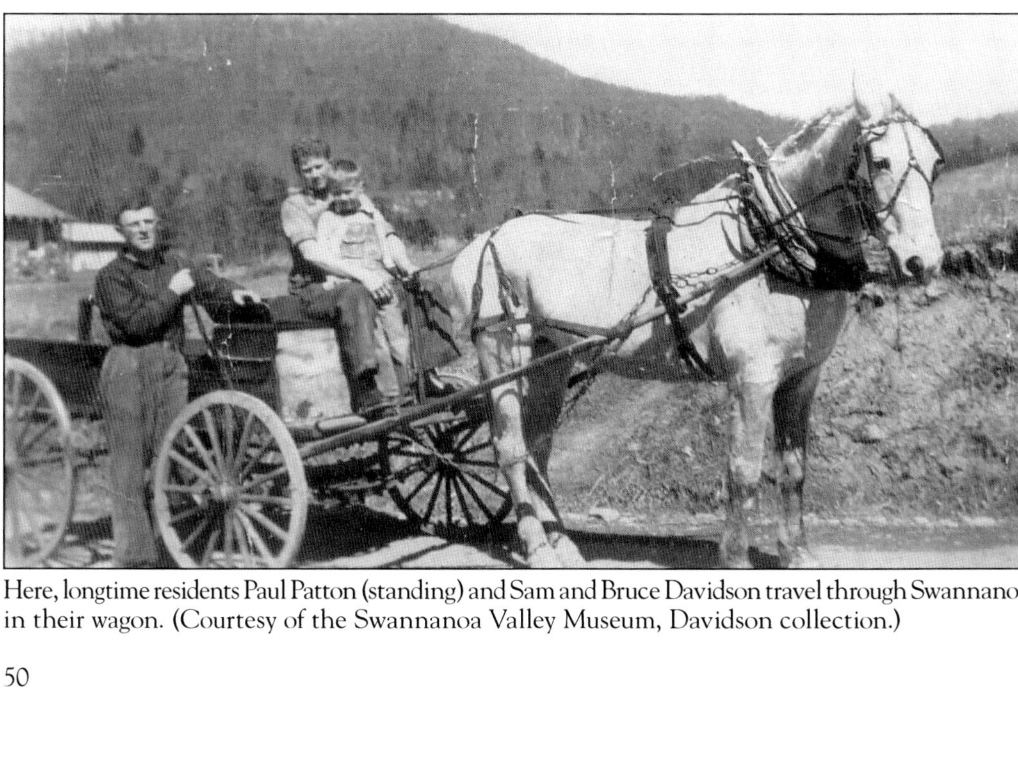

Here, longtime residents Paul Patton (standing) and Sam and Bruce Davidson travel through Swannanoa in their wagon. (Courtesy of the Swannanoa Valley Museum, Davidson collection.)

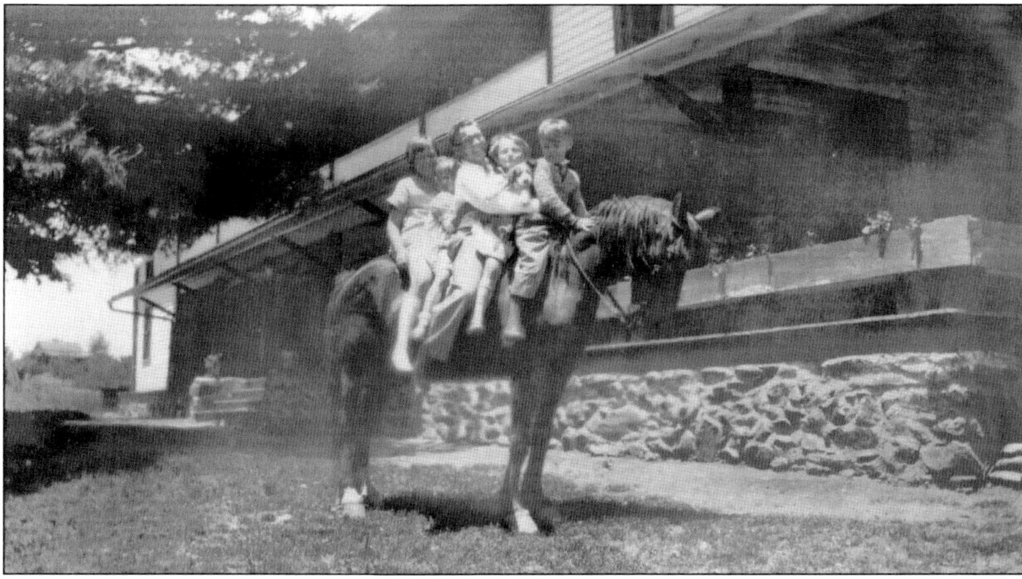

Oliver "Spec" Alexander (adult in center) sits bareback in front of the Alexander Inn with some of the children of the inn's summer boarders and Sandy the dog. (Courtesy of the Western Regional Archives, State Archives of North Carolina.)

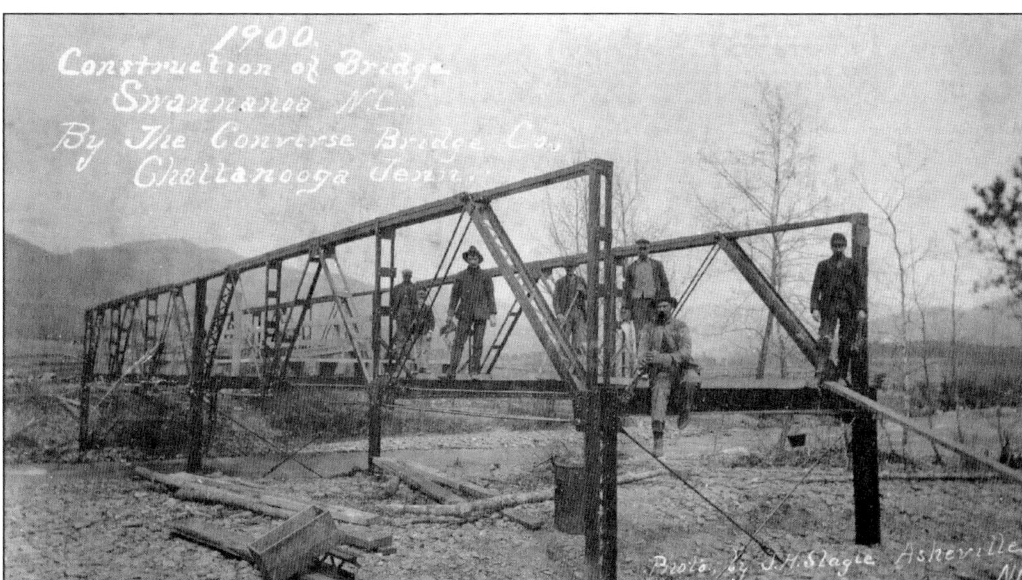

One of the earliest bridges across the Swannanoa River, seen here, was built in Swannanoa in 1900 by the Converse Bridge Company of Chattanooga, Tennessee. (Courtesy of the Swannanoa Valley Museum.)

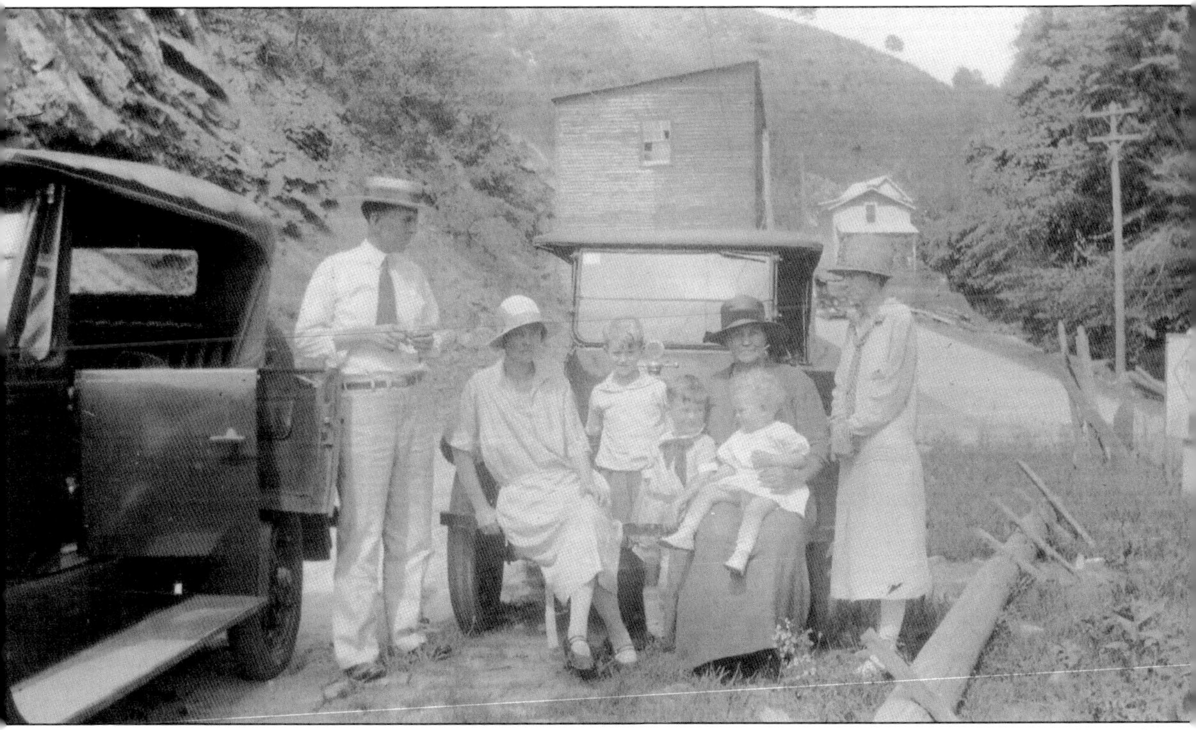

Trails up the mountains originally cleared by animals like buffalo, bear, and deer were followed by Native Americans. Soon after that, the trails became stagecoach and wagon roads, and then were converted into railroad beds when the railroad came to the valley in 1879. The railroads brought great changes to the Swannanoa Valley that lasted for decades. But as the automobile became an increasingly affordable and convenient alternative, much of the original rails were torn up to make way for improved automobile roads. Tourists soon preferred the control of taking their own vehicles on scenic drives through the mountains. Even today, the original buffalo route crossing the Blue Ridge at Swannanoa Gap and following the Swannanoa River remains the busiest artery connecting western North Carolina to the Piedmont region. (Courtesy of the Swannanoa Valley Museum, Penland Burgin collection.)

Four

Daylight Enters Buncombe County

The Railroad Brings Business

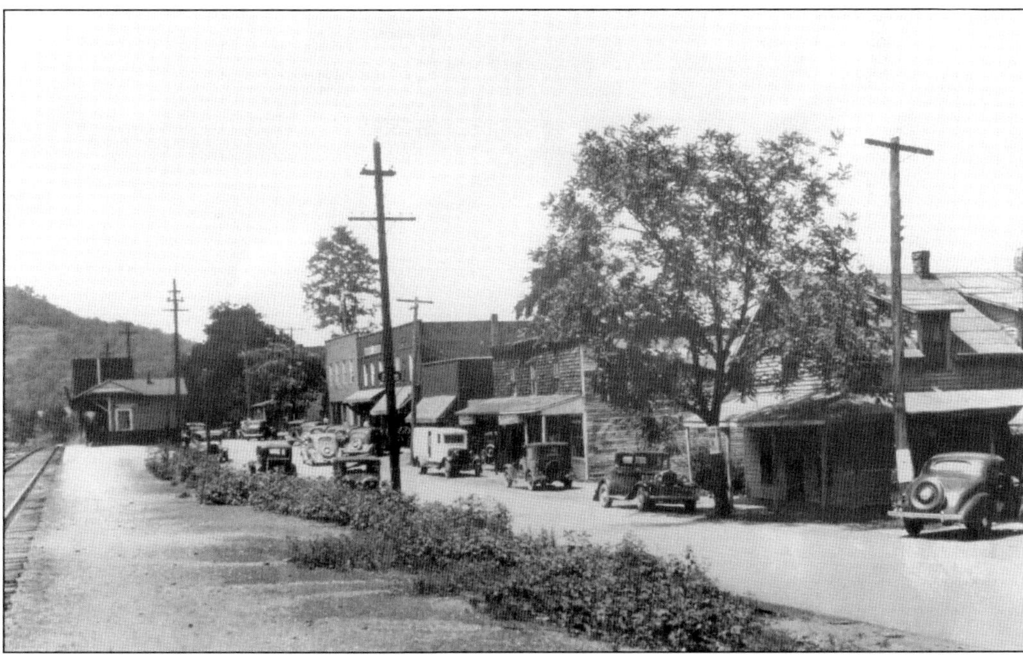

Because of the steep grade between Old Fort and Black Mountain, as well as the disruption of the Civil War, the railroad did not come to Swannanoa until the late 1870s. Constructing the railroad up the mountain was a feat of human engineering that took the lives of more than 100 of the approximately 500 convicts who worked in chain gangs to complete the line. Seven tunnels—the longest of which, Swannanoa Tunnel, is 1,822 feet long—and 70 miles of track later, "daylight entered Buncombe County," as was telegraphed to Gov. Zebulon B. Vance upon completion of the tunnel, and Swannanoa was connected by rail to the rest of North Carolina on March 11, 1879. With the coming of the railroad, businesses migrated to the rail centers. Railroad Street in downtown Swannanoa, seen in this Herbert W. Pelton photograph, was the business hub for the town in 1933. (Courtesy of the Swannanoa Valley Museum.)

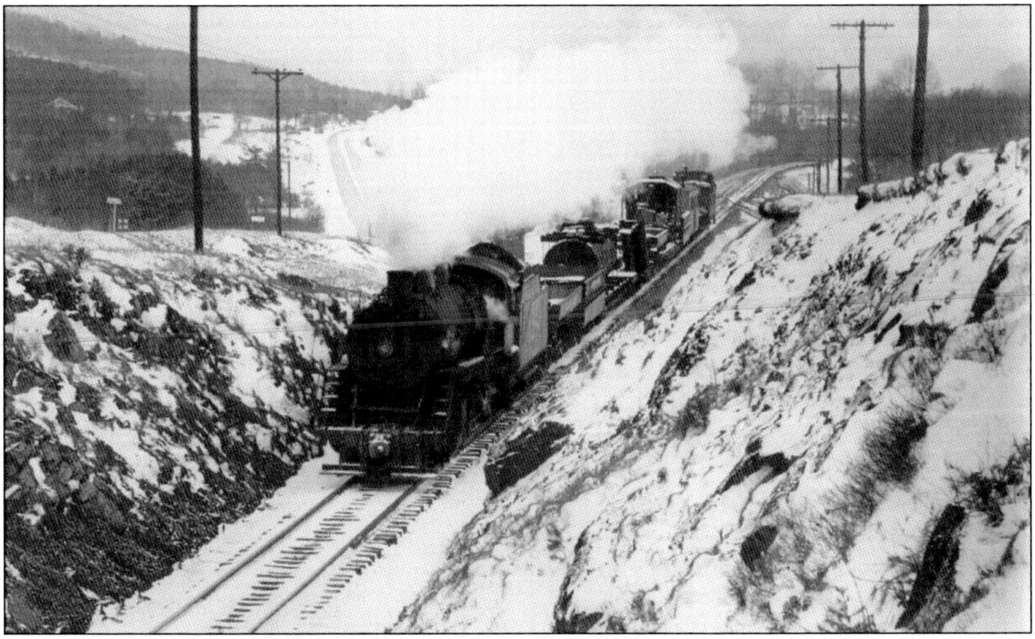

Many passenger trains arrived and departed daily in Swannanoa. Most commercial goods were also transported via railroad. In fact, the impetus for extending the railroad into western North Carolina was the drought of 1845, which resulted in crop failure for many mountain farms and left many families without enough food to survive the cold winter. Because of the lack of train service, families were not able to import enough goods from outside of the region. Political leaders demanded the state pursue linking western North Carolina via rail with the rest of the state. In this photograph taken by Noah Rozzell, a train passes through Buckeye Cove in Swannanoa. (Courtesy of the Swannanoa Valley Museum, Noah Rozzell collection.)

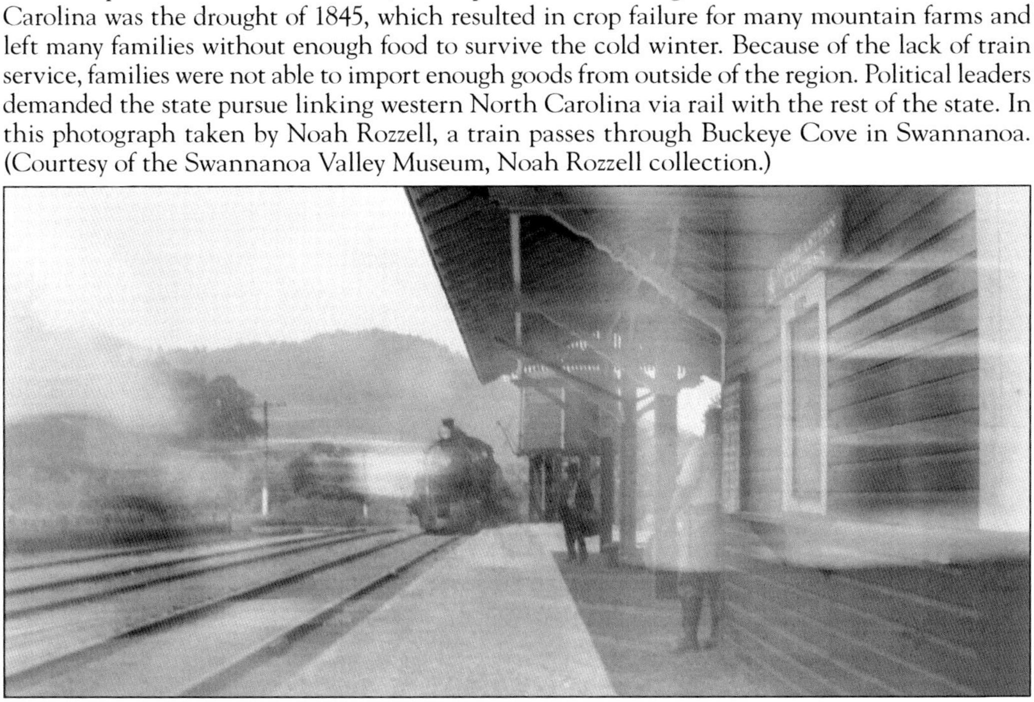

During the first 16 years of its existence, the Swannanoa train station was known as Cooper's Station, the name of the old stagecoach stop at the Alexander Inn. On February 6, 1895, a petition filed by the residents of Swannanoa requested a name change so that the station and the town would have the same name. Here, a train approaches the station in the early 1900s. (Courtesy of Brenda Parks Hughes.)

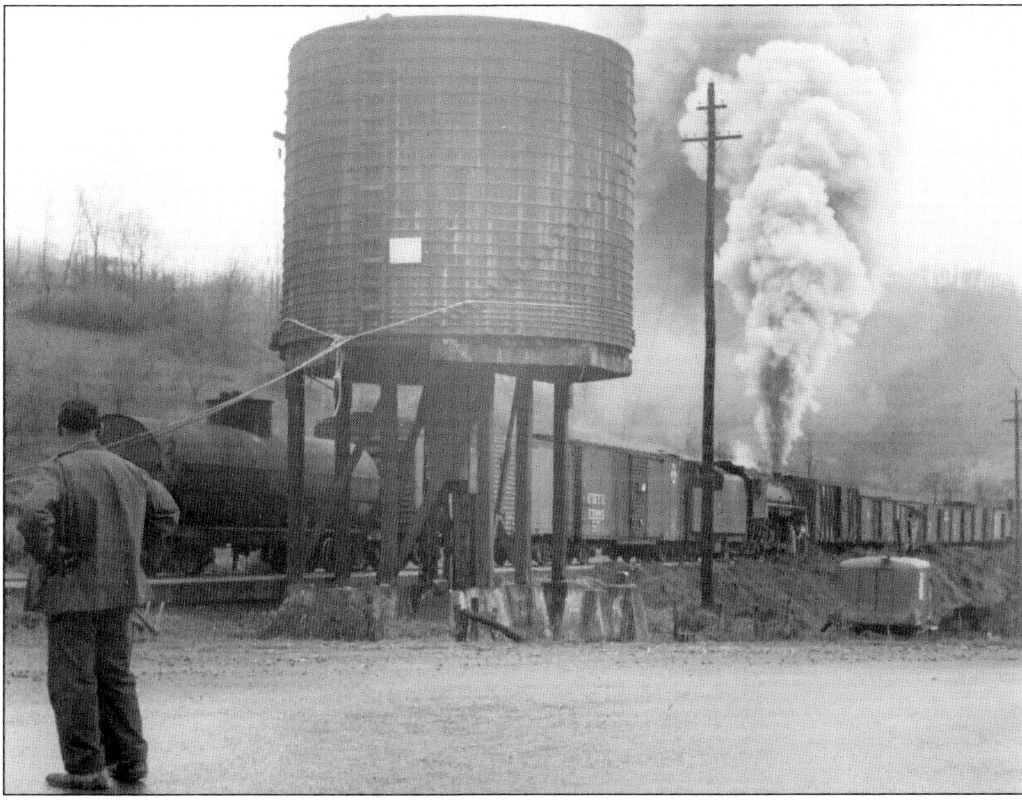

To the west of Swannanoa station was a water tower. This Noah Rozzell photograph shows a station worker watching a Southern Railway train run past the water tower around 1950. Water towers originated with the steam engine and were used to replenish the train with water. (Courtesy of the Swannanoa Valley Museum, Noah Rozzell collection.)

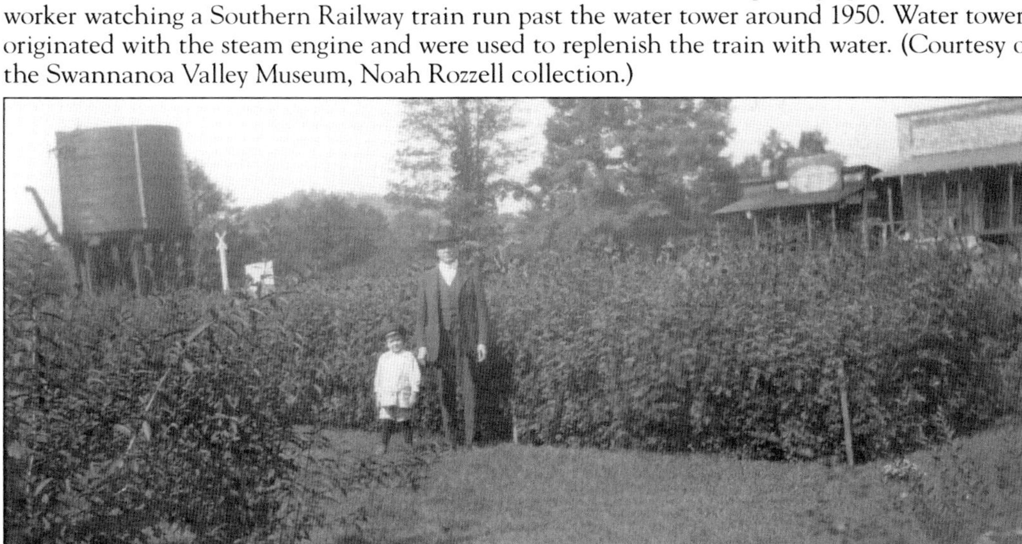

Stationmaster W.J. Parks and his son, James, stand in the flower garden planted between Swannanoa station and the water tower. Before the station's name changed in 1895, there were two general stores in Cooper's Station, one owned by George Hyams and the other by William Wilson, according to an oral history given by G.A. Burgin in 1955. Residents could sell things to Hyams, but they would only be paid in goods from his store. (Courtesy of Brenda Parks Hughes.)

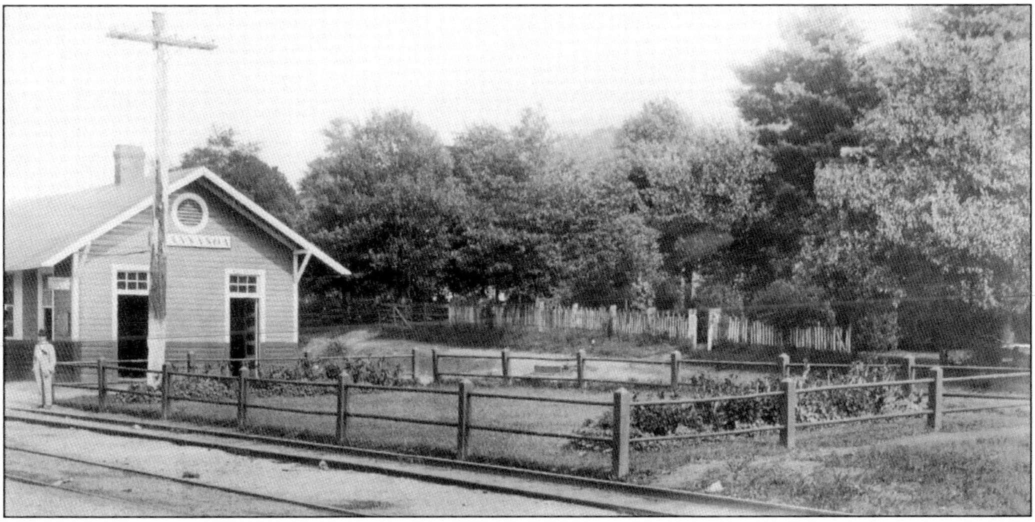

This photograph was taken for a December 1918 *Southern News Bulletin* article about the Swannanoa station and its stationmaster, Walter J. "W.J." Parks. The article reads, "Beautiful Garden in Swannanoa: An excellent example of what can be accomplished in the way of improving station grounds is illustrated in the picture above showing the attractive flower garden planted by Agent W.J. Parks at the Southern Railroad station at Swannanoa. When Mr. Parks was placed in charge of this station a few years ago, the grounds were in a very unkempt condition but by untiring efforts he has improved them until this year his flower garden was considered the most beautiful of any on the Asheville Division. Mr. Parks takes great pains in keeping his station grounds clean and his office tidy and has been highly commended for his efforts. His flowers are not only enjoyed and appreciated by the local community but he has received a great many compliments from the traveling public and from the railroad officials. Entering the service of the Southern in 1906 as bill clerk at Thomasville, NC, Mr. Parks was promoted to agent at Davidson, NC in May, 1907, and since has served in that capacity continuously at Davidson and Swannanoa. He has established a record for courtesy to the public, never having had a single complaint or suit to arise at his station during his twelve years of service as agent." (Courtesy of Brenda Parks Hughes.)

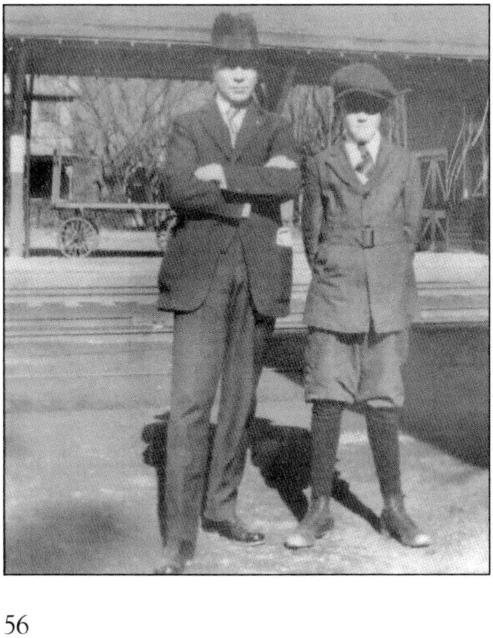

Parks is seen here with his son Walter Jr. near the entrance to the Southern Railroad station in Swannanoa in 1921. The passenger shed in the right background was built in 1919 to serve the increasing volume of summer visitors that began coming following World War I. The Wilson residence is in the left background. (Courtesy of Millie Parks Ogletree.)

W.J. Parks was one of the many businessmen to take advantage of the new train stop in Swannanoa and the shoppers it brought. He opened several businesses on Railroad Street, including a grocery store and a coal company, both of which are noted in this advertisement. (Courtesy of Brenda Parks Hughes.)

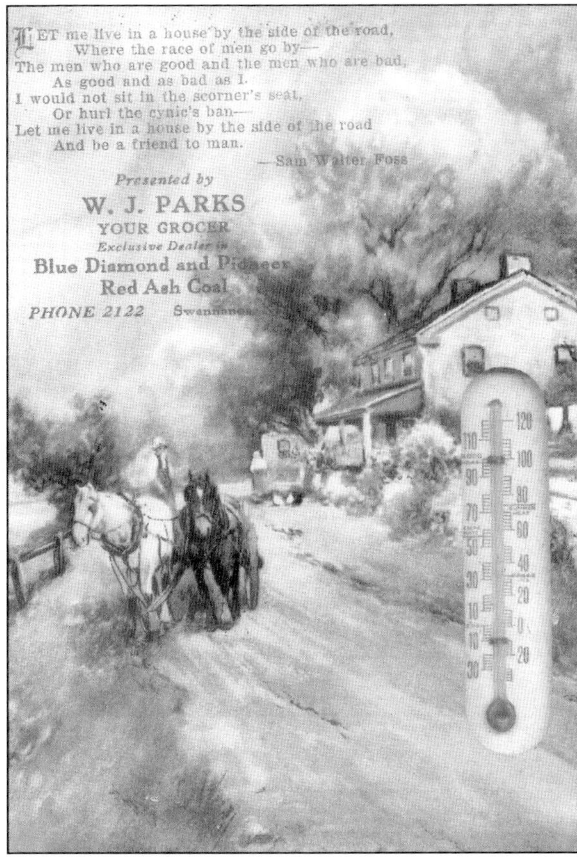

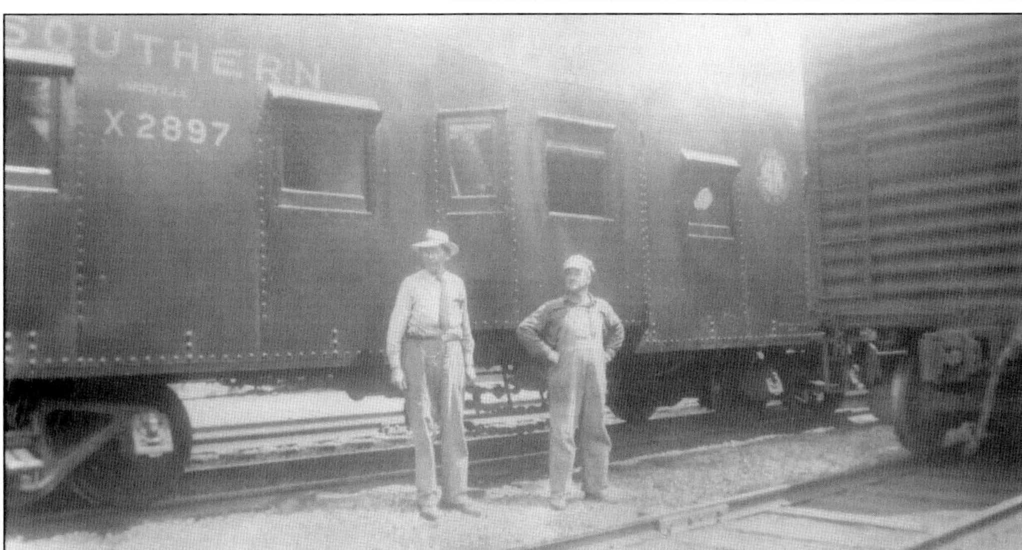

The Western North Carolina Railroad operated until 1886, when it was taken over by the Richmond & Danville Railroad. In 1896, the Southern Railway Company took control of the railroad. Jack Hughes (right) was an engineer for the Southern Railway Company. (Courtesy of Brenda Park Hughes.)

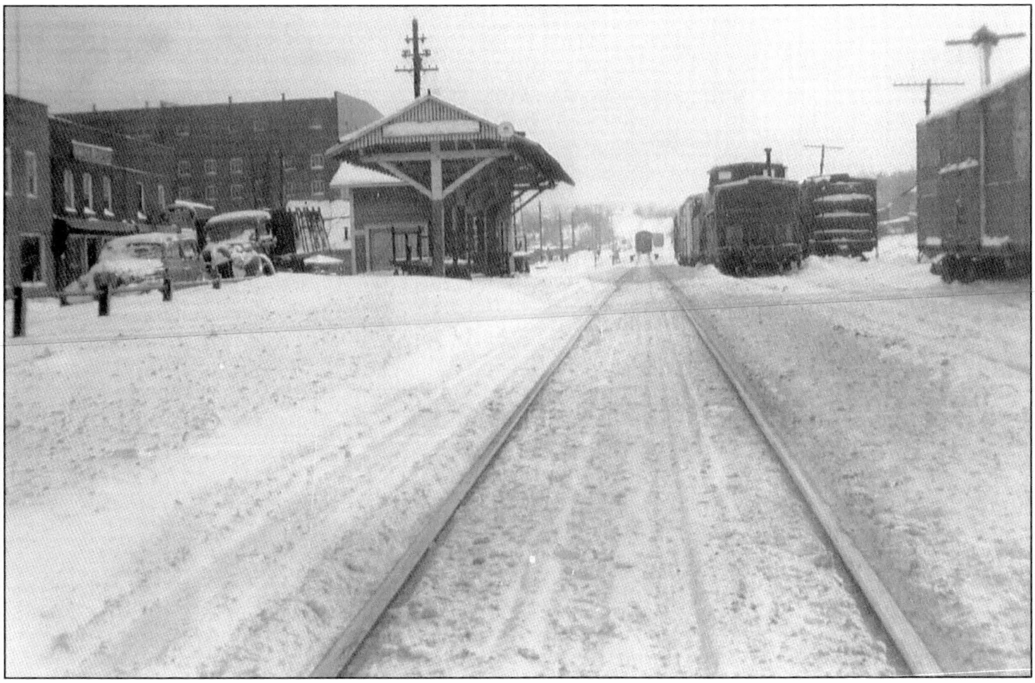

Regular passenger service to Asheville ended in 1975, but the area still attracts hundreds of thousands of visitors each year. This photograph of the train tracks covered in snow shows the station as well as several Railroad Street businesses. (Courtesy of Brenda Parks Hughes.)

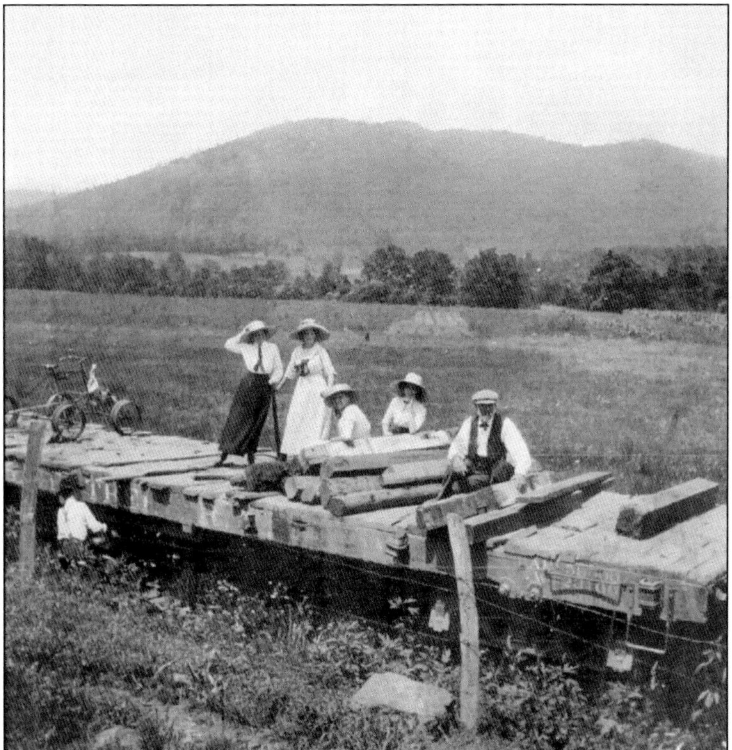

The railroad was and continues to be a source of fascination for tourists to the area. In 2013, the railroad began to sponsor a steam-engine passenger-train trip from Asheville to Old Fort, which follows the railroad line that transported tourists to the area for almost a century. Here, members of the Penland and Burgin families enjoy riding the rails. (Courtesy of the Swannanoa Valley Museum, Penland Burgin collection.)

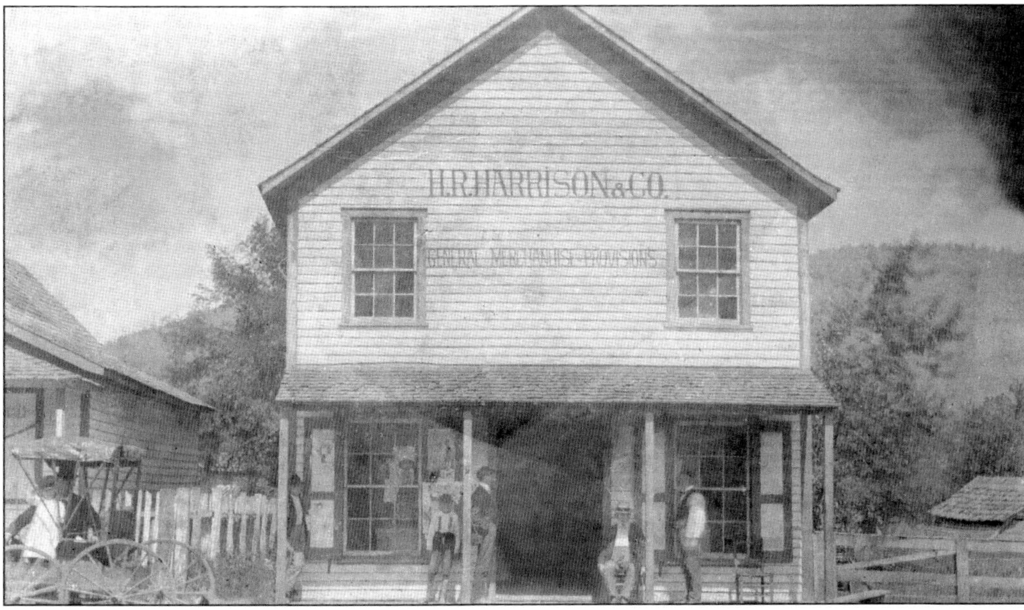

After getting off the train, tourists needed to buy supplies for their summer stays, so many general provision stores operated near the train stations. There were also often several stables within walking distance of the train, to provide wagon and carriage transport to tourists from the station to their boardinghouse or hotel. H.R. Harrison & Co., a general merchandise and provision store near the Swannanoa station, is seen here in 1890. (Courtesy of the Swannanoa Valley Museum.)

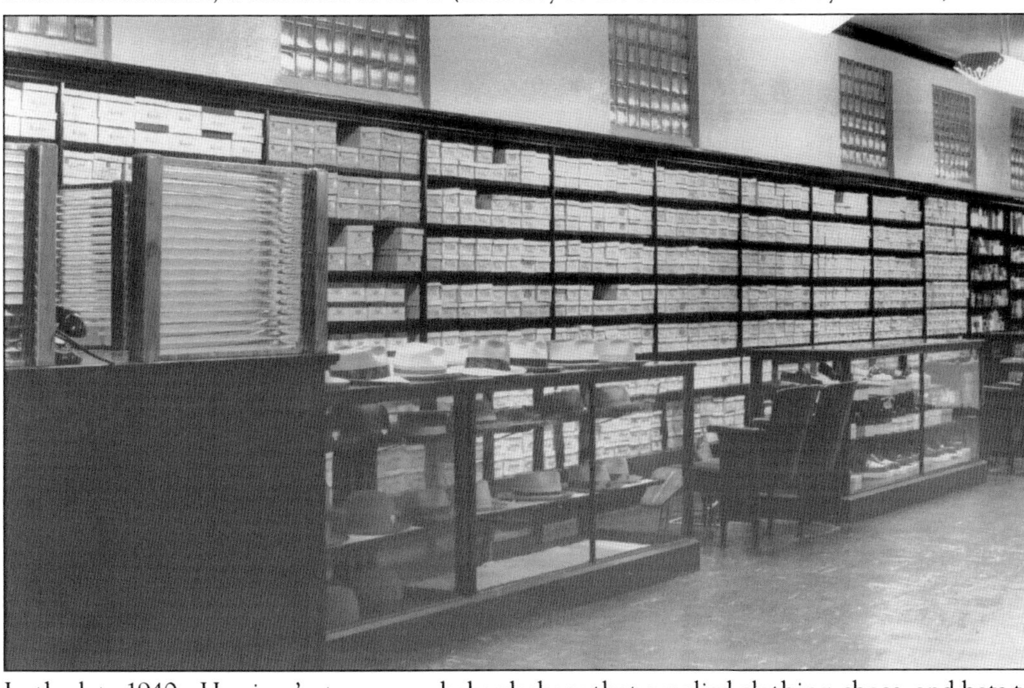

In the late 1940s, Harrison's store was a haberdashery that supplied clothing, shoes, and hats to visitors and locals. H.W. Harrison also had a furniture store in the same building, located directly across Railroad Street from the train station. (Courtesy of the Swannanoa Valley Museum, Noah Rozzell collection.)

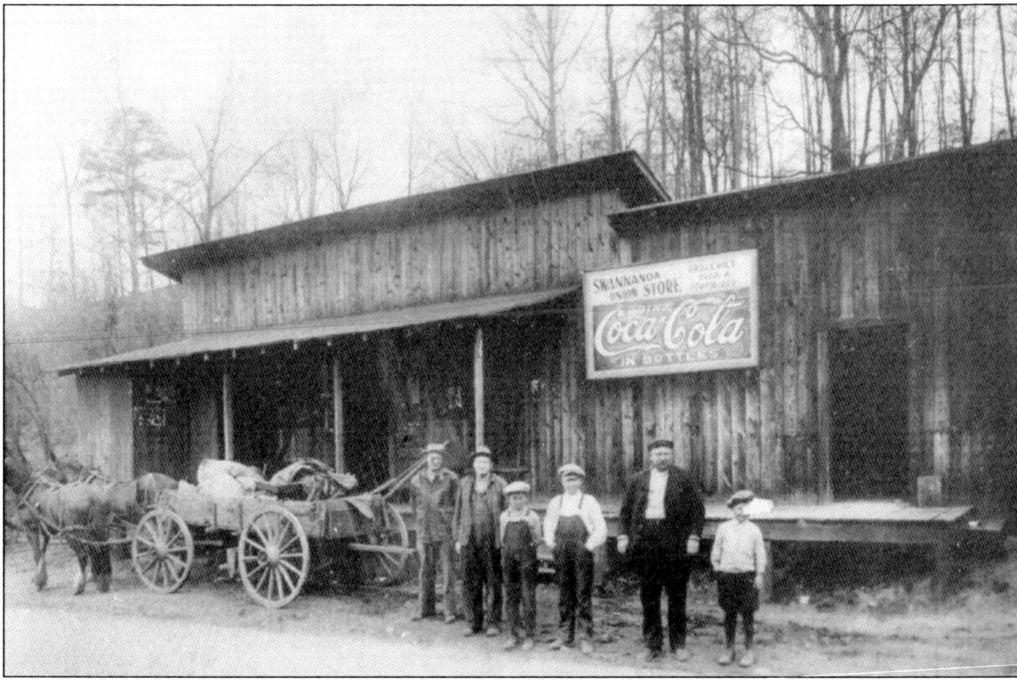

Another general provision store in early Swannanoa was the Swannanoa Union Store, which sold groceries, feed, and fertilizer. Coca-Cola became one of the first corporate sponsors in the area by providing signs to country stores. (Courtesy of the Swannanoa Valley Museum.)

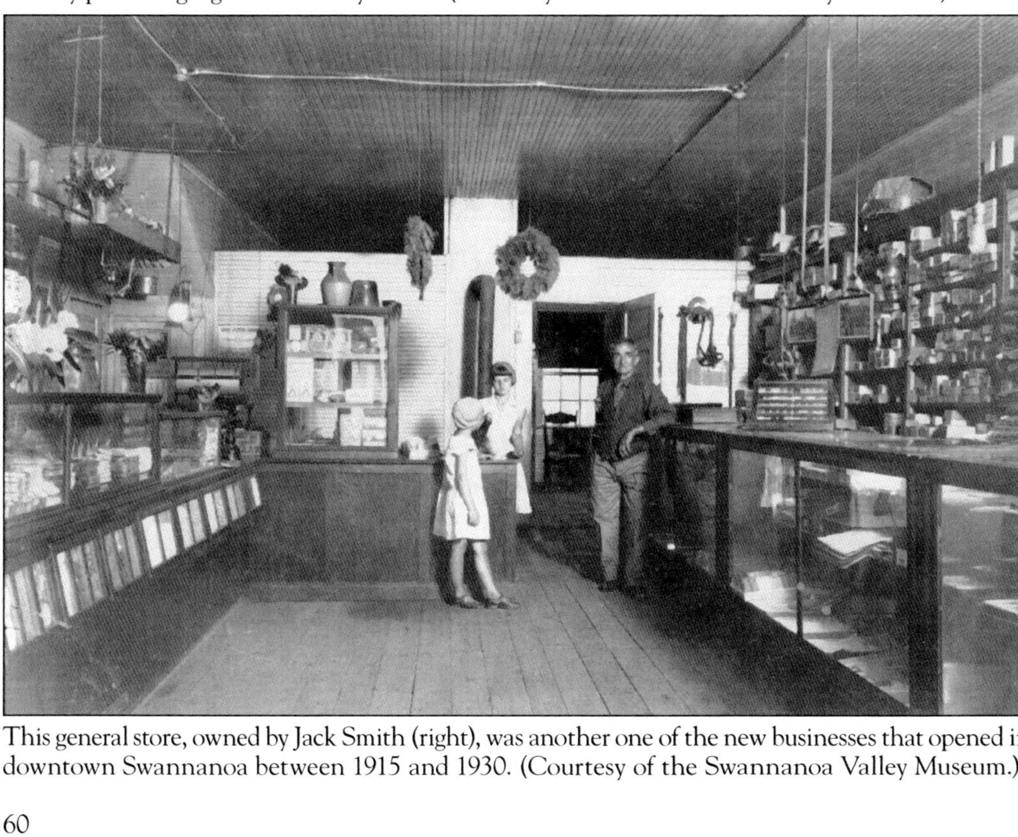

This general store, owned by Jack Smith (right), was another one of the new businesses that opened in downtown Swannanoa between 1915 and 1930. (Courtesy of the Swannanoa Valley Museum.)

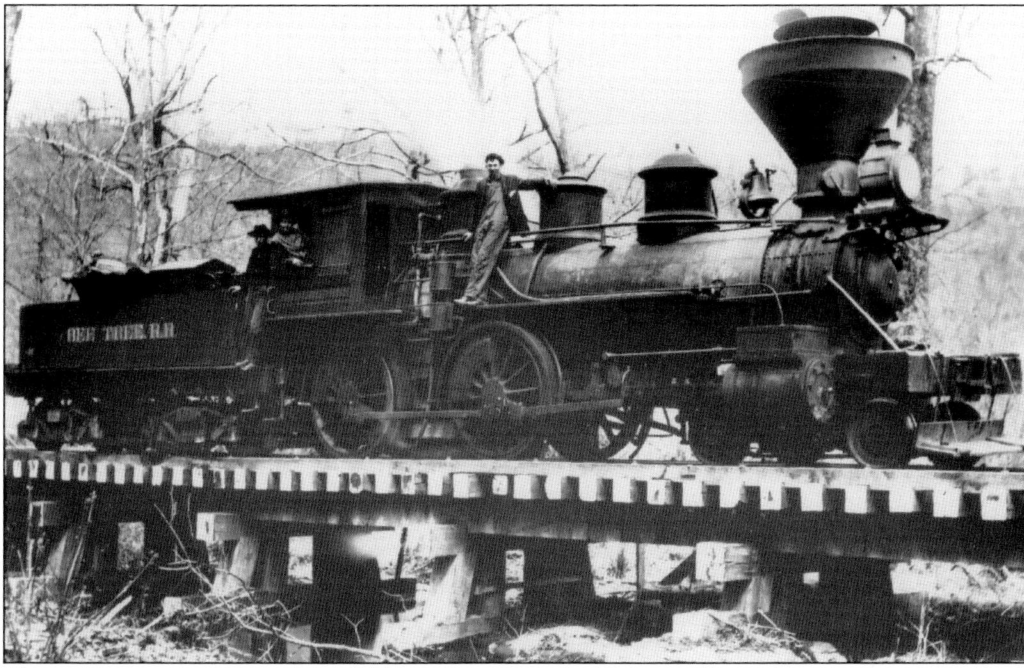

The Swannanoa Valley, while emerging as a mecca for tourists seeking a healing climate, was also becoming known for its harvestable timber. Many logging companies built rail lines up to previously untouched valley land. One of these was the Bee Tree Lumber Company. Seen here is one of the engines that pulled carloads of timber up and down the mountain. (Courtesy of the Swannanoa Valley Museum.)

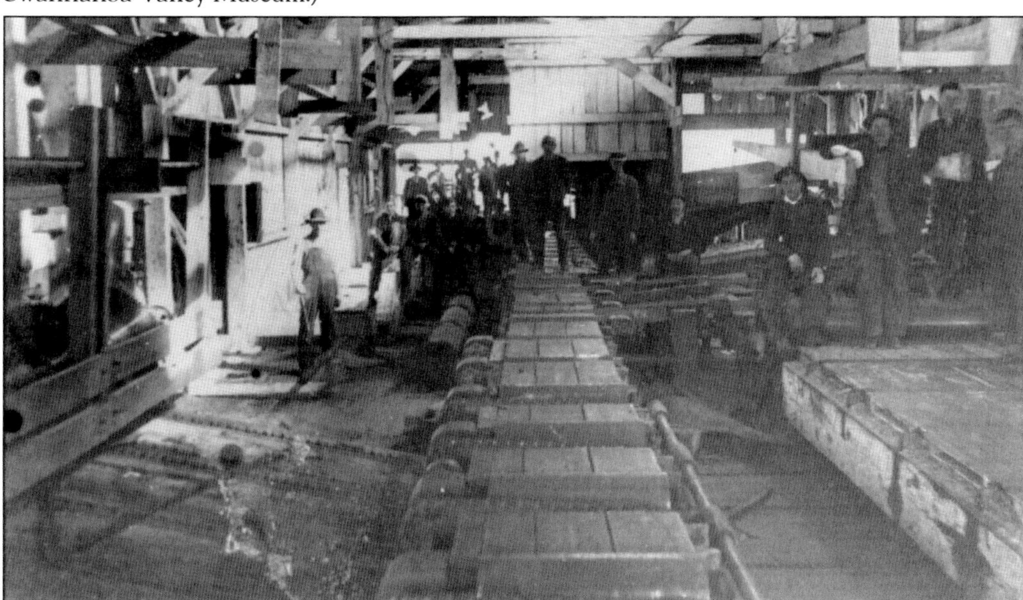

The Craggy Lumber Company was established in the Bee Tree community in 1903 and was replaced by the Bee Tree Lumber Company in 1910. The lumber mill was at the base of the Craggies, at the head of the Bee Tree Valley. The interior of the Bee Tree sawmill is seen here in 1913. (Courtesy of the Swannanoa Valley Museum, Catherine Pruett collection.)

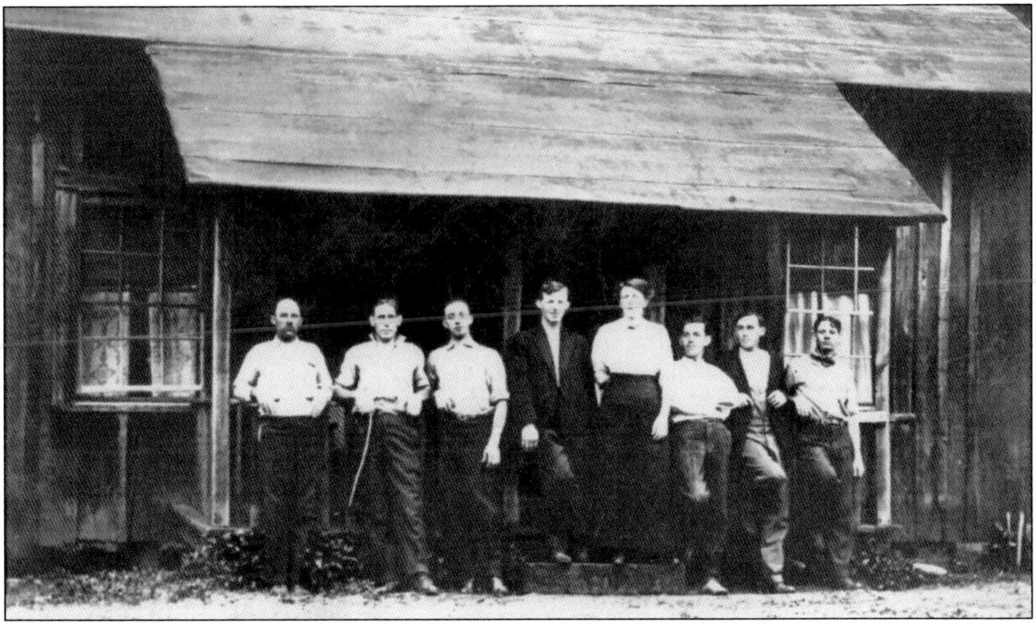

With the logging railroad came the company store, advertised as "a large general store, a meat market and a post office, all under one roof." These 1913 photographs show the company's mill, located at the confluence of Bee Tree Creek and Spruce Fork, which contained a post office and the store. The company also had a camp kitchen and a boardinghouse. The Bee Tree Lumber Company was in operation until the great flood of 1916, which washed away most of the railroad, submerged or destroyed most of the mill, and successfully ended most of the logging operations in the Swannanoa Valley. (Above, courtesy of the Swannanoa Valley Museum, Catherine Pruett collection; below, courtesy of the Swannanoa Valley Museum.)

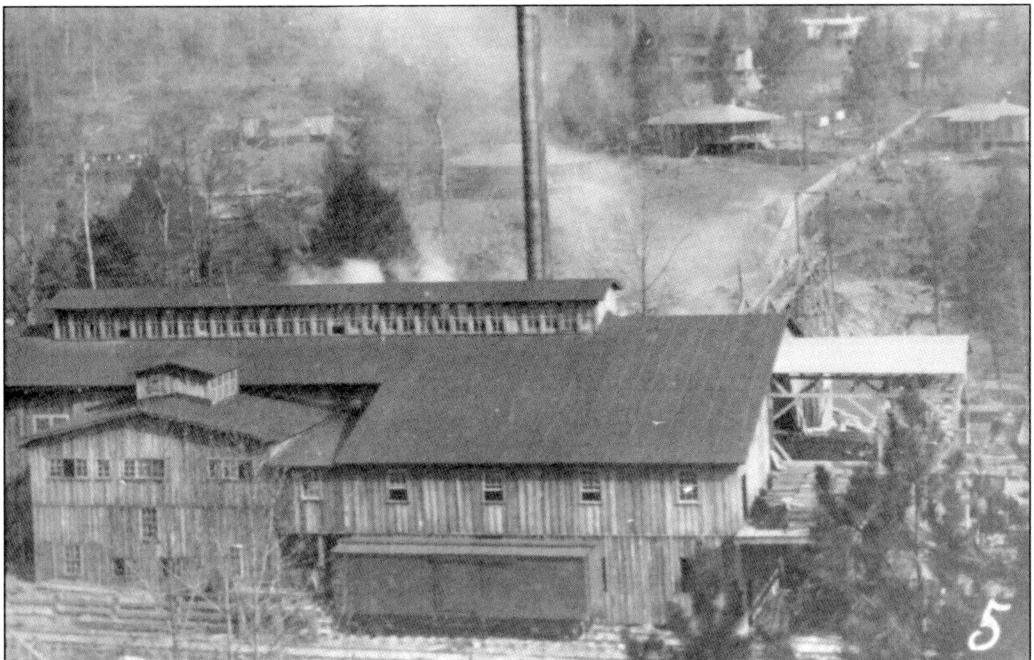

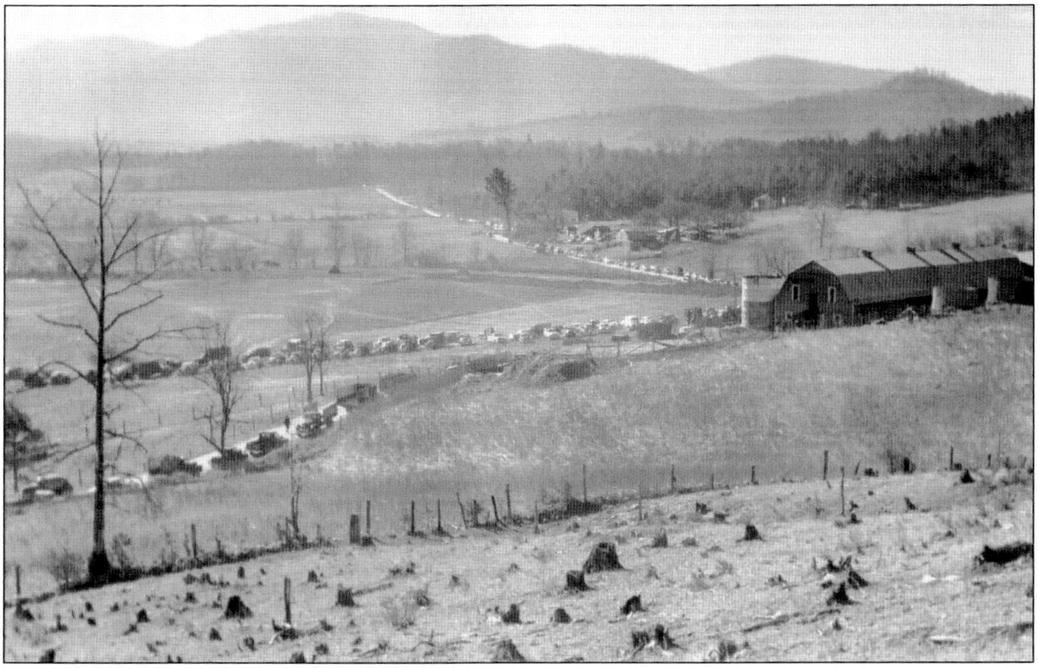

The land in the Swannanoa Valley, like in much of Appalachia, was often exploited, and not just for its timber or mineral wealth. In 1951, W.C. Shope auctioned his dairy and farm equipment after selling his land, on Greggs Branch in the Bee Tree community of Swannanoa, to Oerlikon Tool and Arms Corporation, a Swiss company. These two photographs offer different views of the dairy auction. The land, which had originally been settled in the late 1700s by the Alexander family, was sold several times before being purchased by Chemtronics in 1978. Chemtronics began to produce hallucinogenic chemical warfare agents and tear gas. Though Chemtronics is now defunct, the land has been declared a Superfund site by the Environmental Protection Agency and is currently unusable due to its dangerous levels of organic compounds, heavy metals, and dissolved solids. In 2013, a community advisory group was formed to address cleaning up the site. (Both, courtesy of the Swannanoa Valley Museum, Noah Rozzell collection.)

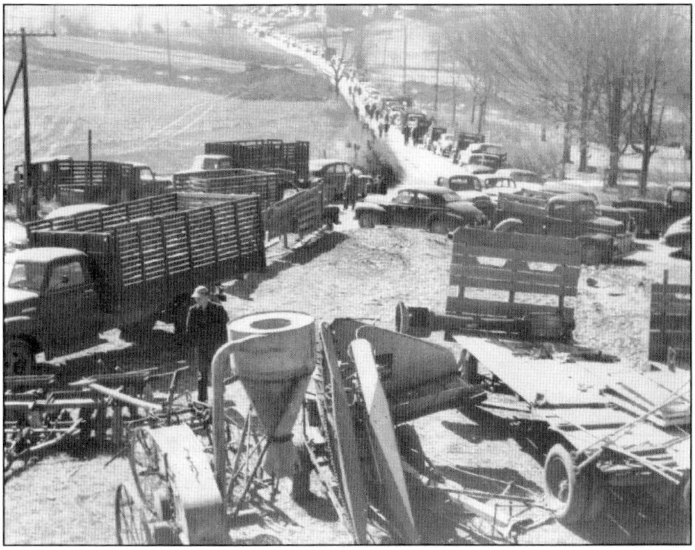

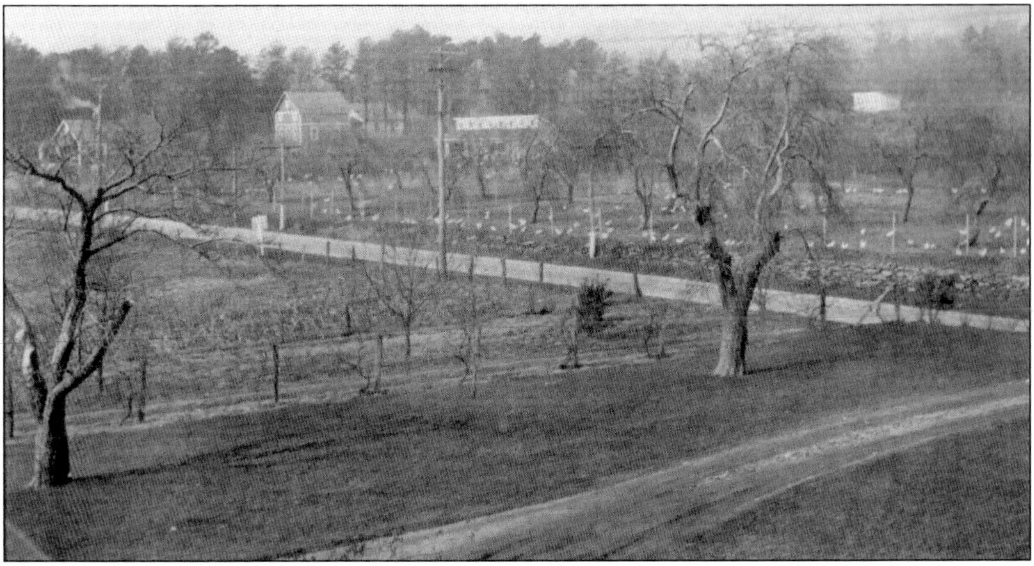

Not all use of the land by large organizations was exploitative, however. Seen here is the Mountain Agricultural Research Station, also known as the North Carolina Agricultural Test Farm, which was established in 1908 on a piece of land purchased from the Alexander family. The programs at the test farm looked to provide mountain farmers information on better ways to raise crops and livestock in a mountain climate. The station was moved to its present 398-acre location in Haywood County during World War II, when the US Army chose the Swannanoa site as a location for a new Army hospital. (Courtesy of the Swannanoa Valley Museum.)

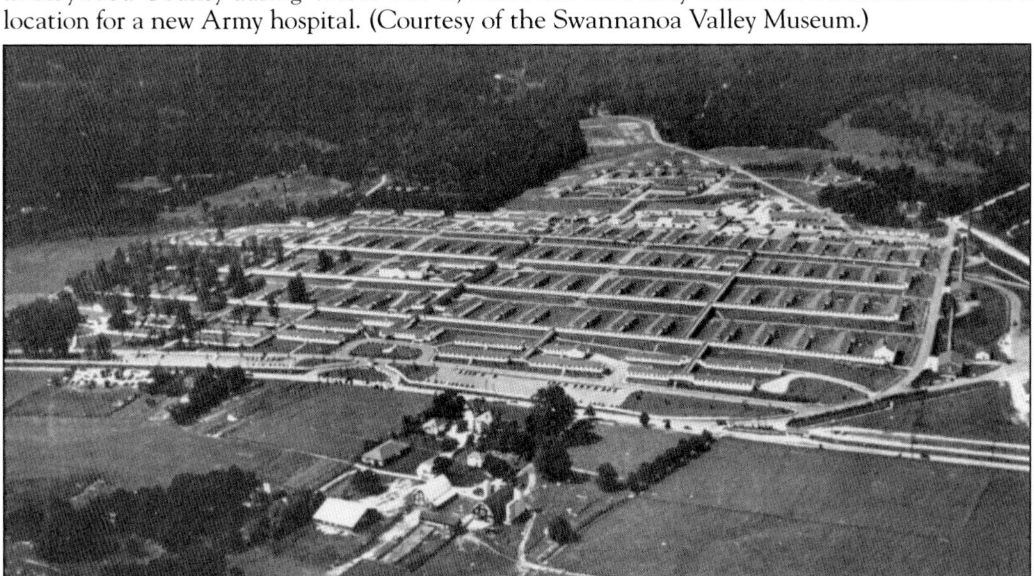

In 1942, the US Army purchased 200 acres from the Mountain Agricultural Research Station to build Moore General Hospital, a 1,520-bed hospital for members of the armed forces wounded in World War II. In the last year of the war, about 250 German prisoners of war were assigned to the facility to relieve a labor shortage. During the worst parts of the war, medical trains carrying wounded soldiers arrived daily at Swannanoa station for transport to the hospital. After the war, the hospital transitioned into a veterans' hospital and then a juvenile detention center. It is presently a women's prison. (Courtesy of the Swannanoa Valley Museum.)

Five

The Model Town
Grovemont-on-Swannanoa

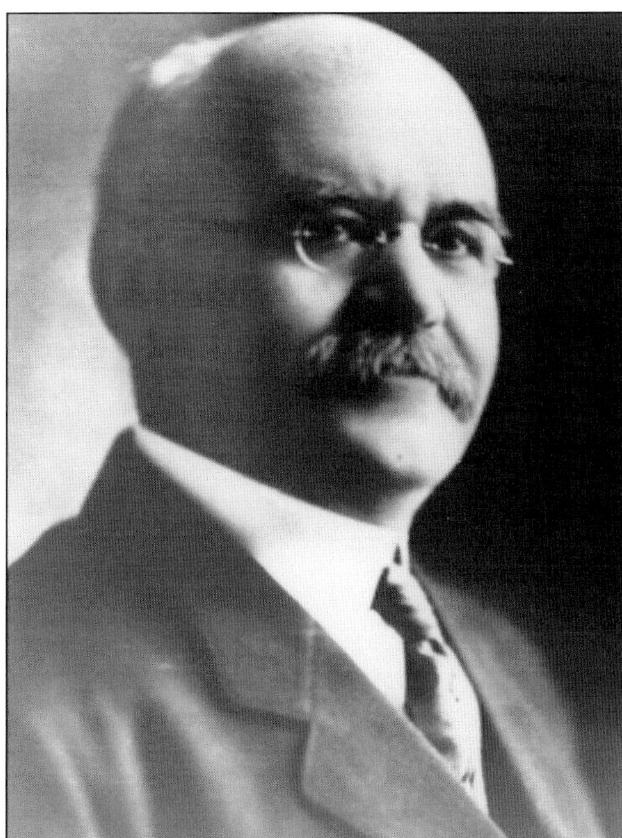

Edwin Wiley "E.W." Grove (1850–1927) was a self-made millionaire most famous for creating Grove's Tasteless Chill Tonic. In 1878, he found a way to bottle a quinine mixture that eliminated the bitter taste normally associated with quinine. The tasteless chill tonic, which many claimed was not all that tasteless, was an improvement over taking straight quinine for the fevers and chills caused by malaria. Some sources claim that, by 1890, more bottles of Grove's Tasteless Chill Tonic had been sold than bottles of Coca-Cola. With the fortune he made through his company, the Paris Medicine Company, Grove built the Grove Park Inn, the Grove Arcade, and the Battery Park Hotel in Asheville. Around 1900, while he was building these western North Carolina landmarks, he became interested in the Swannanoa area. He is seen here in 1925, when he was 65 years old. (Courtesy of the Swannanoa Valley Museum.)

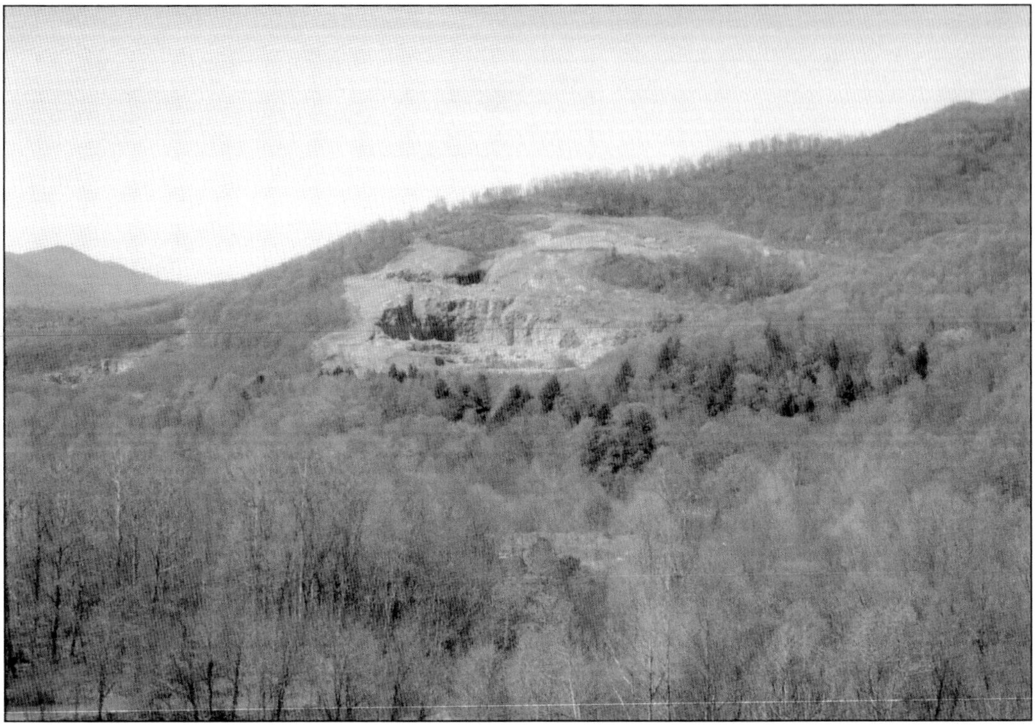

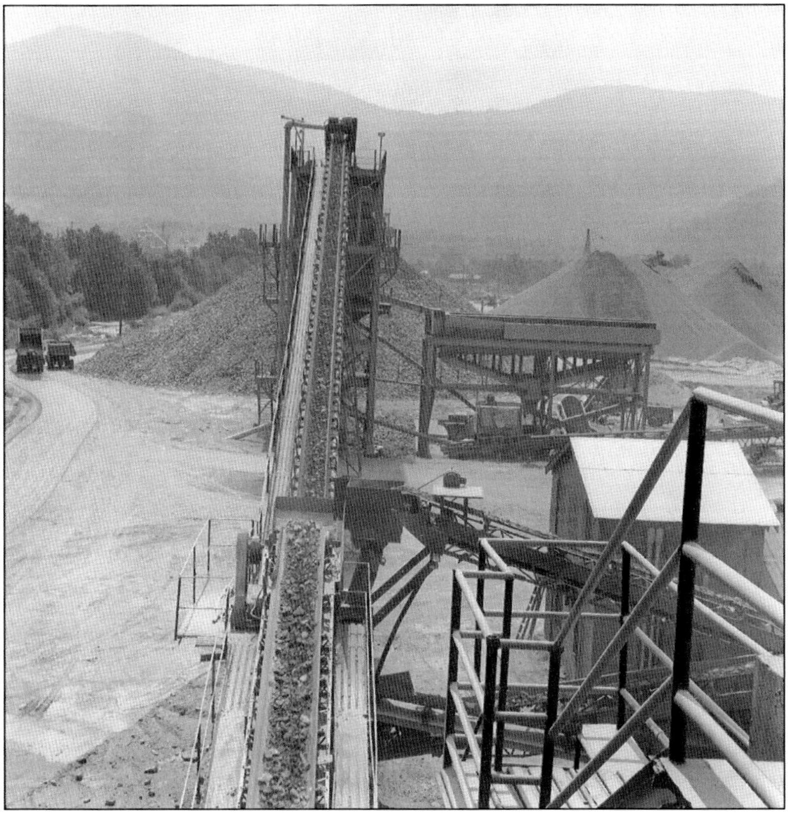

E.W. Grove's first venture in the Swannanoa Valley was to build the Grove Stone & Sand Company, a rock quarry, which still operates on Old Route 70. The quarry supplied material for his buildings, including the Grove Park Inn, in Asheville. The same quarry was later used to supply rock for Grove's Swannanoa building projects. (Both, courtesy of the Swannanoa Valley Museum.)

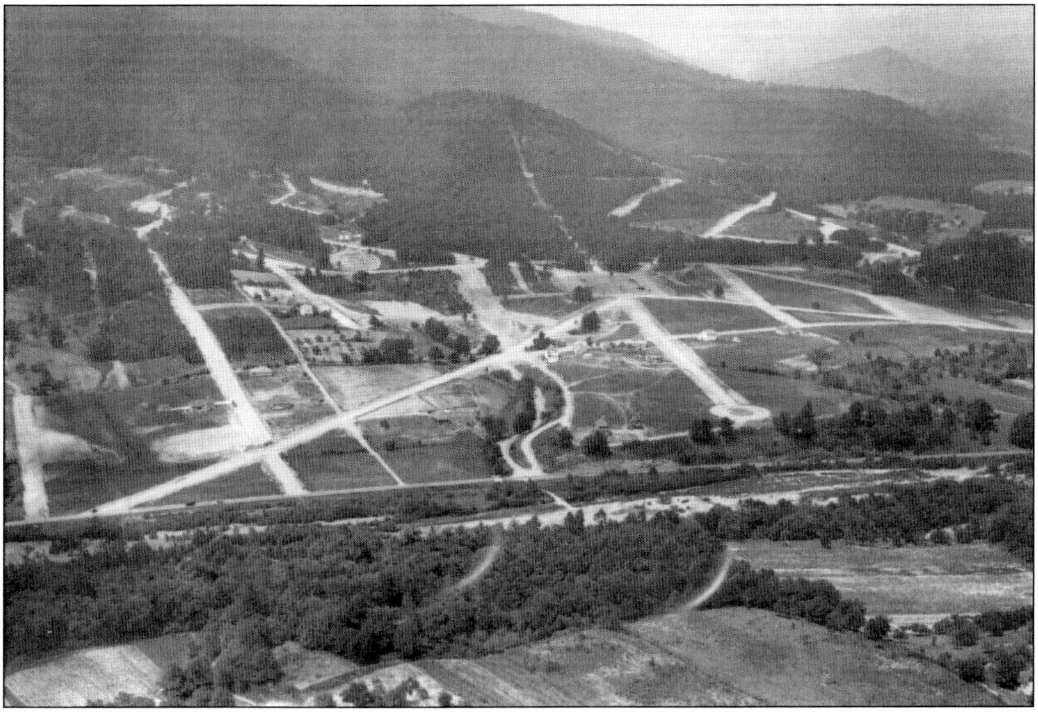

In the early 1920s, Grove began negotiations with the owner of a large tract of land in Swannanoa, Carrie Alexander, who operated the Alexander Inn. Though he paid more than he intended to acquire the land, Grove began planning immediately to build his dream community, which he called Grovemont-on-Swannanoa. This aerial photograph shows the roads and land that were cleared to begin the new community. (Courtesy of the Swannanoa Valley Museum.)

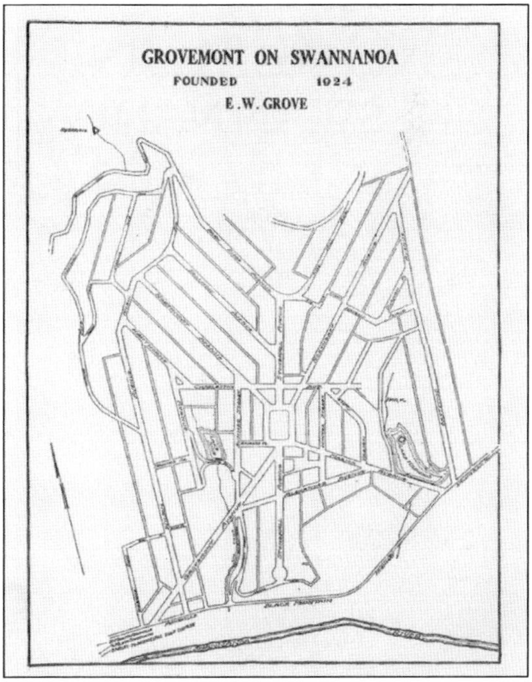

By 1924, Grove had begun the development of Grovemont-on-Swannanoa, which was billed as America's first planned community, where, Grove advertised, "people of moderate means could secure large lots at reasonable prices." Grove intended to recreate the English town his grandparents had lived in. This 1924 map shows that the original community was to be centered around a green and had two lakes. (Courtesy of the Swannanoa Valley Museum, Bill Alexander collection.)

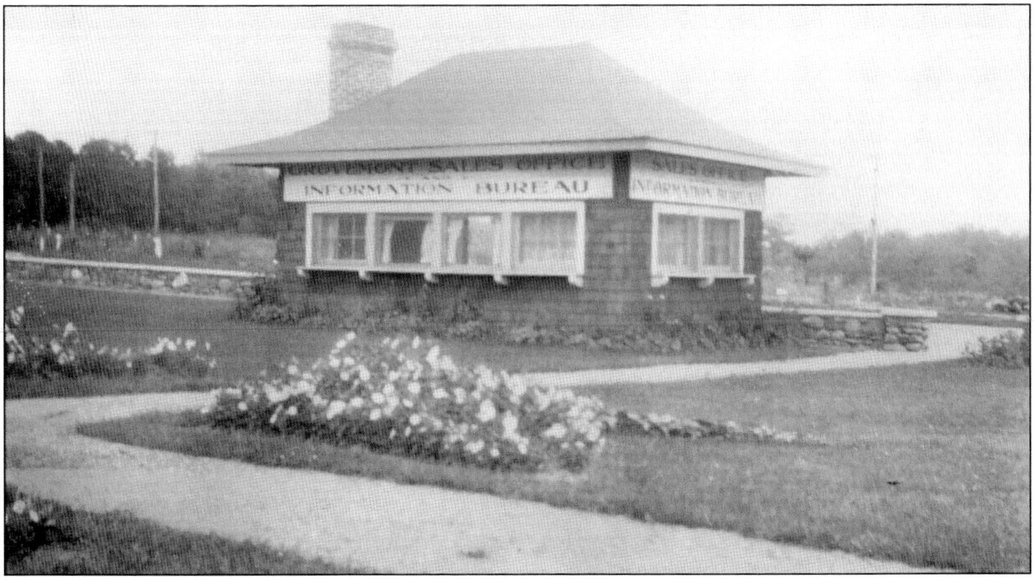

Lots and homes in the Grovemont community were sold through advertisements, real estate brochures, and the Grovemont Sales Office and Information Bureau, one of the small buildings built in 1925 on the corner of the square. One brochure expounds on the desirable qualities of the community, reading, "It is located just 12 miles from Asheville, in the center of much coveted surroundings of natural beauty. The paved State Highway touches its Southern Boundary with the Southern Railway nearby. The town rises in a gentle slope on a plateau overlooking the river until it reaches into the woods on the hillsides. Due to its natural facilities and highway connections Grovemont-on-Swannanoa is geographically right." (Courtesy of the Swannanoa Valley Museum, Barbara Davidson collection.)

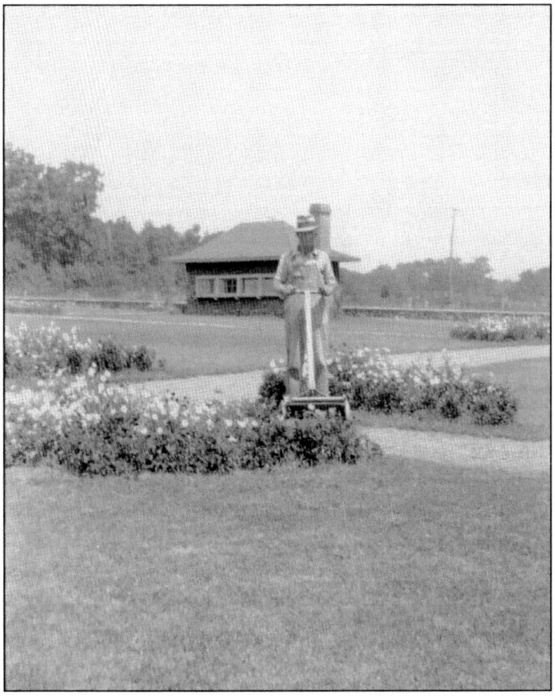

Though Grove had lofty goals, his death in 1927 stalled the plan, and the stock market crash of 1929 killed the remainder of the project. The original blueprint, drawn in 1924, shows houses, shops, a hotel, a post office, a library, and a town hall, as well as lakes, roads, and a water system—much of which was never realized. The civic center of Grovemont was completed, with four small buildings, one situated at each corner of the square. These buildings were meant to be home to a haberdashery, a sales office, a mercantile, and an apothecary. The building seen here behind gardener Wash Tomlin, on the northeast corner of the square, was to be the mercantile. (Courtesy of the Swannanoa Valley Museum, Barbara Davidson collection.)

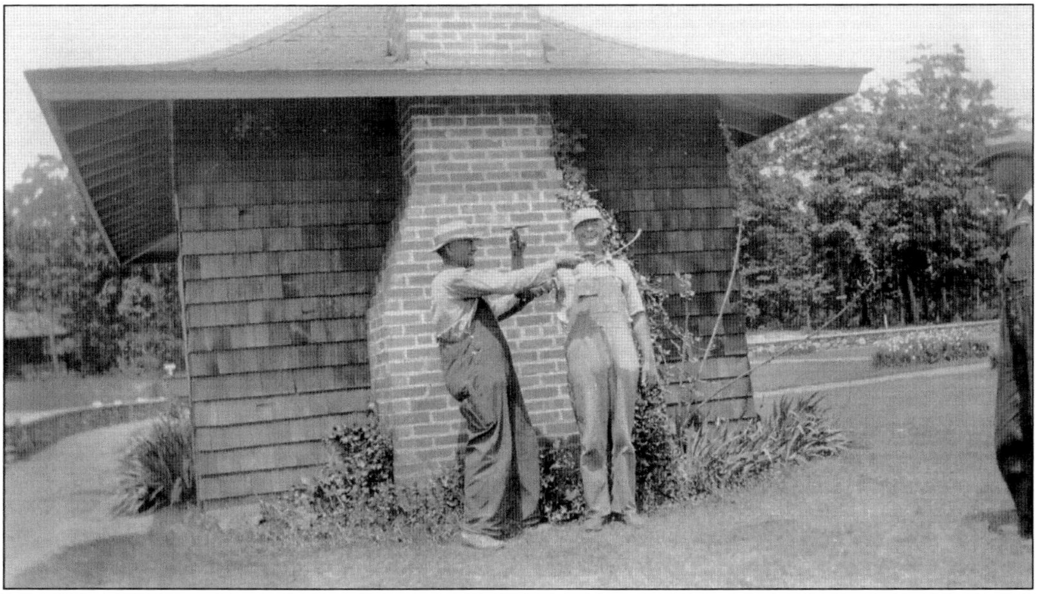

With a maintenance crew at work daily, the entire property—even the smallest garden—was kept in the best condition. This photograph shows Mitch Creasman (left, with reap hook), Wash Tomlin (right, with cigar), and Sam Davidson (far right) in front of one of the main plaza buildings around 1930. (Courtesy of the Swannanoa Valley Museum, Barbara Davidson collection.)

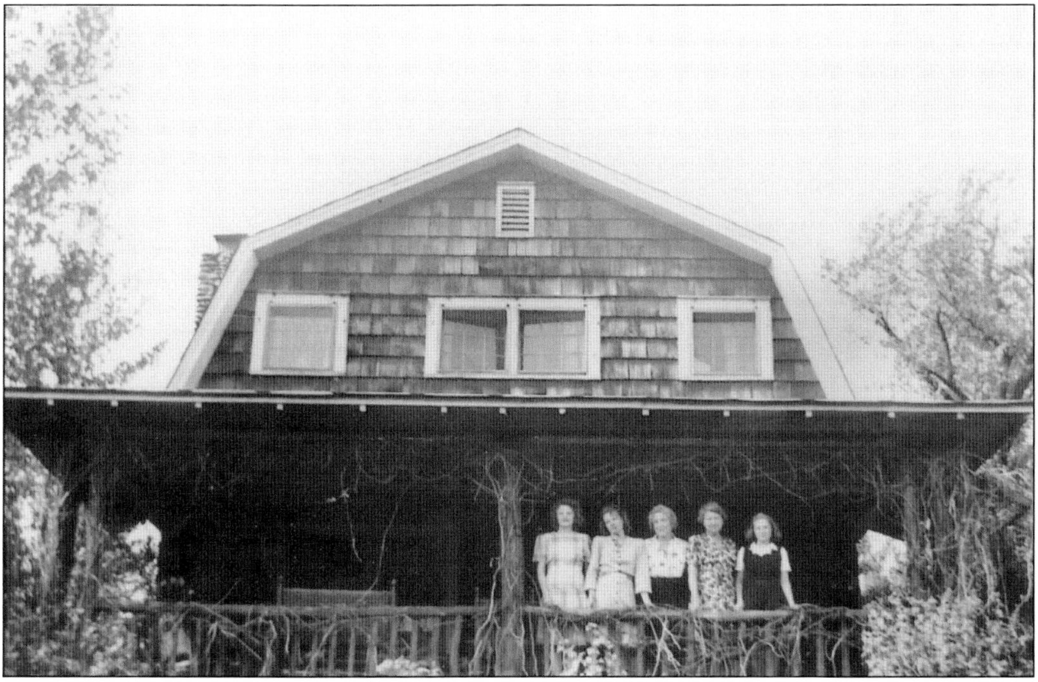

The Lainer Cottage, in Grovemont, was a summer residence used by Swannanoa's many visiting tourists. Seen here in 1941 are, from left to right, Jane Davidson Haskell, Mary Lou Davidson Caceres, an unidentified guest from Florida, Janie Davidson, and Mary Alexander Garner. (Courtesy of the Swannanoa Valley Museum, Bill Alexander collection.)

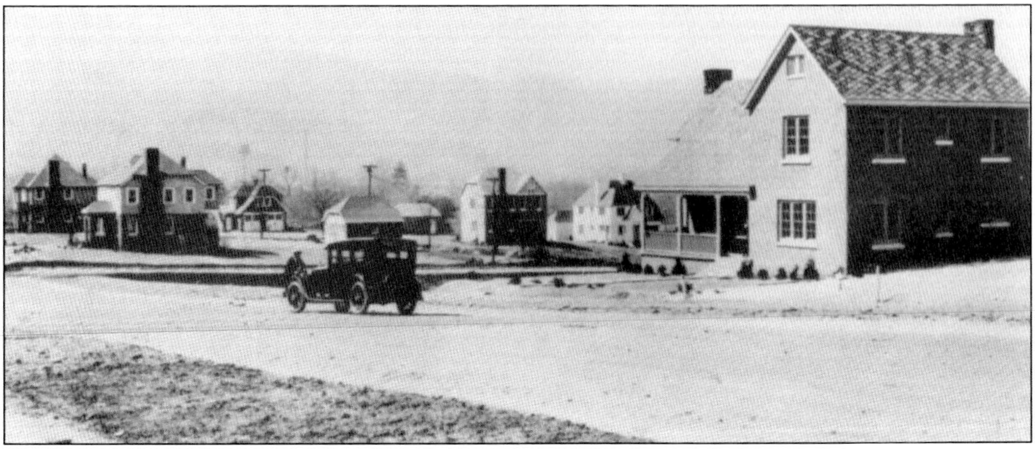

Before his death at the Battery Park Hotel in 1927, E.W. Grove built 19 homes in Grovemont, many of which are seen in this 1920s photograph of Stonewall Avenue. Today, 15 of these houses still stand in the Grovemont community. (Courtesy of the Swannanoa Valley Museum.)

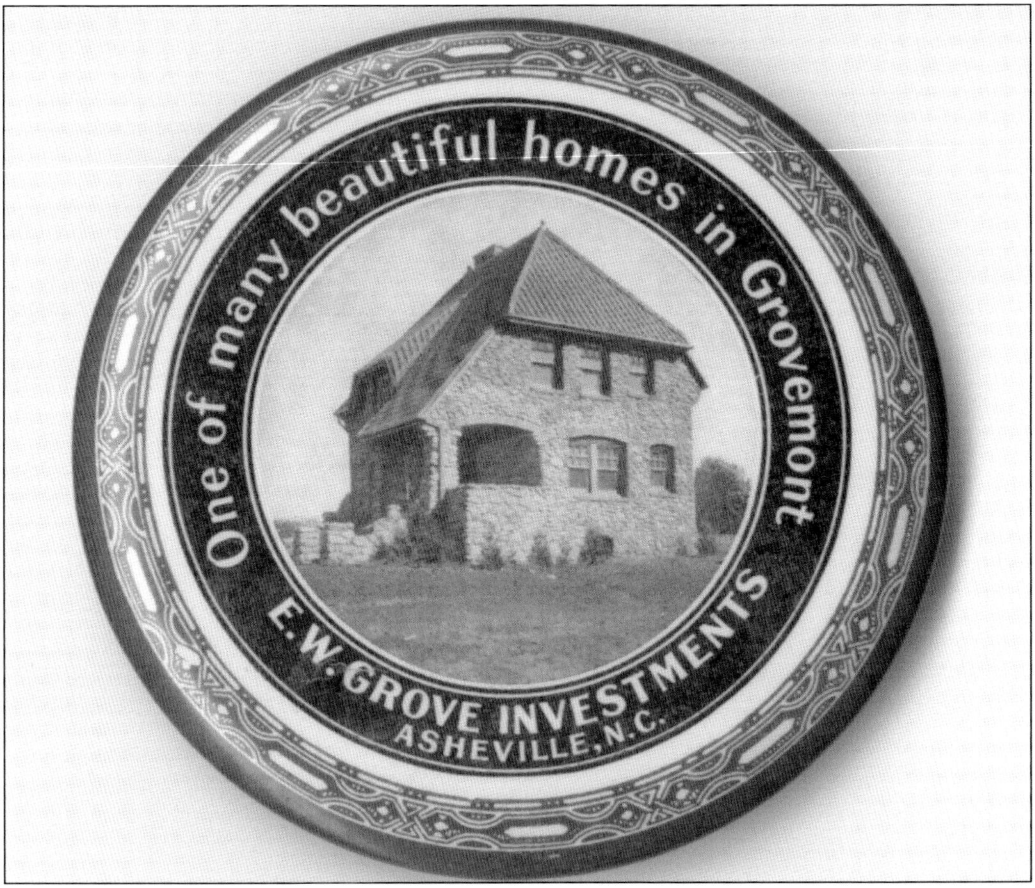

As a gift, E.W. Grove gave new Grovemont homeowners mirrors with photographs of their new homes on the front, like the one seen here. This home, owned by George D. and Winnie Young, was built on Parker Drive in 1925. (Courtesy of the Swannanoa Valley Museum, Bill Alexander collection.)

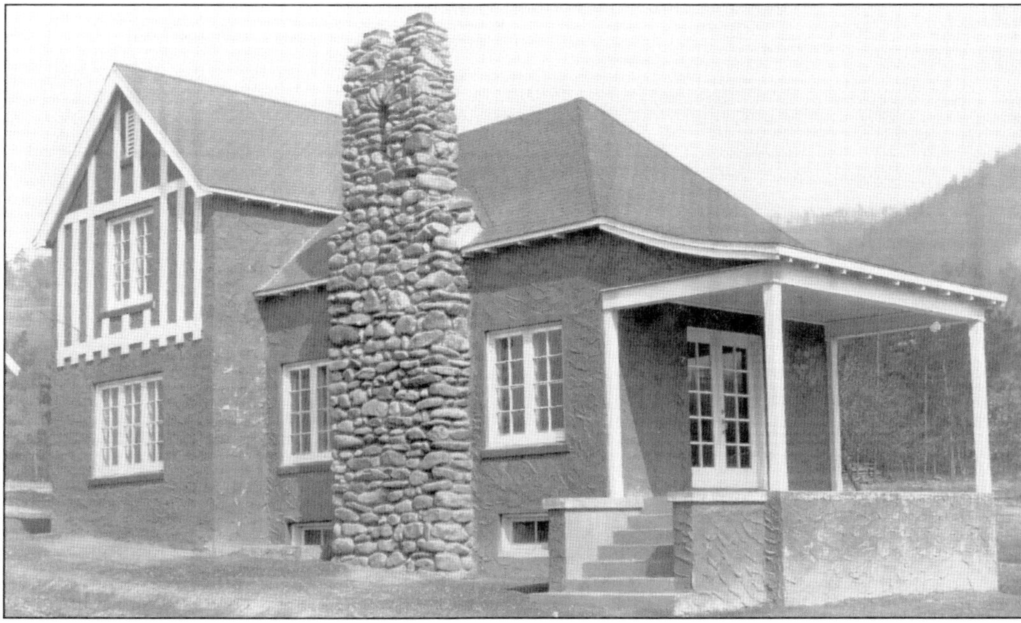

Grovemont's residential lots were large in order to provide ample room for lawns, gardens, and garages. The residential lots averaged 80 feet wide and 160 feet deep, while the business properties ran 25 feet wide and 100 feet deep. Unimproved lots ranged in price from $750 to $1,250, while the improved properties, with residences, were priced from $8,500 to $13,000. (Courtesy of the Pack Memorial Library, North Carolina Collection.)

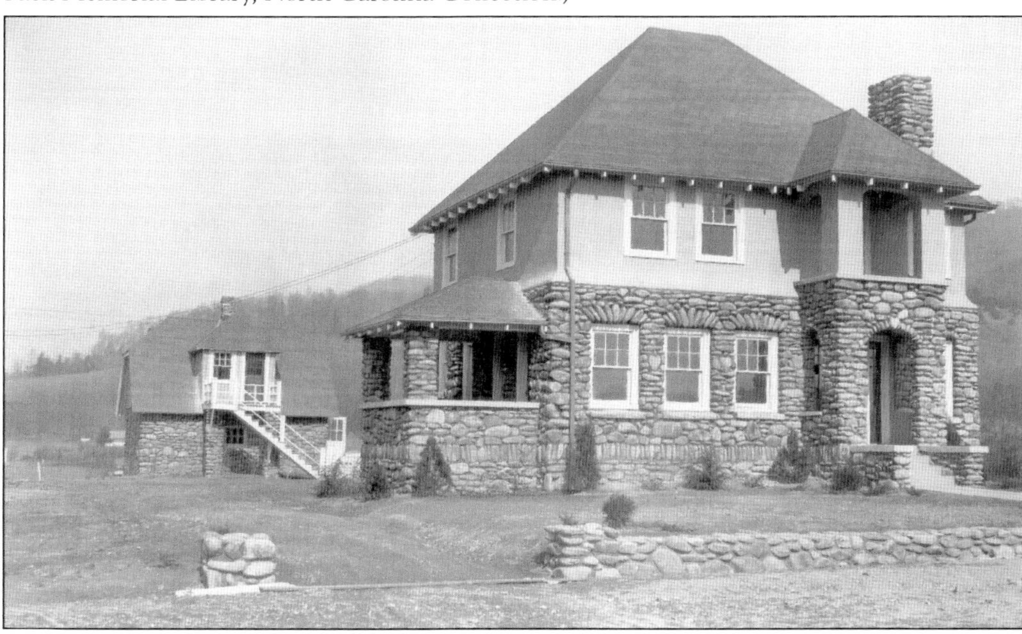

Grove's houses, with only one exception, were built using either stucco, river rock, or a combination of the two. Grove's consistent use of rock from the Swannanoa River made his buildings in Grovemont, Lake Eden, and Asheville easily identifiable. The only exception is one home in Grovemont, which was covered in brick to appease the executives from Beacon who purchased the pre-built home. (Courtesy of the Pack Memorial Library, North Carolina Collection.)

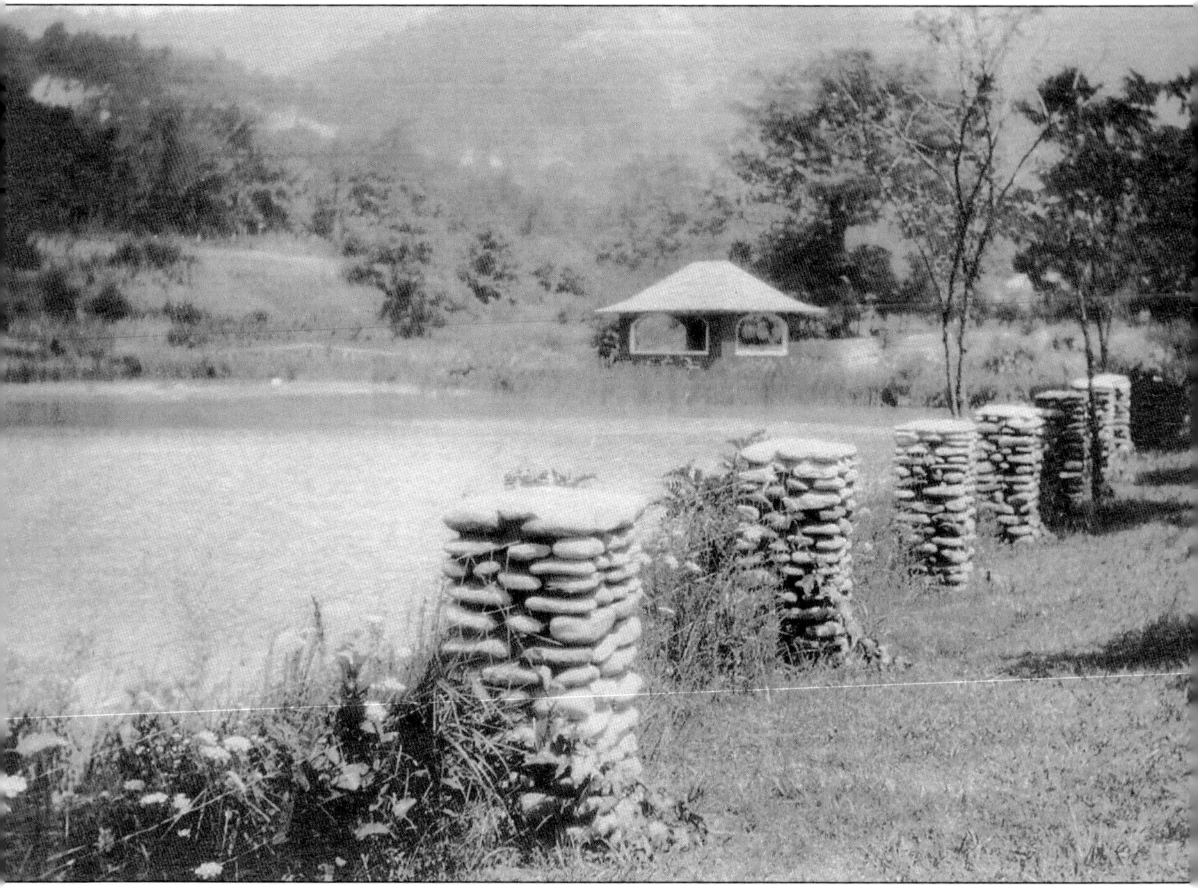

Grovemont originally had two lakes, neither of which still exists. Lake June, seen here, was west of the main plaza. Lake Wildwood was near the entrance to Grovemont, at the intersection of Old Route 70 and Marion Avenue. According to Grove, the lakes were meant to "add additional beauty and appeal to a setting that would have been attractive without them." (Courtesy of the Swannanoa Valley Museum, Barbara Davidson collection.)

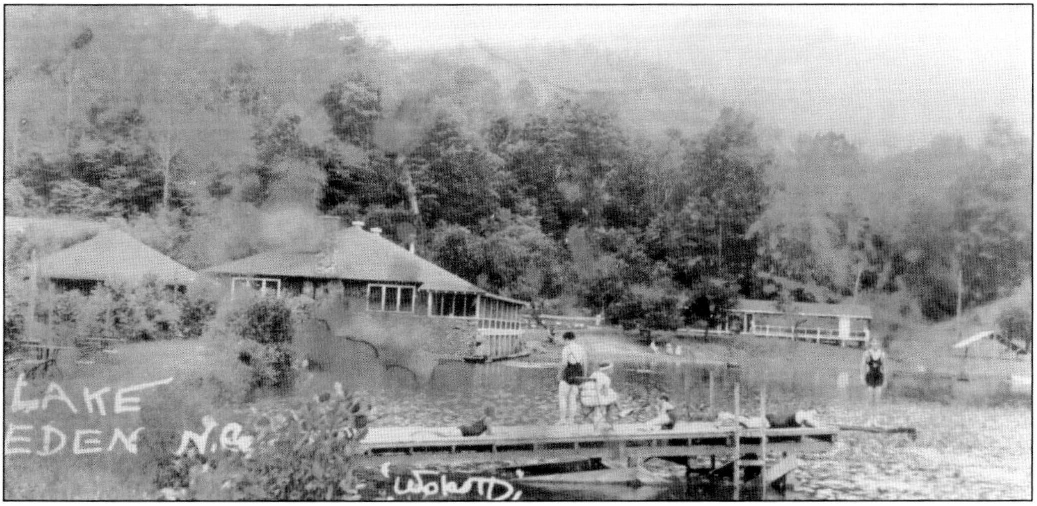

E.W. Grove's interests first developed Lake Eden as a country club for Grovemont-on-Swannanoa residents. A promotional brochure for the property reads, "Lake Eden was developed by Mr. Grove with the idea in mind of creating an amusement center for Asheville as well as Grovemont. The location is slightly separated from The Model Town." In 1923 and 1924, the site served as a girls' camp. The property then became a summer resort hotel. By 1934, Gertrude C. Sprague was operating Lake Eden, which by then had a bathhouse, a large pavilion, tennis courts, a baseball field, cottages, and hotel buildings, with "all the modern conveniences." This site later became home to Black Mountain College and Camp Rockmont, a Christian summer camp for boys. (Courtesy of the Swannanoa Valley Museum.)

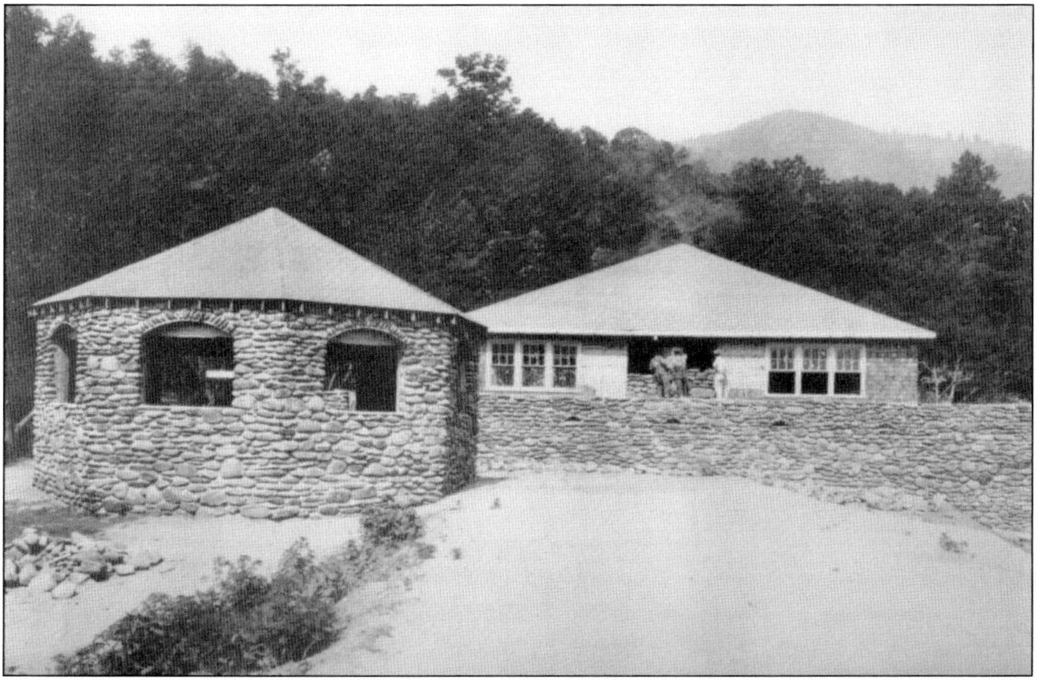

E.W. Grove's river rock buildings can still be seen throughout Lake Eden, and the style is apparent in this photograph of the construction of Lake Eden's "low rambling stone casino," which served as a dance and recreation hall. (Courtesy of the Swannanoa Valley Museum.)

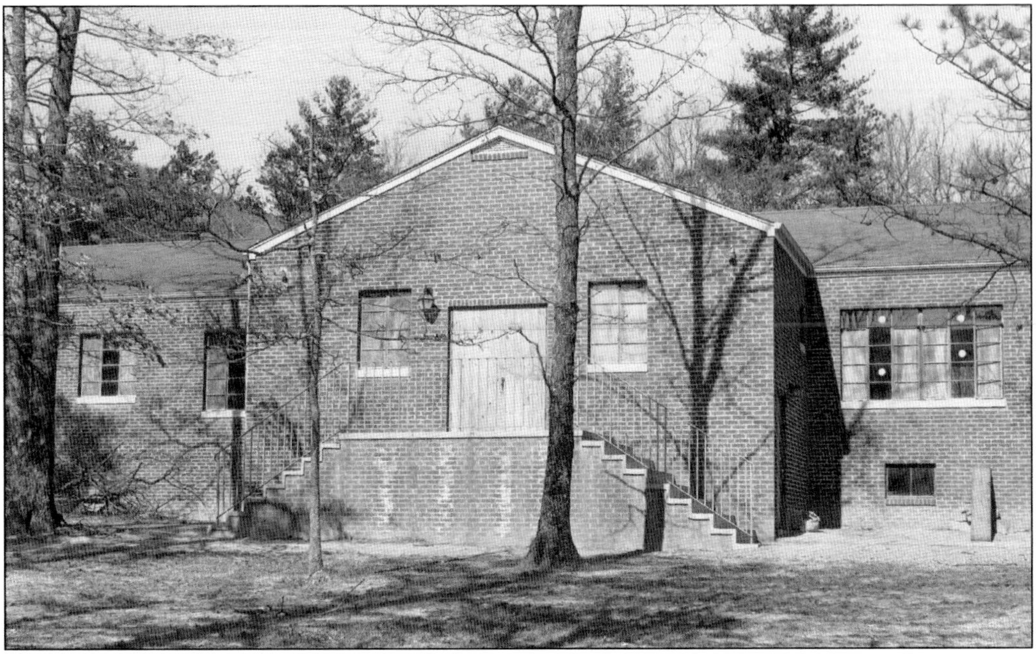

The Swannanoa clubhouse, seen here, was originally built in 1952 and sits on the northern end of Grovemont's main plaza. The community center building is now owned by the Swannanoa Community Council and is home to the very active Swannanoa Public Library. (Courtesy of the Swannanoa Valley Museum.)

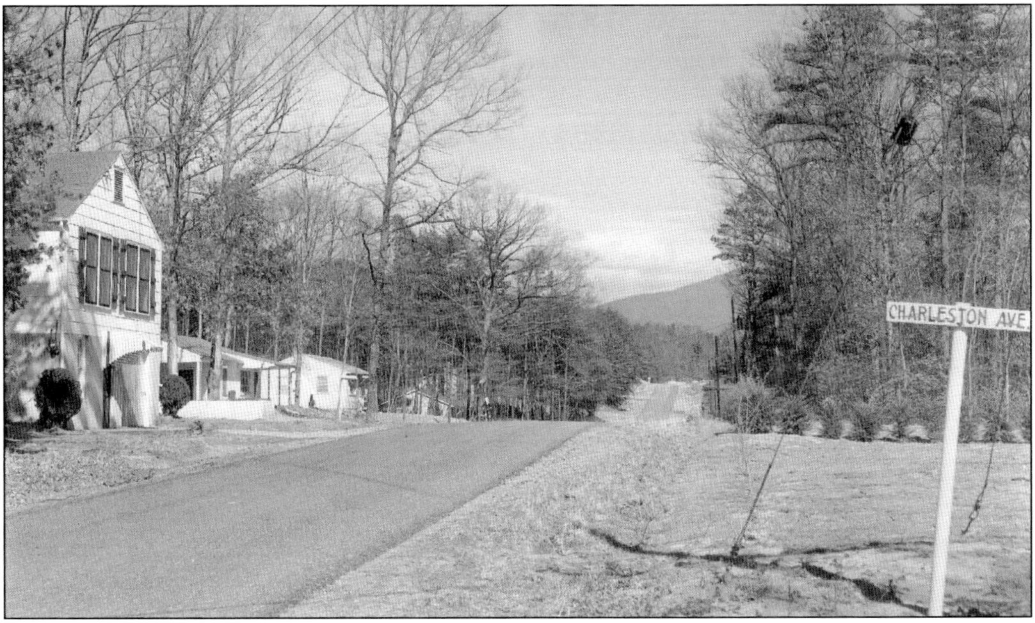

Though E.W. Grove's dream of a quaint English village like the one his grandparents lived in was never fully realized, the Grovemont of today is still a web of streets anchored by a central park, which has been rebuilt to feature a playground, a walking path, and a playing field. Today, the inclusive community is known for its popular summer programs, including Groovin' on Grovemont, a weekly free outdoor concert series. (Courtesy of the Swannanoa Valley Museum.)

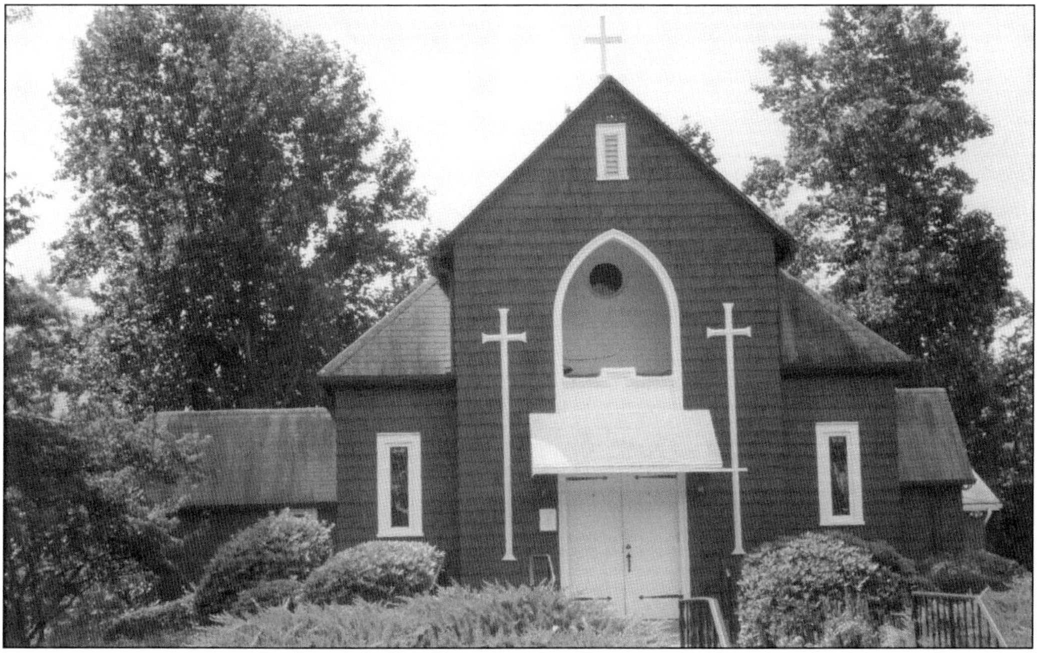

St. Margaret Mary's Catholic Church has served Catholics in eastern Buncombe County since its dedication on October 11, 1936. The two acres of undeveloped land on which the church now sits, in the Grovemont community, were purchased from E.W. Grove's son by the church in the spring of 1936 for $500. The property had originally been slated for a hotel. (Courtesy of the Swannanoa Valley Museum.)

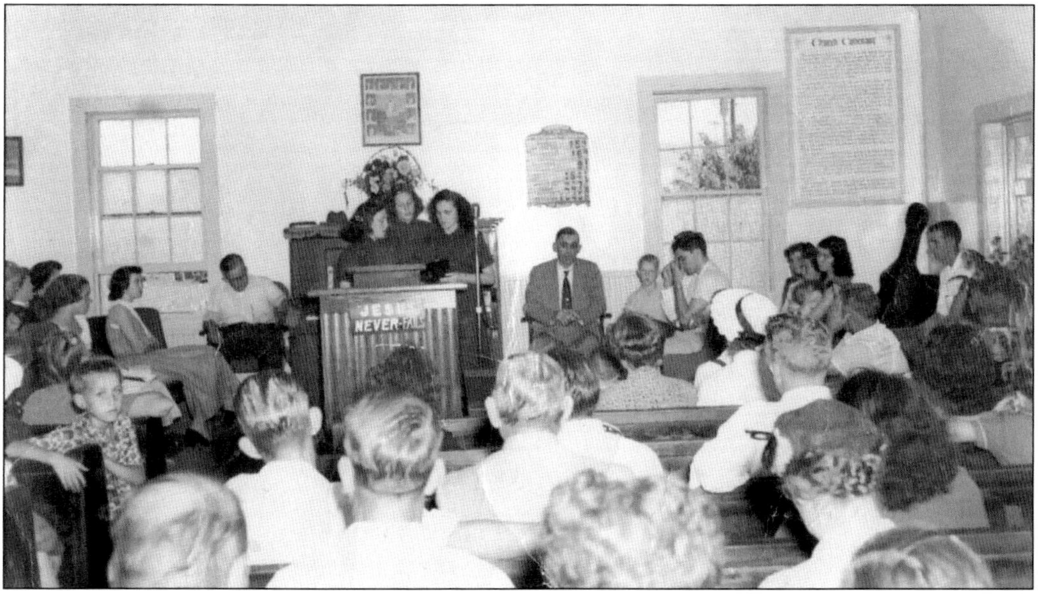

Just outside the Grovemont and Lake Eden communities is Grove Stone Baptist Church, which began in the spring of 1935 as the Grove Stone Mission of the Swannanoa First Baptist Church and was officially formed on June 25, 1938. In 1942, the church leased its first building from the Morgan Manufacturing Company. This photograph shows a church service around 1950. (Courtesy of the Swannanoa Valley Museum, Eddie Frizsell collection.)

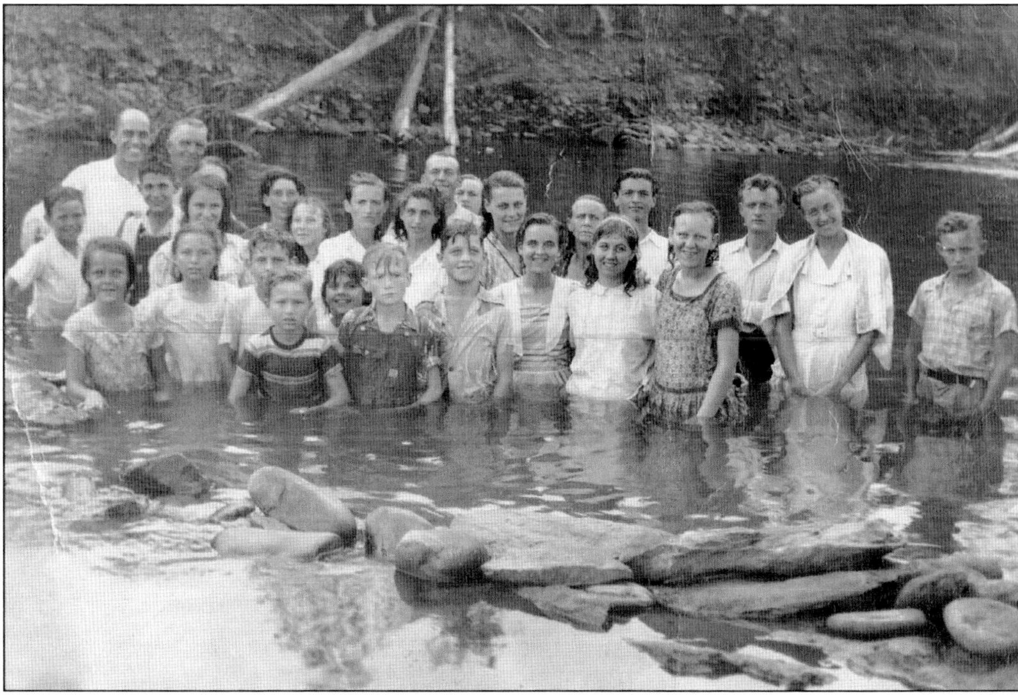

In 1962, property for the present Grove Stone Baptist Church was purchased, and construction on its new building began. This 1950s photograph shows new members being baptized into the Christian faith in the Swannanoa River. (Courtesy of the Swannanoa Valley Museum, Eddie Frizsell collection.)

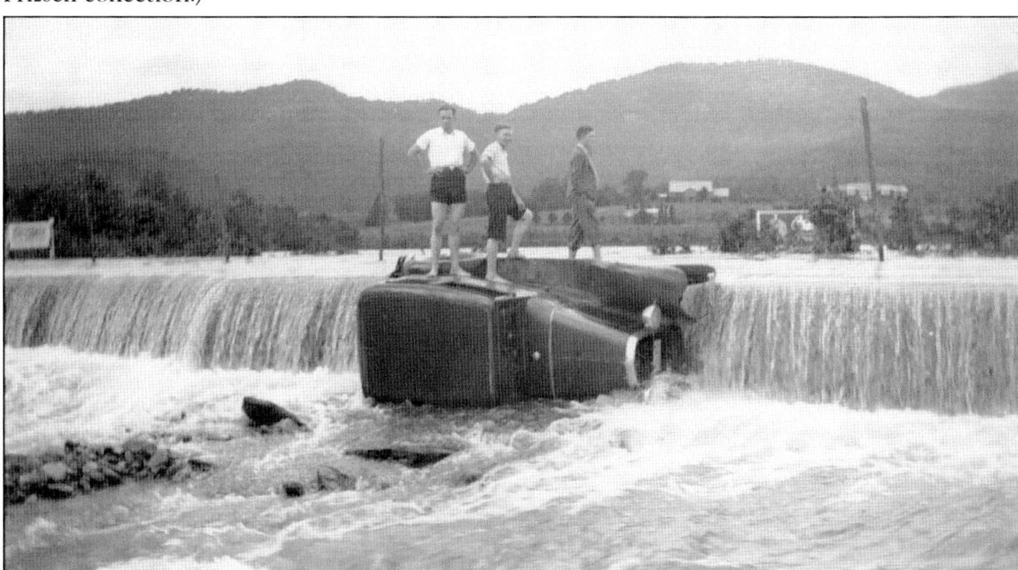

Living on the banks of a river is beautiful, but it is also unpredictable. Floods have plagued home and business owners since the first recorded flood in August 1796. Floods in Swannanoa have resulted in tragic deaths, damage to railroads and bridges, compromised water supplies, ruined homes, and devastated crops. These three men stand on a car tipped over during the August 30, 1940, flood of the Swannanoa River in Grovestone. (Courtesy of the Swannanoa Valley Museum.)

Six

Beacon Blankets Make Warm Friends

Industry Moves to the Mountains

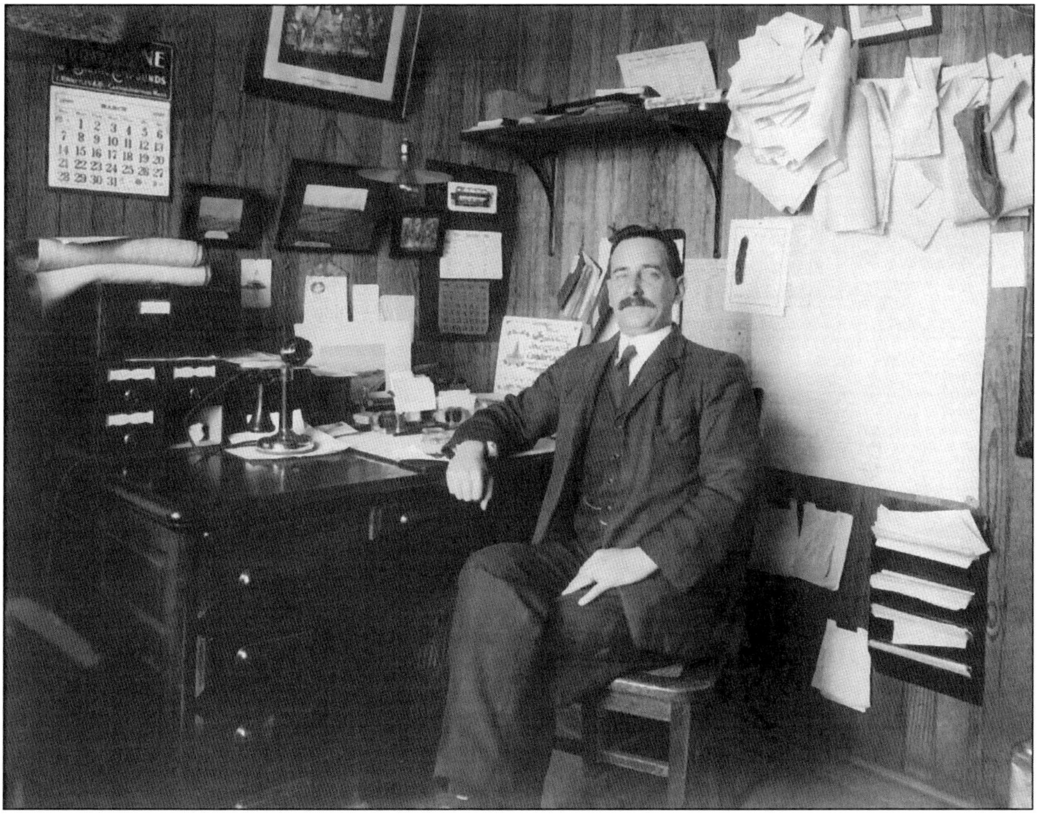

In 1923, from the window of a train traveling from Asheville, Charles D. Owen II spotted a piece of flat land adjacent to the Swannanoa station that he thought would be a perfect location for his family's business, the Beacon Manufacturing Company, to build a new plant on. Later that year, he purchased the land, 160 acres of rich farmland that belonged to Mr. and Mrs. Charles P. Whitson. The plant eventually grew to cover approximately 1,300 acres and was billed as "the largest blanket manufacturing plant in the world." Charles D. Owen is seen here in his Massachusetts office in 1909. (Courtesy of the Swannanoa Valley Museum.)

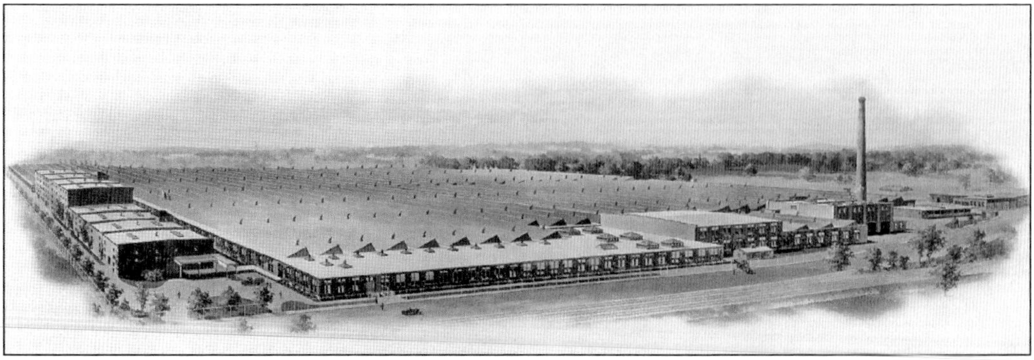

Before moving to Swannanoa, the Beacon Manufacturing Company had been operating in New Bedford, Massachusetts, since 1905, with Charles D. Owen leading the company. The New Bedford plant is seen here in the late 1910s. (Courtesy of the Swannanoa Valley Museum.)

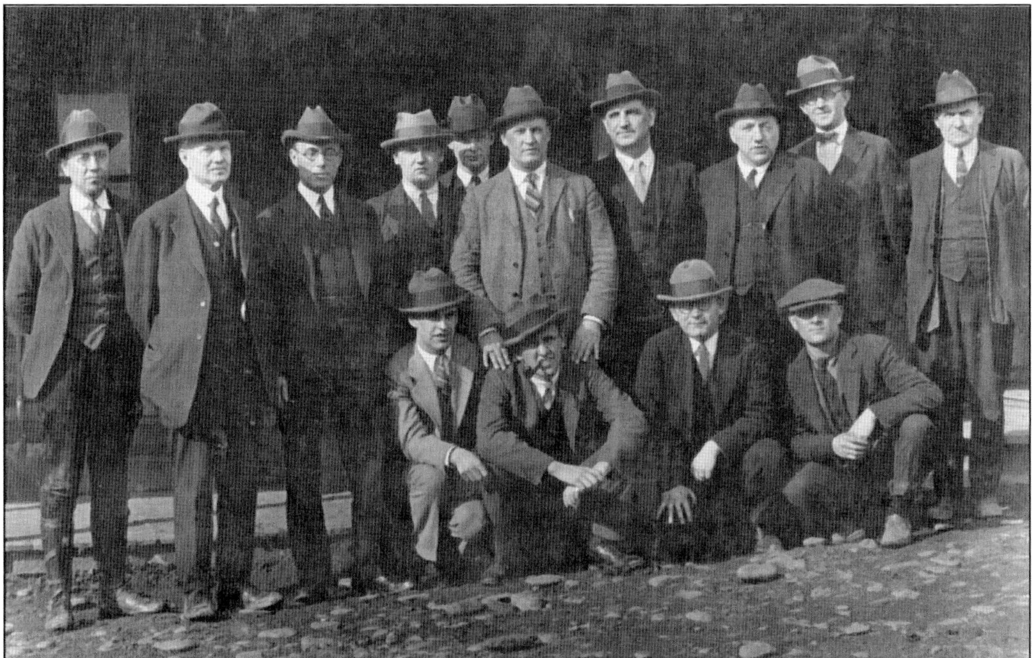

Charles D. Owen II (standing, third from left) is seen here with his executive staff at the New Bedford plant in 1918. (Courtesy of the Swannanoa Valley Museum.)

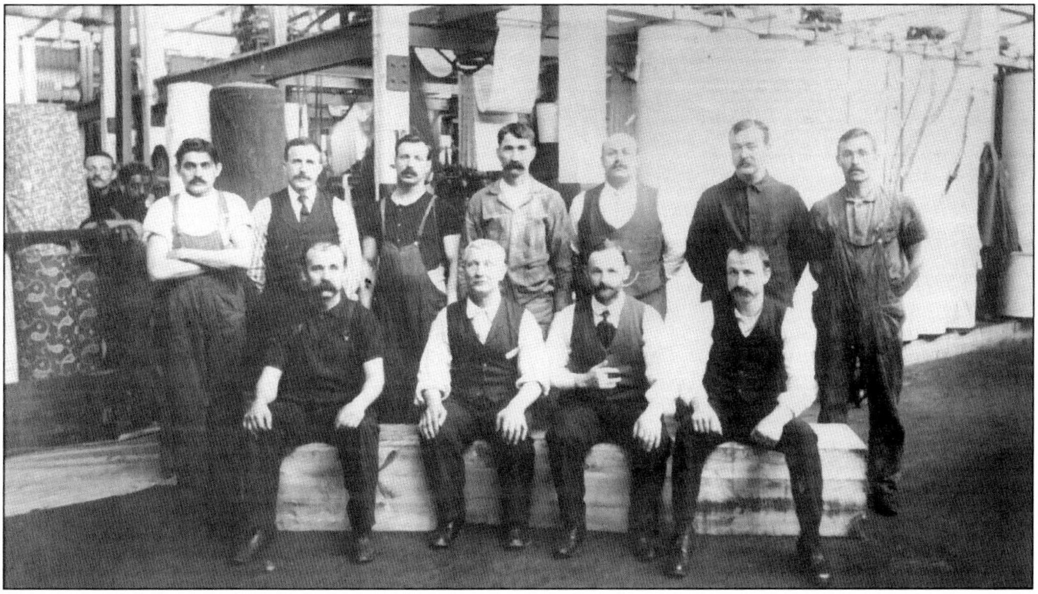

Before the New Bedford plant was erected, Charles D. Owen II traveled extensively through Europe, studying methods of using cotton threads on woolen machinery. He discovered that as long as he used the rough cottons grown in China's mountains, rather than the weaker American cottons, the same type of manufacturing used to create woolen fabrics would be suitable for making cotton fabrics. A group of employees is seen here in the New Bedford weaving room. (Courtesy of the Swannanoa Valley Museum.)

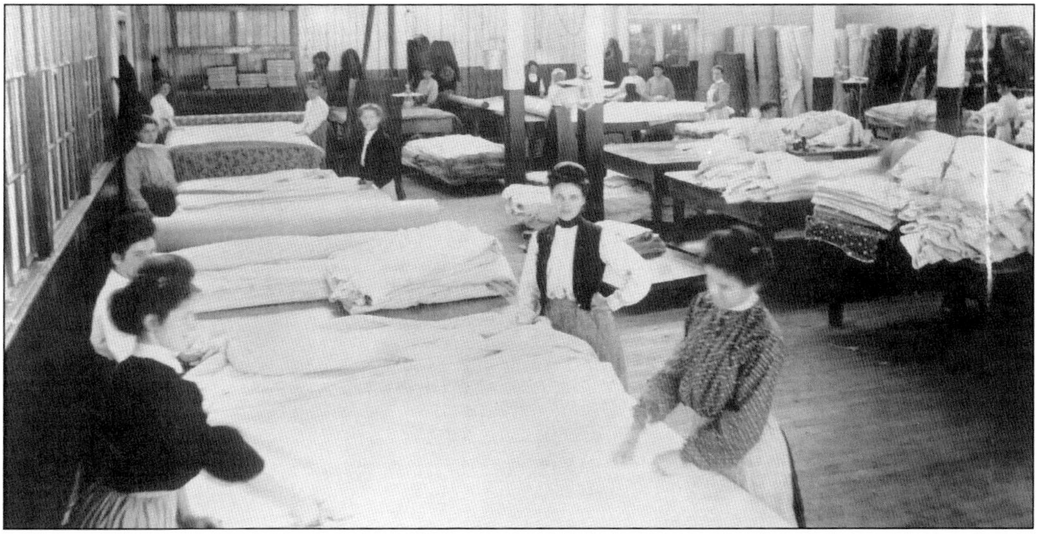

Convinced that he could make cotton blankets and bathrobes on machinery previously used only to process wool, Charles D. Owen II returned to America and, with his father, began manufacturing fabrics. Since most homes in the early 1900s had no heating systems, Beacon blankets and bathrobes quickly became very popular, and, by 1912, the plant was three times its original size. By then, the plant was not only producing a large volume of products and shipping them throughout the country, but it had also expanded to manufacturing everything from pastel-colored baby blankets to heavy jacquard blankets in an array of colors. Here, women cut and fold the cotton fabrics at the New Bedford plant. (Courtesy of the Swannanoa Valley Museum.)

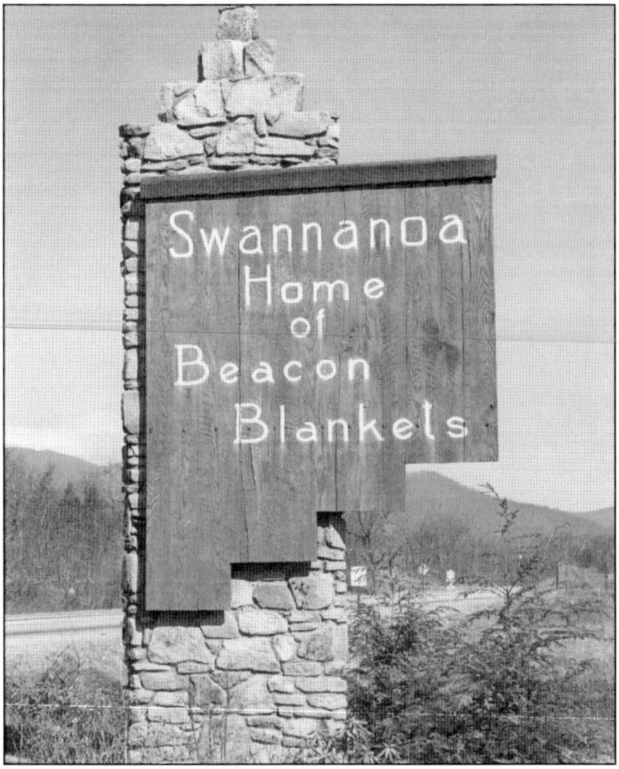

Charles D. Owen died in 1915 at the age of 72, and his son Charles D. Owen II took over all operations of the company, expanding the plant yet again in 1917 and in 1919, making it the largest blanket manufacturing plant in the United States. In the 1920s, Charles D. Owen II felt that it was time to expand the plant outside of Massachusetts in order to access cheaper Southern labor, deal with fewer unions, and have better railroad service, which had been discontinued at the New Bedford plant. The construction of the plant in Swannanoa began in 1924, and Charles D. Owen III traveled to Swannanoa to supervise the project and get to know the community. Swannanoa then became the home of Beacon Blankets. (Courtesy of the Swannanoa Valley Museum.)

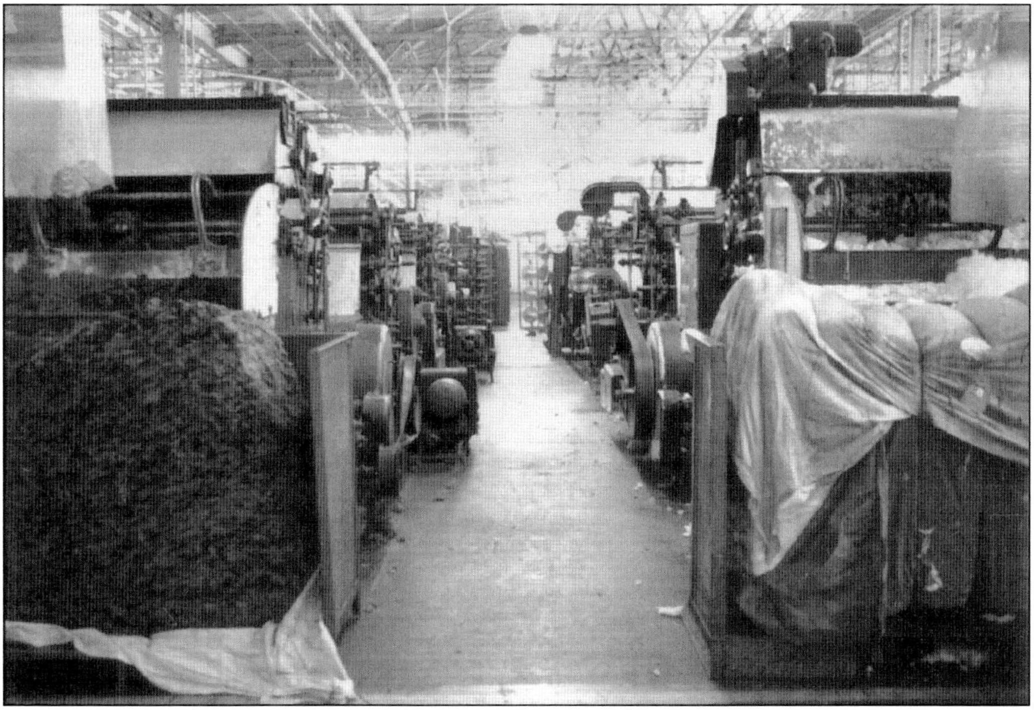

The new Swannanoa plant began operating in 1925, but it only produced three types of material in its early years. (Courtesy of the Swannanoa Valley Museum.)

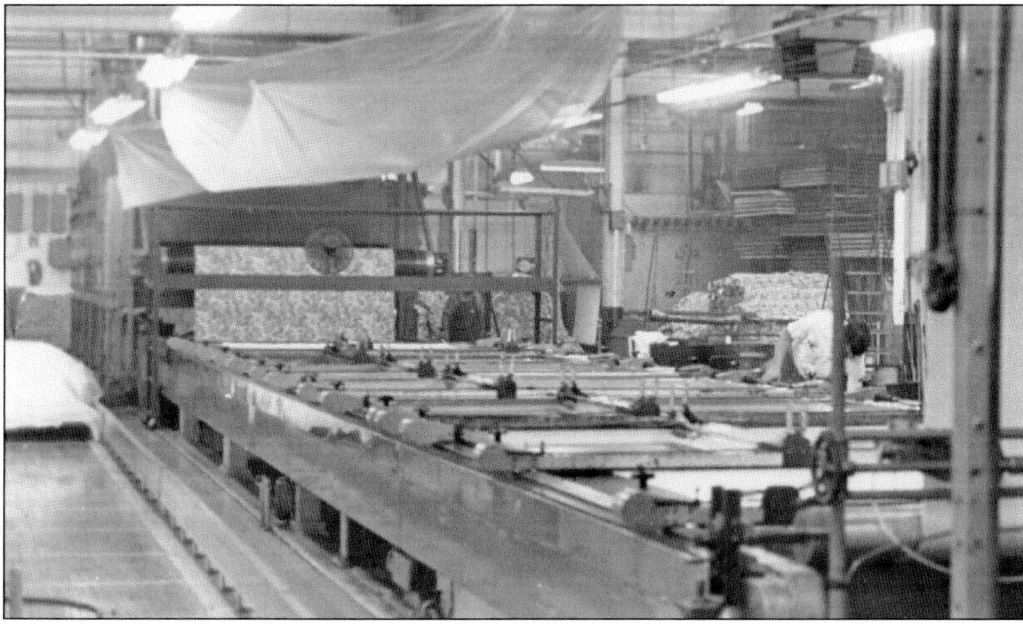

Before Beacon arrived in Swannanoa, most of the area was farmland. Even near the train station, "there was only a lumber mill and a couple grocery stores," according to Bill Barnwell, who moved to Swannanoa in 1921, just before the mill was built. "When Beacon came in everything changed. [Swannanoa] started growing when they started production." (Courtesy of the Swannanoa Valley Museum.)

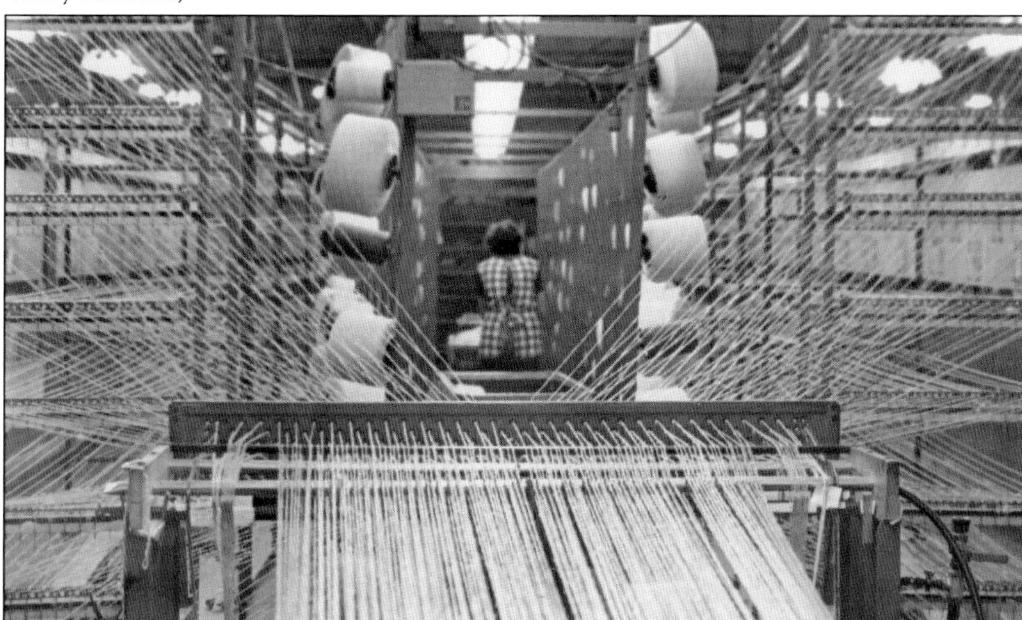

The plant was not the only part of Beacon Blankets that moved south. Many of the New Bedford employees made the move to Swannanoa as well, following their jobs. While getting settled, most of them stayed nearby at Ma Stanton's boardinghouse until they could bring their families down. (Courtesy of the Swannanoa Valley Museum.)

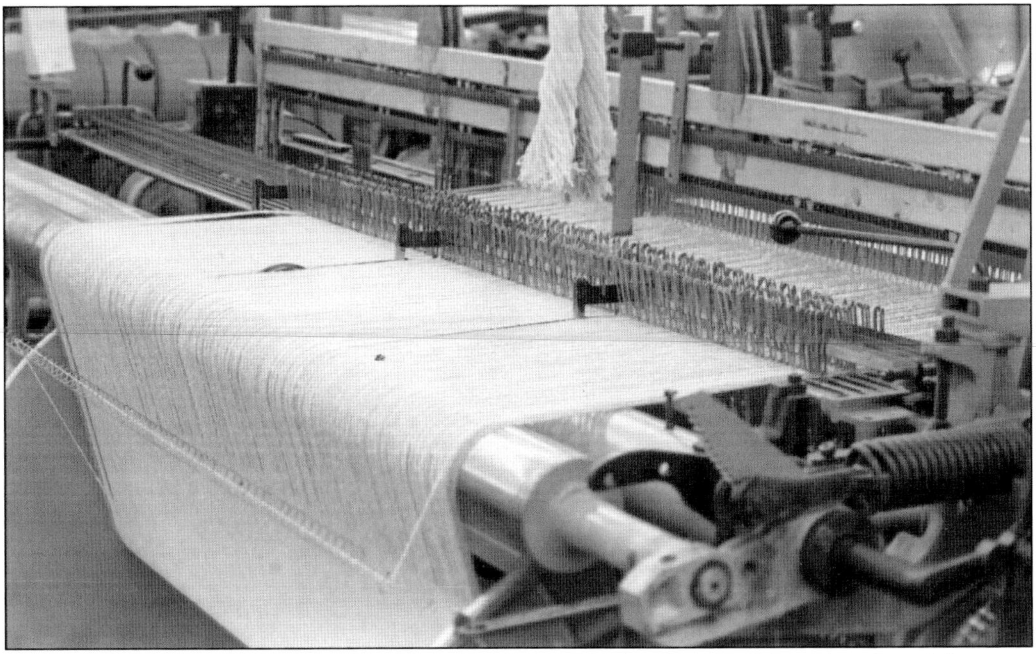

From 1925 to 1927, many Swannanoa natives were trained to begin work at the plant. Most new employees had no background in textiles, but they were eager for jobs with steady paychecks, as farming as an occupation was becoming less predictable. (Courtesy of the Swannanoa Valley Museum.)

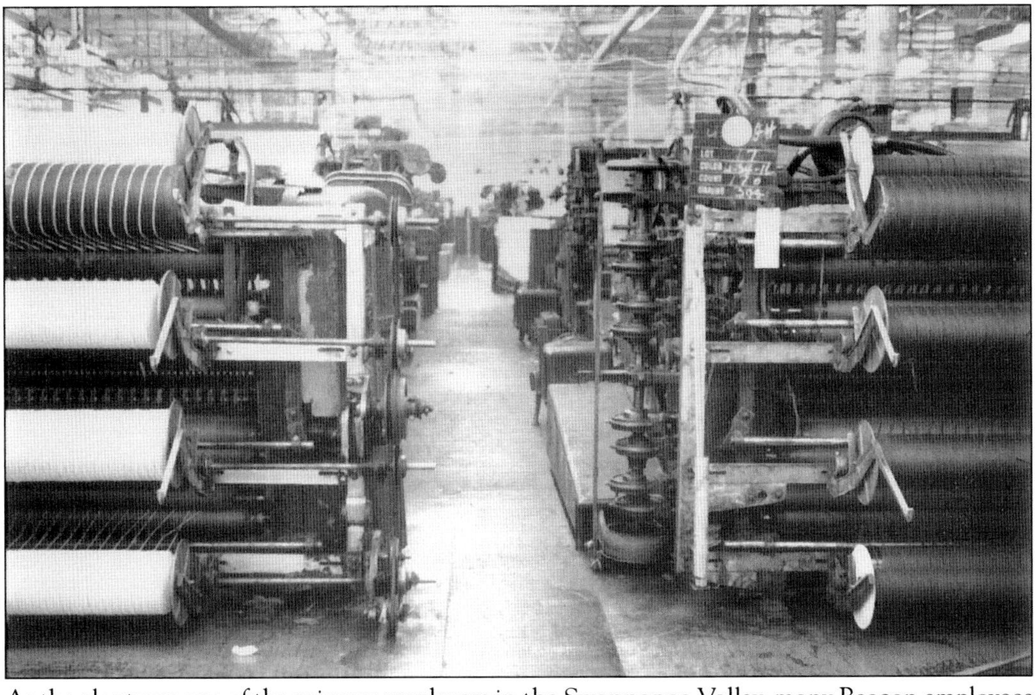

As the plant was one of the primary employers in the Swannanoa Valley, many Beacon employees remained at the company for decades. In some cases, two and even three generations of the same family worked at Beacon. (Courtesy of the Swannanoa Valley Museum.)

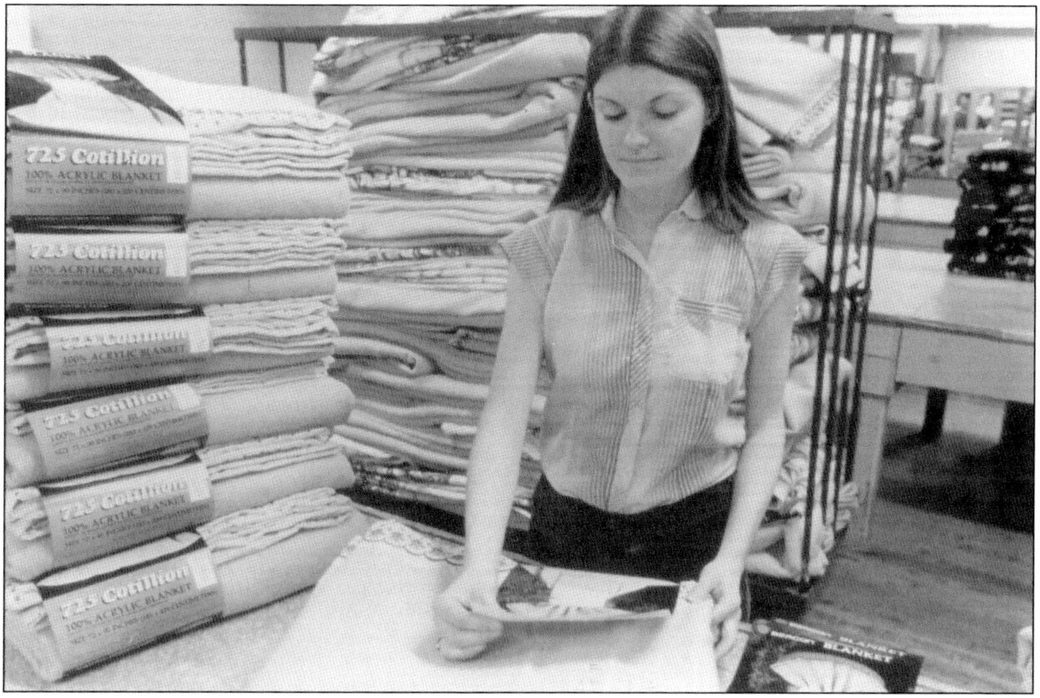

Above, Lynn Marett, who worked at Beacon for 23 years, applies tickets to blankets. Many workers attributed Charles D. Owen II's open-door policy as being key to their happiness. The policy made it possible for any worker to come speak with Owen if he or she was having problems on the job or at home. As the company expanded, Owen also enlisted his assistants to ensure that there was always someone available. Below, Beacon executives stand inside the plant. (Both, courtesy of the Swannanoa Valley Museum.)

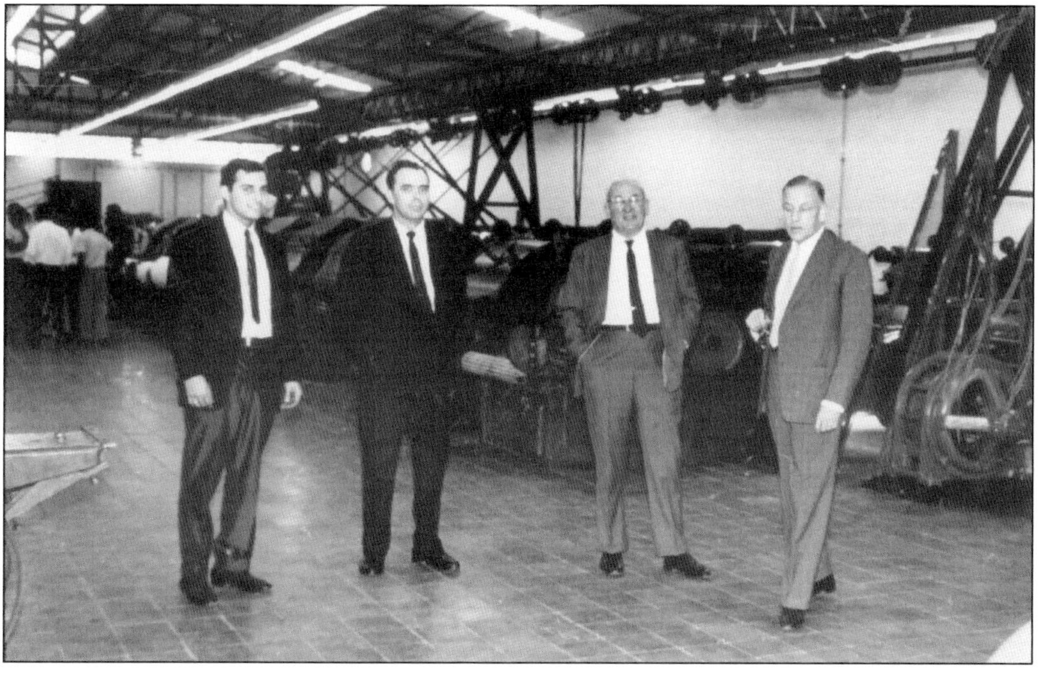

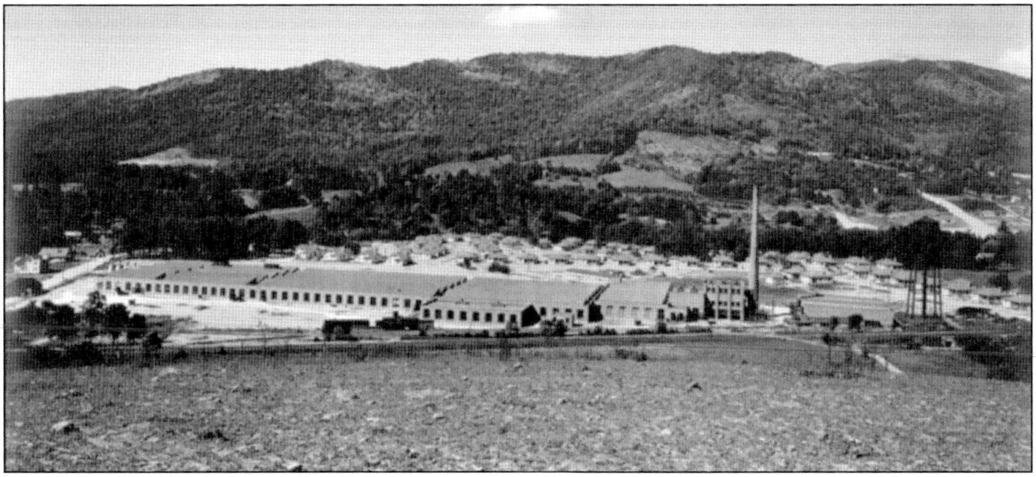

The plant continued to grow until the Great Depression hit the country in 1929. The Owen family had a difficult decision to make, needing to close either the Swannanoa plant or the original New Bedford plant. They chose to close the New Bedford plant and move all of their machinery and equipment via train the 950 miles from Massachusetts to North Carolina. (Courtesy of the Swannanoa Valley Museum, Hill collection.)

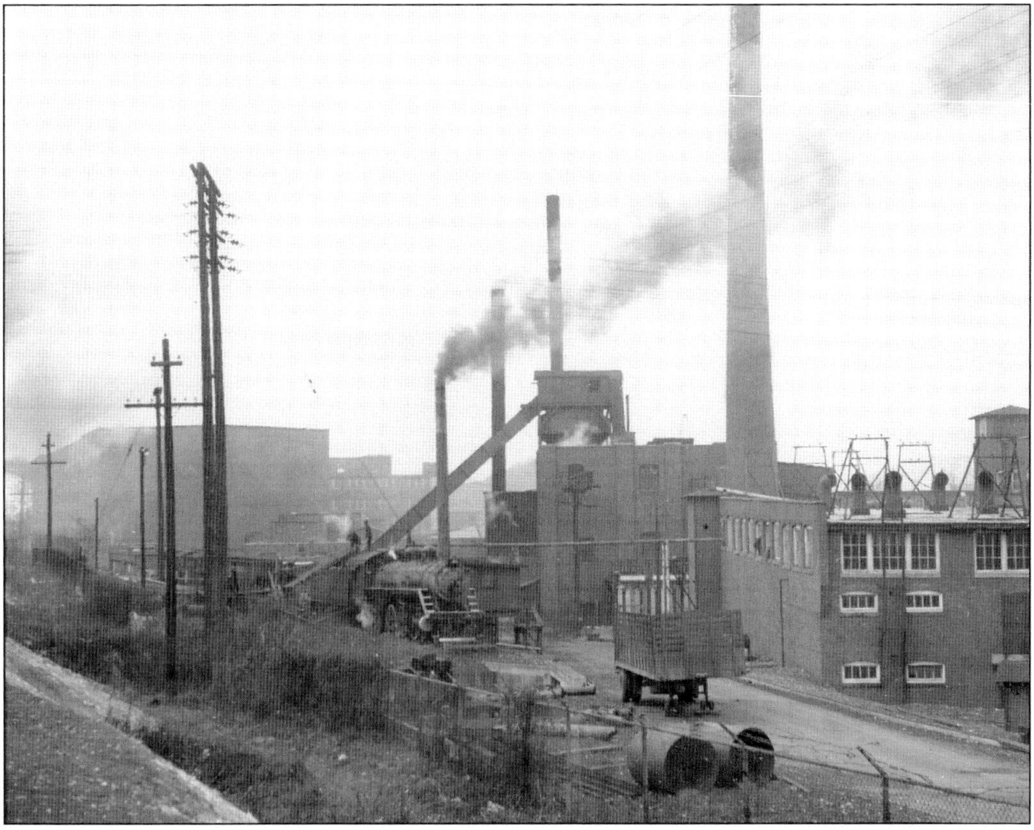

In 1933, the complete New Bedford plant was moved, brick by brick, to Swannanoa. All of the machinery and equipment was taken down, placed on thousands of freight cars heading south, and then reassembled in the new five-story plant. (Courtesy of the Swannanoa Valley Museum.)

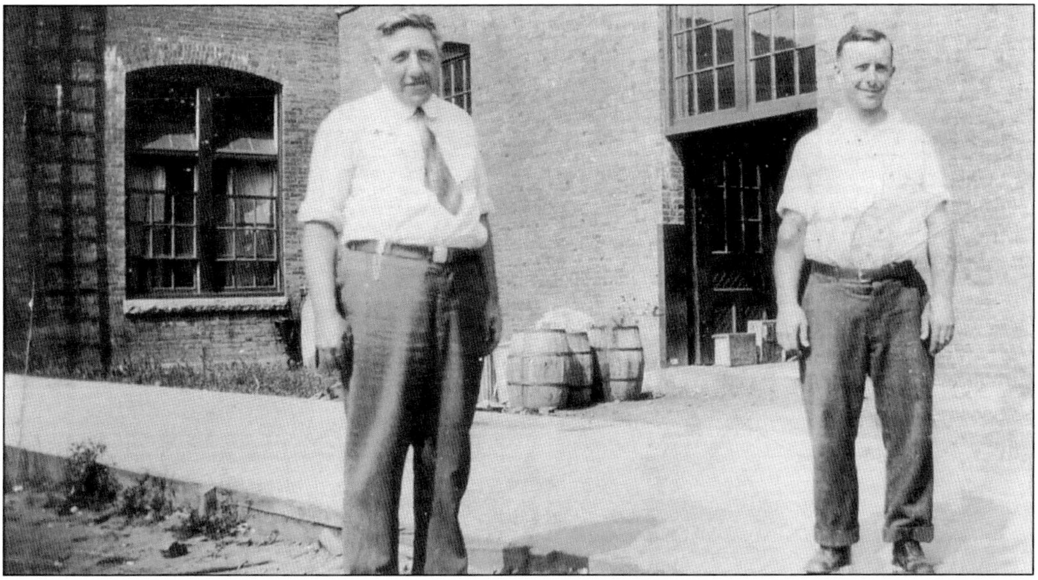

While the plant was being relocated, Pres. Franklin D. Roosevelt ordered a moratorium on all banks for two weeks, during which no one could deposit or withdraw money. The Owens family had hired many new employees to help move and reassemble the mill, so, to ensure that these workers would be able to shop at local stores to buy necessities while the banks were closed, Charles D. Owen II issued scrip money to each employee, noting that Beacon would honor all scrip used in the stores. Here, two employees stand in front of one of the mill's entrances. (Courtesy of the Swannanoa Valley Museum.)

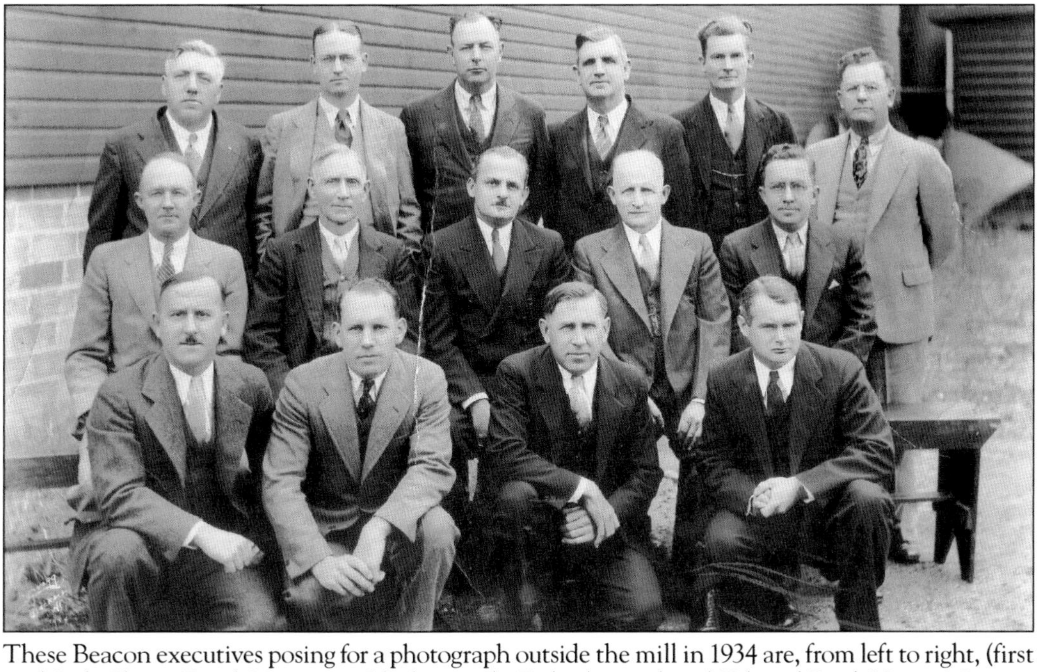

These Beacon executives posing for a photograph outside the mill in 1934 are, from left to right, (first row) Jade Shore, Frank Vincent, ? Blecher, and ? Daly; (second row) Edward Deal, Henry Morgan, A.J. Magnant, ? Gibbs, and ? Mallory; (third row) Jack Smith, ? Cleveland, George D. Young, "Boog" Powell, Charles Edwards, and John Vailancourt. (Courtesy of the Swannanoa Valley Museum.)

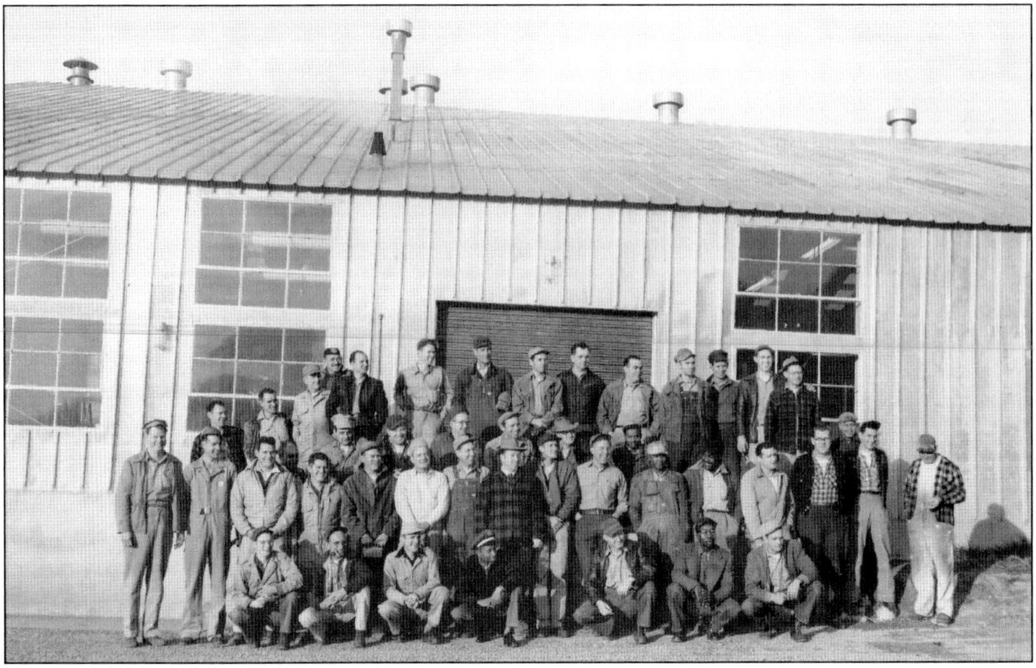

After the despair of the Depression passed, the prosperity of the mill and the surrounding community began to slowly increase once again. The US armed forces began to require more new products and materials, and Beacon quickly adapted to the new demands. With increased productivity came the need for more employees. Just before the beginning of World War II, Beacon had just over 2,200 employees on its payroll. Above, Beacon employees pose for a group photograph outside of the machine shop. Below, the men from Beacon's pipe shop gather for a group photograph. (Both, courtesy of the Swannanoa Valley Museum, Bryant collection.)

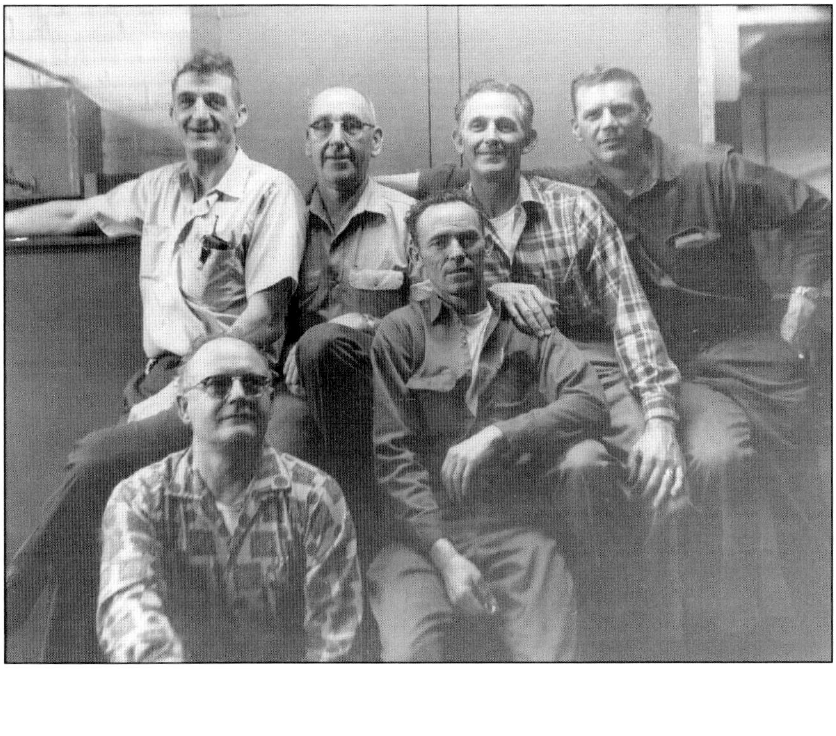

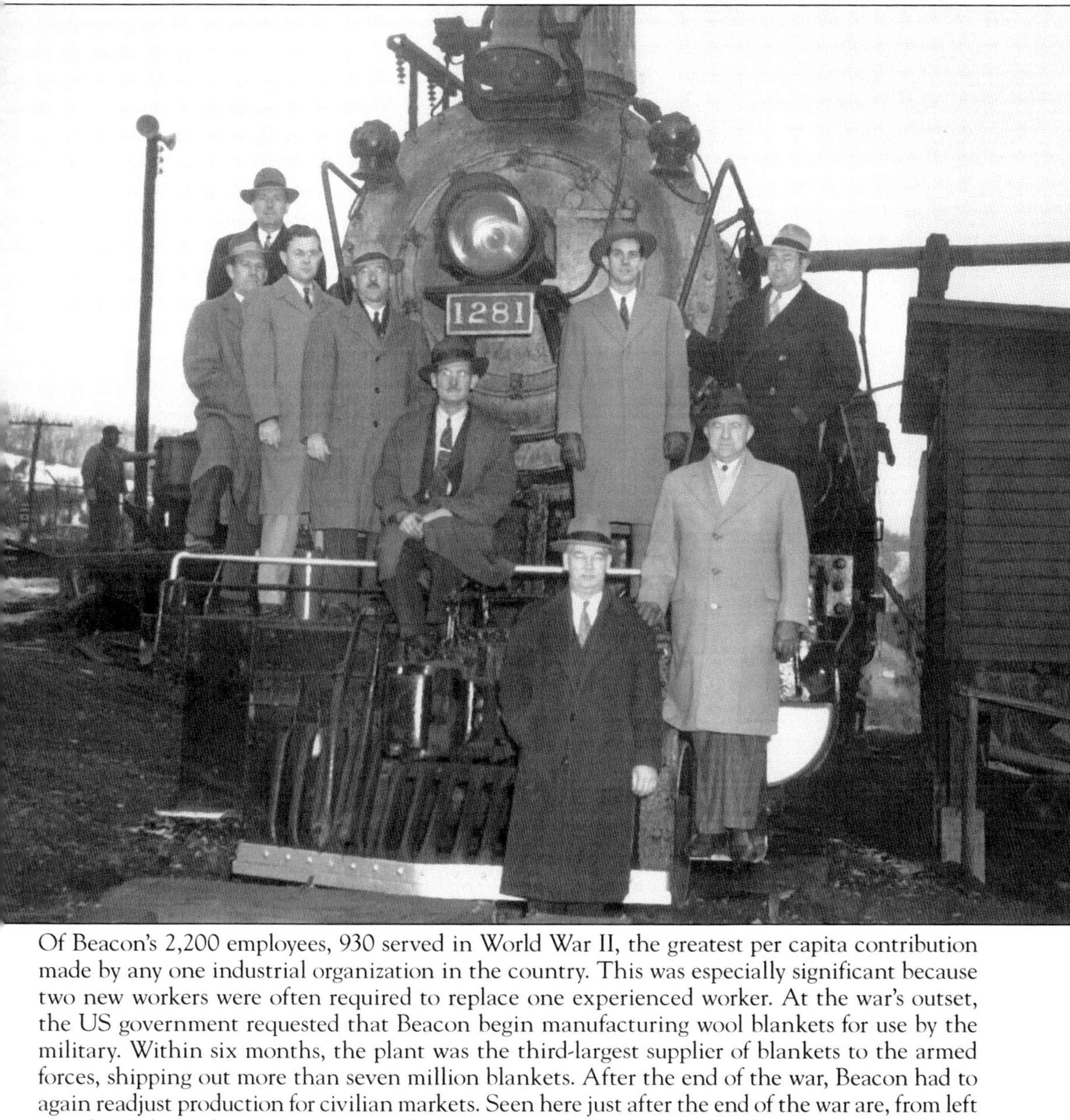

Of Beacon's 2,200 employees, 930 served in World War II, the greatest per capita contribution made by any one industrial organization in the country. This was especially significant because two new workers were often required to replace one experienced worker. At the war's outset, the US government requested that Beacon begin manufacturing wool blankets for use by the military. Within six months, the plant was the third-largest supplier of blankets to the armed forces, shipping out more than seven million blankets. After the end of the war, Beacon had to again readjust production for civilian markets. Seen here just after the end of the war are, from left to right, Bob Darden, Frank Vincent, Bill Johnson, Jade Shore, Charles Edwards, Alden Gifford, Hal Cory, ? Lawrence, and ? Oliver. (Courtesy of the Swannanoa Valley Museum.)

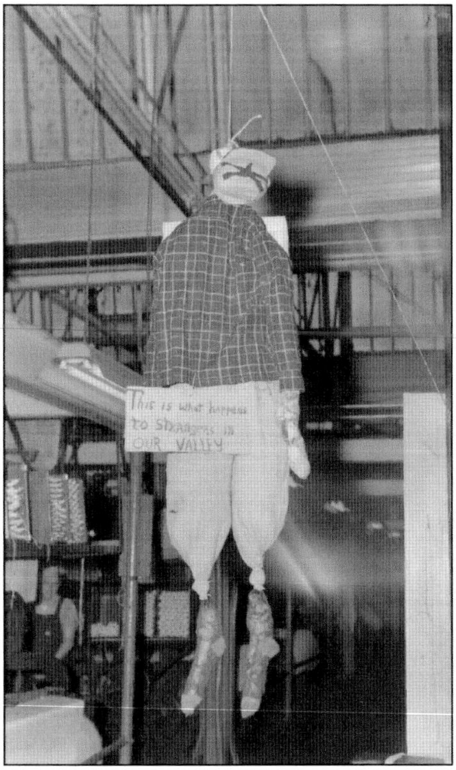

One of the primary reasons for Beacon's move to the South was to get away from the unions that were active in the Northeast. Shortly before Beacon made the move to Swannanoa, a strike in a New Bedford mill lasted six months. When the Owen family relocated the plant, they did their best to ensure that they would have few problems with employees attempting to unionize. They did so by providing services to their workers, like inexpensive housing, help with hospital bills, credit at company stores, and recreational opportunities. Beacon was involved in almost every aspect of its workers' daily lives, and approximately 75 percent of families in the town had at least one family member working at Beacon, which made it very difficult for any talk of unionizing to progress. These two photographs illustrate how some Beacon employees felt about unions. The sign above the makeshift coffin below reads, "St. Peter, this man is coming to you're [*sic*] door. He has tried this 3 times before. This is what we think of this stupied [*sic*] Jerk who came to our valley to mess up our work. Youre [*sic*] the judge if it's there or below. But keep in mind, he was a member of the AFL-CIO." (Both, courtesy of the Swannanoa Valley Museum.)

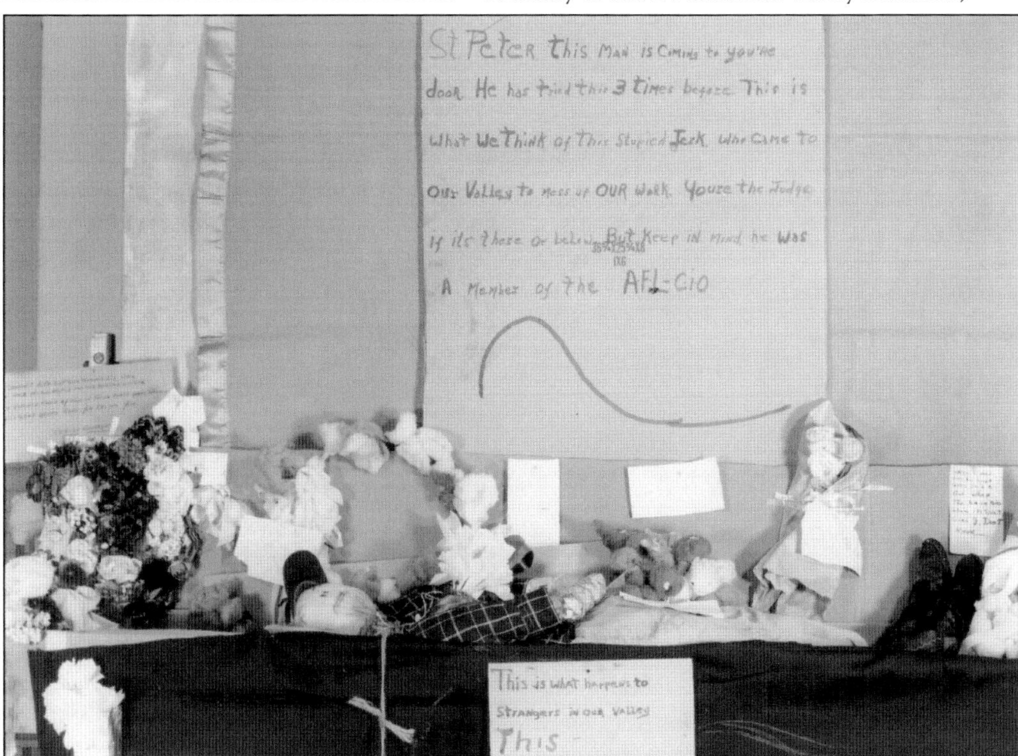

Seven

Mr. Owen's Mill Community

Businesses, Services, and Recreation

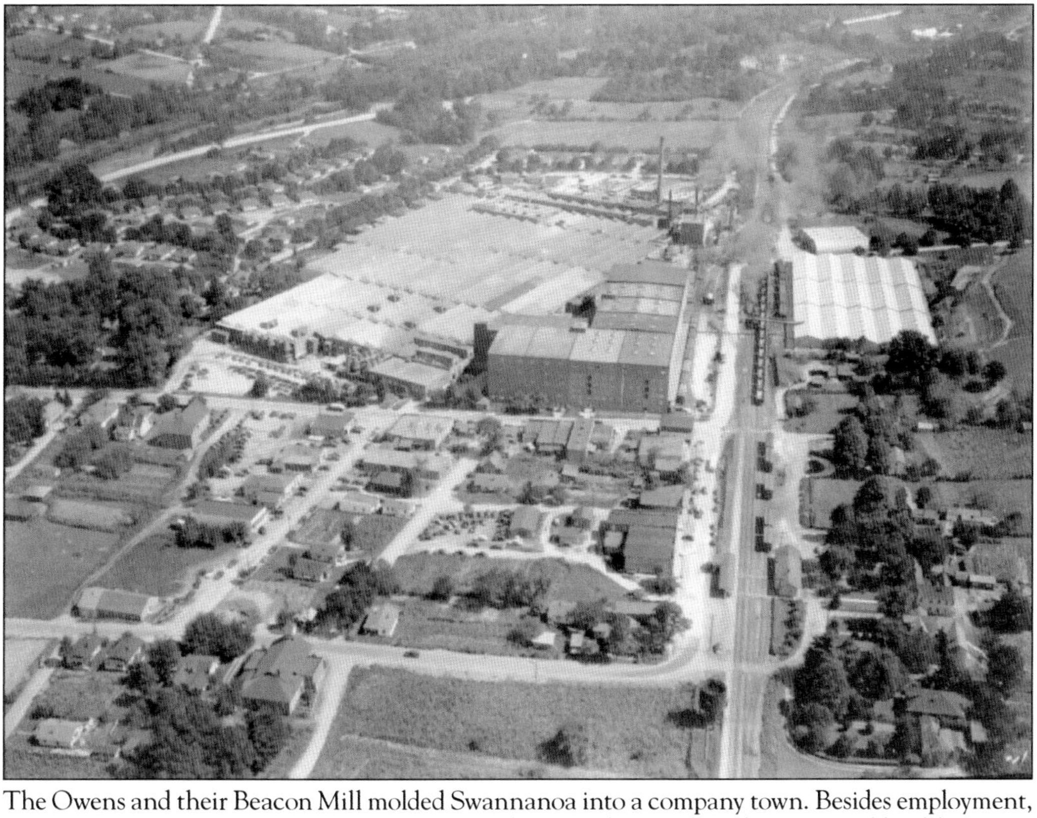

The Owens and their Beacon Mill molded Swannanoa into a company town. Besides employment, Beacon also provided a number of services to their employees, from housing and health care to basic town infrastructure. In this aerial photograph from September 1948, the enormity and central location of the plant reflects the large role it played in the lives of its employees and of all residents of Swannanoa. (Courtesy of the Swannanoa Valley Museum.)

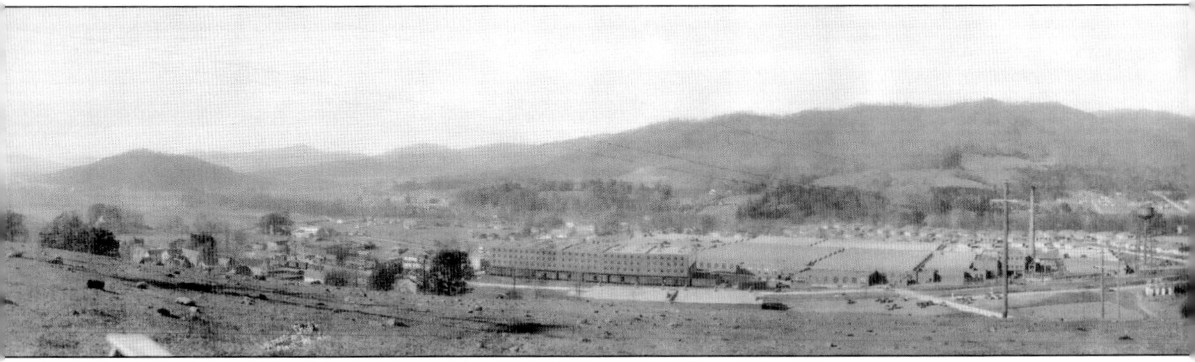

Because many Beacon employees relocated to Swannanoa either from New Bedford or from rural farms in western North Carolina, the availability of housing across from the mill was a significant draw for many workers. In this 1940s panoramic photograph of downtown Swannanoa, both the old and new mill villages are seen. The old village, located directly across from the mill,

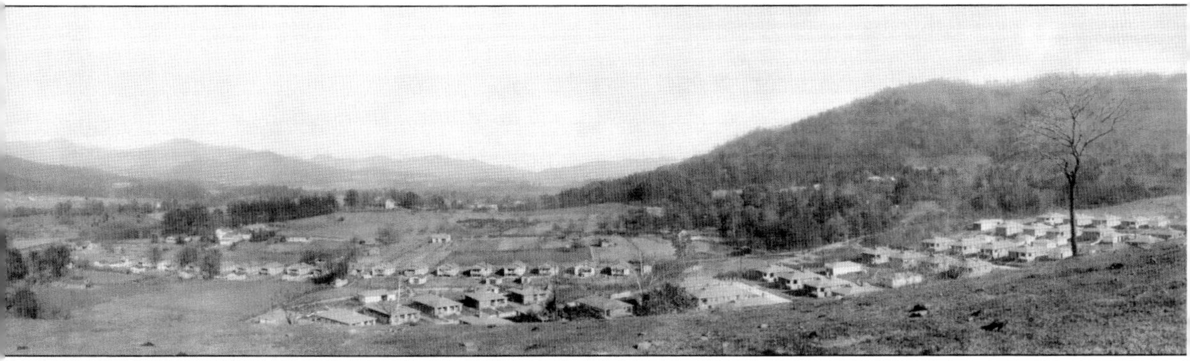

was constructed in 1924 for the mill's first workers. It consisted of 49 two-bedroom houses. The new village's brick duplexes were built across the railroad tracks from the mill. (Courtesy of the Swannanoa Valley Museum.)

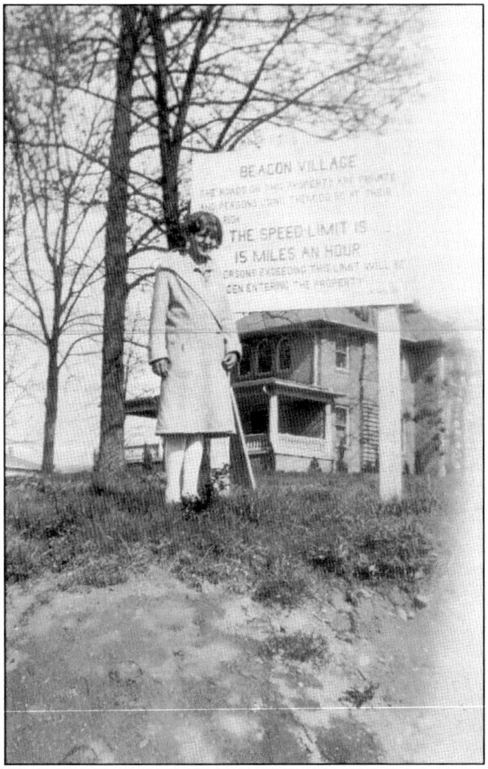

Owen rented out homes in the mill villages by the room, at a going rate of 25¢ per room. Though the pay at Beacon was fairly low—about $40 a week for a 45-hour workweek—the number of services provided to Beacon employees allowed employees to live comfortably. (Courtesy of the Swannanoa Valley Museum.)

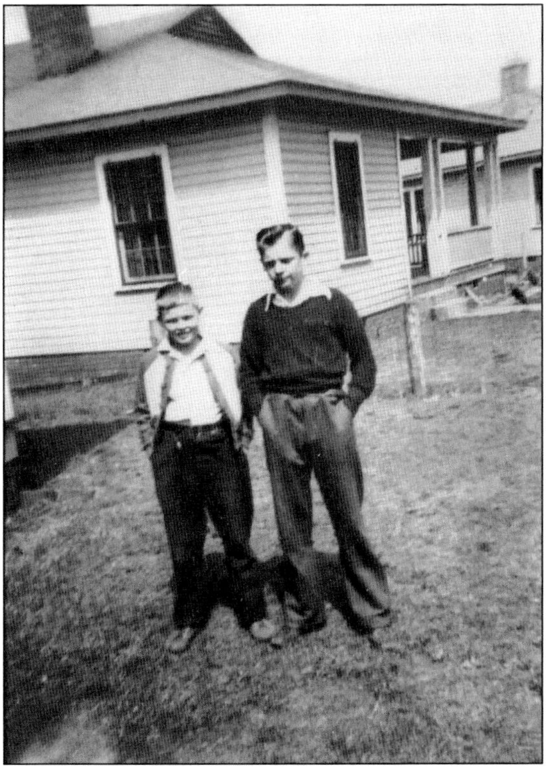

Many children remember the villages as idyllic places in which to grow up. Their playmates were always nearby in the small, closely-knit town. Wade Martin recalled, "When I was a young boy . . . if during the play day I felt I wanted a drink of water or a bite to eat I could almost go into any house in the village and get me a drink of water or a jelly biscuit. We was village kids and village kids was part of the Beacon family." (Courtesy of the Swannanoa Valley Museum, Betty Babb collection.)

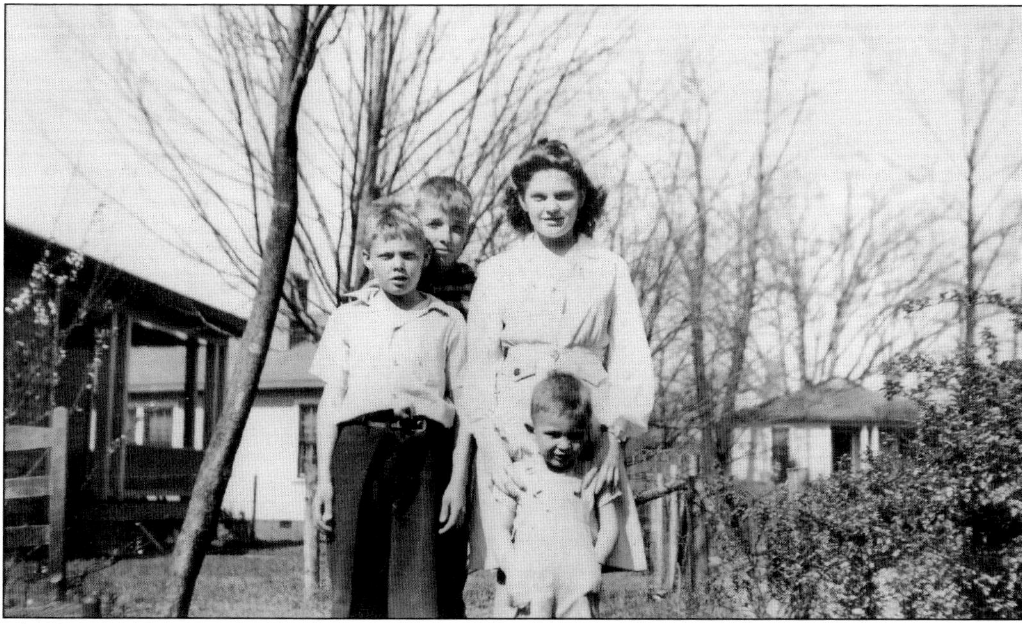

The houses in each village were constructed in a nearly identical style, which helped create a sense of equality between the workers, though African American workers were not allowed to live in the village until much later. Some Beacon executives lived in the villages, but many constructed larger homes outside of the community, with some making their homes in the new Grovemont community across the Swannanoa River. In 1948, the mill began to sell off the homes to the families who had been renting them for the past two decades, for about $1,000 per room. In these photographs, villagers stand outside their homes in the old village. (Both, courtesy of the Swannanoa Valley Museum, Betty Babb collection.)

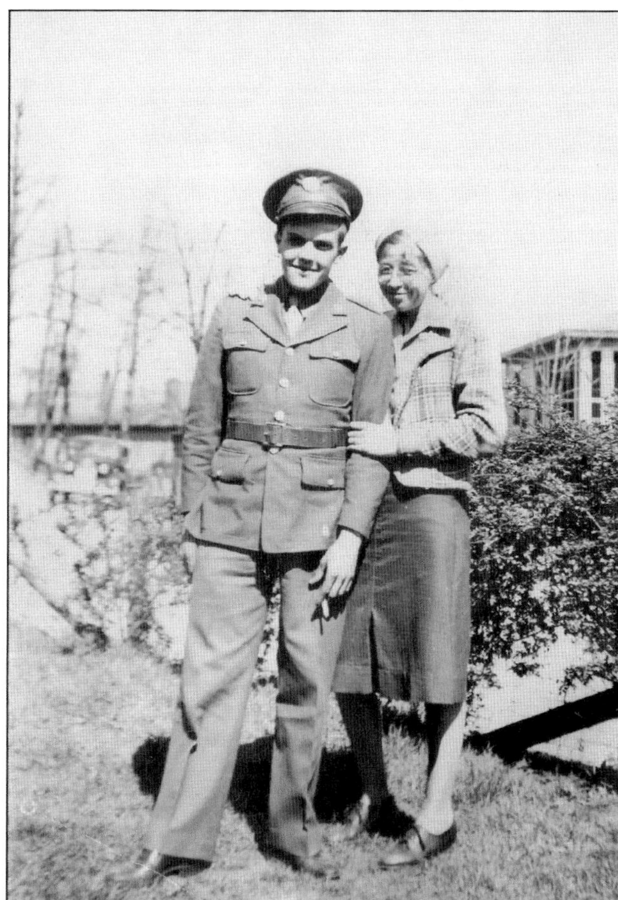

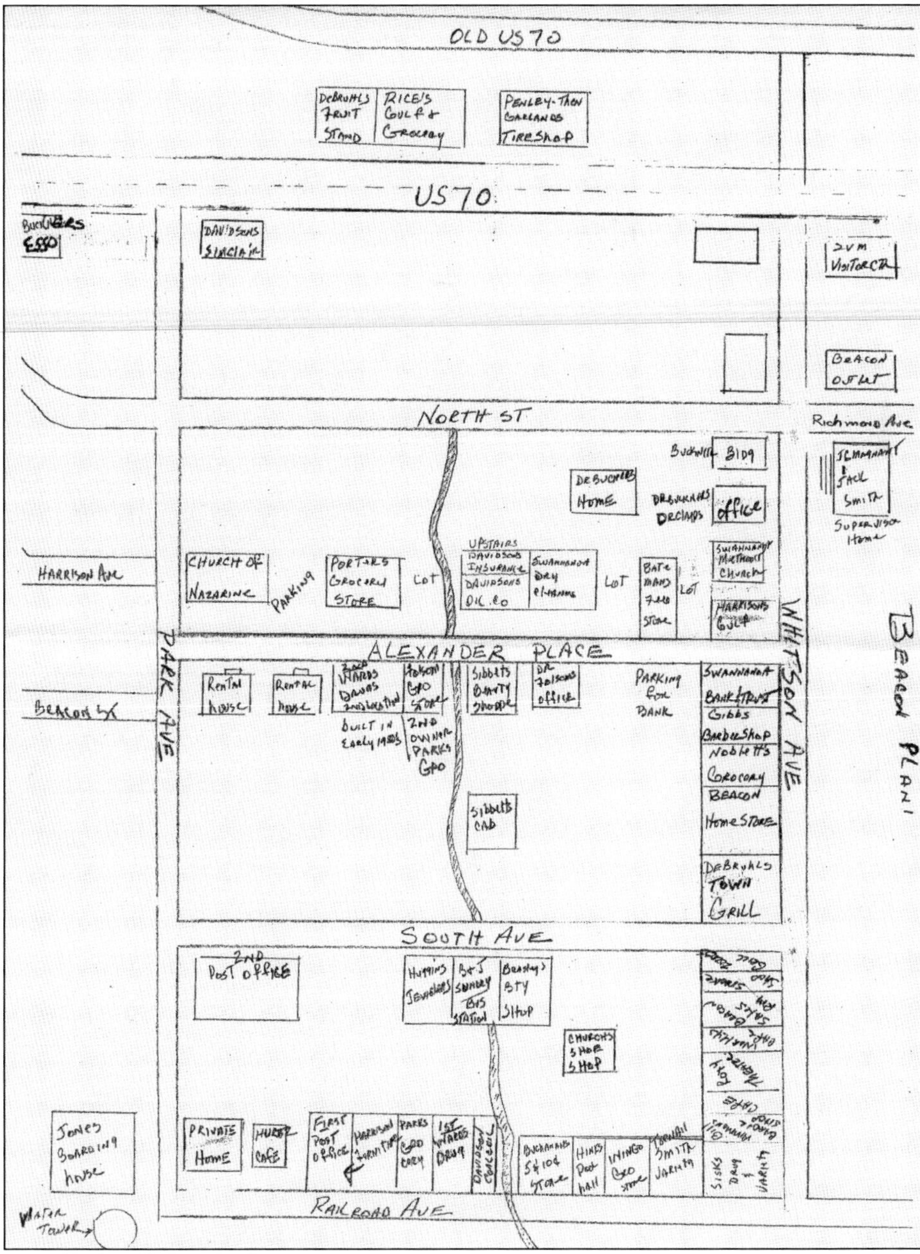

This sketch of downtown Swannanoa, drawn by Bill Alexander, who grew up in Swannanoa, shows the businesses that were present during the heyday of the Beacon Manufacturing Company. Another resident and the author of a memoir about growing up in Swannanoa, Gene Mills, remembers, "The Mill controlled everything in Swannanoa from the price of haircuts to the price of groceries. When The Mill gave a raise, these prices were raised accordingly. The pay in The Mill was adequate. It provided a fairly good living in very hard times. The Mill provided the fire department, maintained the streets, provided water and electricity, and just about every other need you could think of. There was even a grocery store owned by The Mill, called The Home Store, where I tasted my first Coca-Cola." (Courtesy of the Swannanoa Valley Museum, Bill Alexander collection.)

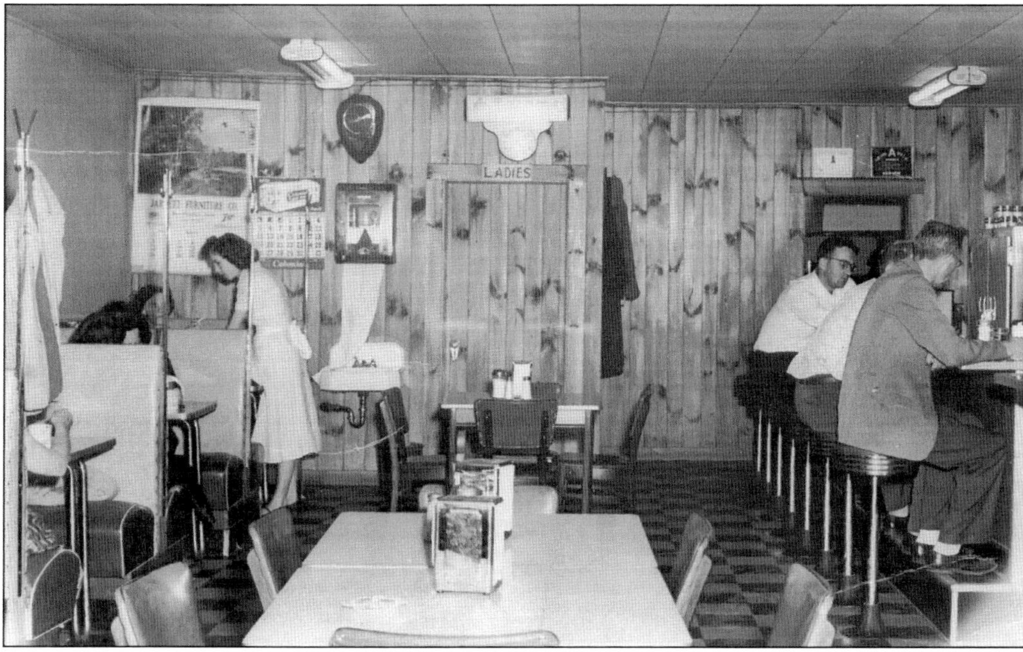

By the 1950s, Swannanoa had several grocery stores, a drugstore, a depot, and its own movie theater. Shown here is the interior of DeBruhl's Town Grill, located on Whitson Avenue across the street from the mill, as it looked in 1954. (Courtesy of the Swannanoa Valley Museum, Bill Alexander collection.)

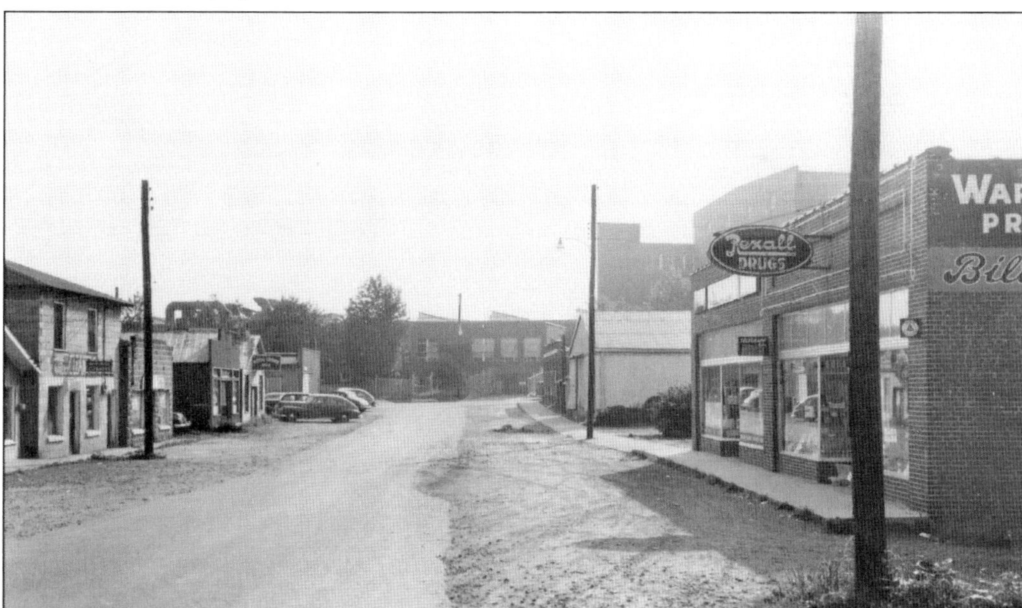

This photograph shows Swannanoa's Alexander Place from the west looking towards Beacon Manufacturing. This road was home to Rexall Drugs, a laundry, and a general store. On Whitson Avenue, perpendicular to Alexander Place, were Smith's Hardware & General Merchandise Store, the Swannanoa Bank & Trust Company, a Shell station, and Swannanoa United Methodist Church. (Courtesy of the Swannanoa Valley Museum, Melton collection.)

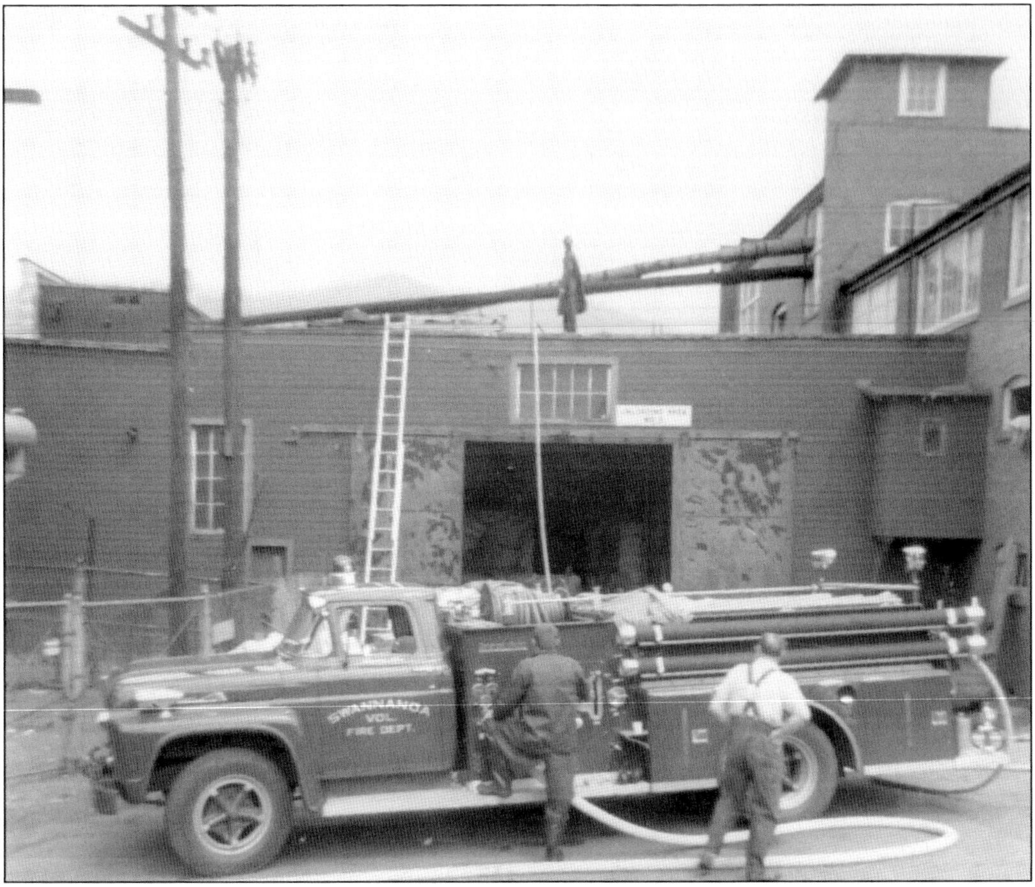

Among the many services provided by the mill was a volunteer fire department. In the photograph above, the fire brigade works on a project at the plant. Below, firefighters pose for a photograph while practicing a drill. (Both, courtesy of the Swannanoa Valley Museum.)

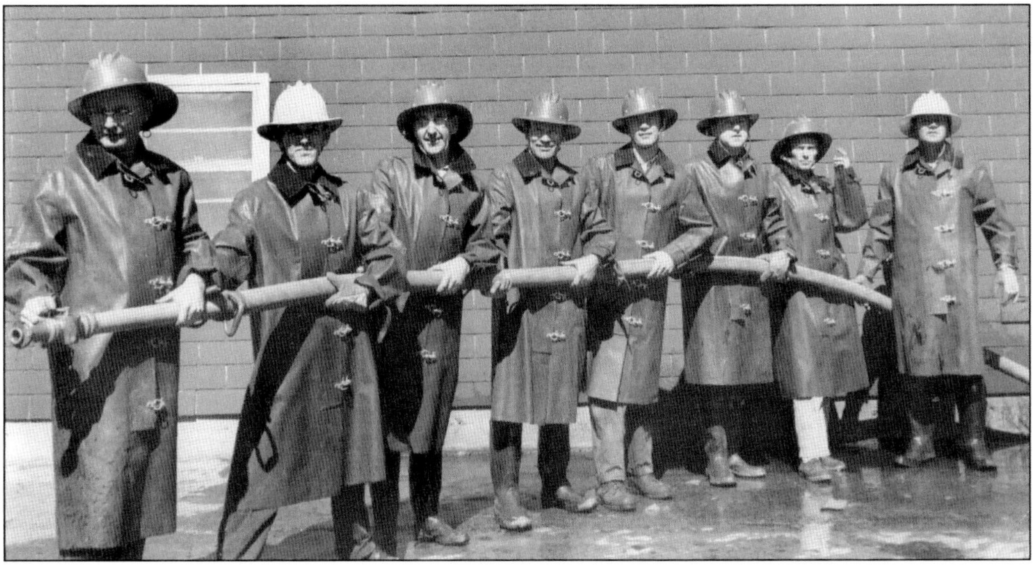

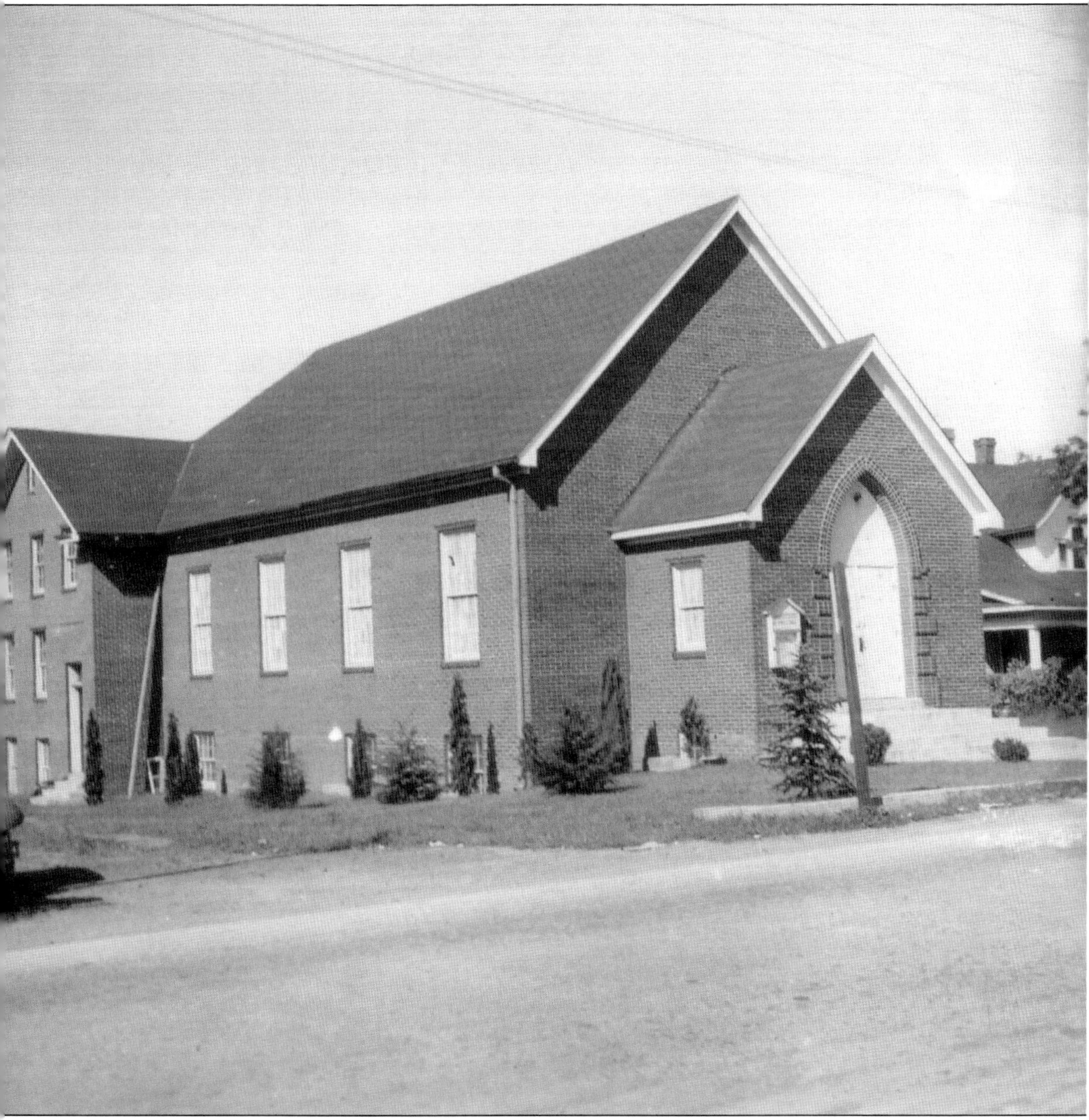

The origins of Swannanoa United Methodist Church, seen here on Whitson Avenue, can be traced back to June 25, 1883, when William F. Davidson sold a two-acre tract of land to the church's trustees for 50¢. A church was built on the property, near where Warren Wilson College is today, and was named Davidson's Chapel. After this original church burned and was rebuilt, it was sold in 1892, and new land was acquired in downtown Swannanoa—still called Cooper's Station at that time—from William H. Wilson and his wife, Hattie E. Wilson. A one-room wooden church building was built south of the train station. The church was lit with oil lamps, and a board fence was constructed out front for the 25 parishioners to tie their horses. The church is now most well known for hosting the Welcome Table, a free meal and fellowship provided every week to members of the community. (Courtesy of the Swannanoa Valley Museum.)

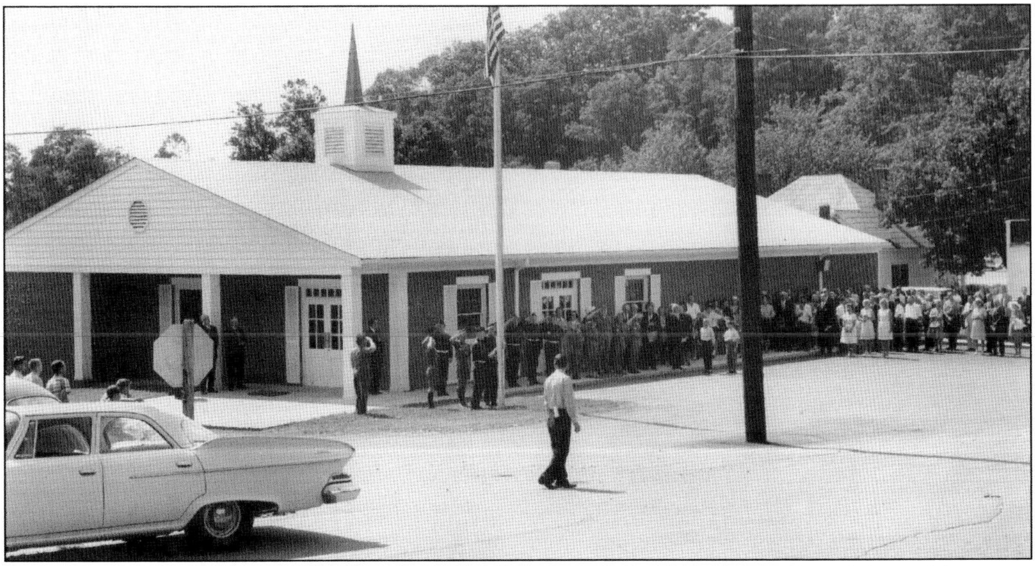

Until 1965, Swannanoa's post office was on Railroad Street, and mail was often delivered by train. On Sunday, June 20, 1965, at 2:30 p.m., Swannanoa's new post office, on Whitson Avenue, was dedicated by Congressman Roy A. Taylor and Hon. W.T. Martin of the post office department. According to the *Black Mountain News*, among those honored and introduced at the ceremony were "our heavy industry owners and managers, all visiting federal, state, county and local officials and others who had a part in making this new postal facility available." The event was open to the community and refreshments were provided. (Courtesy of Brenda Parks Hughes.)

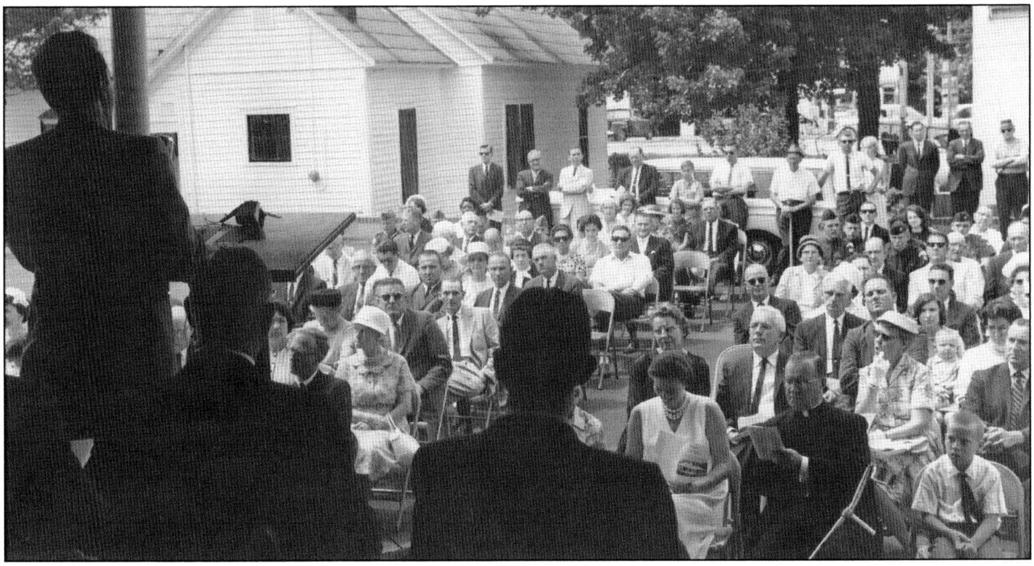

Congressman Roy A. Taylor gave a speech at the 1965 post office dedication in which he recognized Beacon Manufacturing as one of the industrial plants that was turning out products and materials in line with the latest scientific achievements in the country. Taylor went on to identify Swannanoa as the industrial hub of Buncombe County and western North Carolina, and to say that with the development of roads into the region, he expected western North Carolina to experience the largest economic boom since the railroad entered the mountain 80 years before. Around 250 people were present at the ceremony. (Courtesy of Brenda Parks Hughes.)

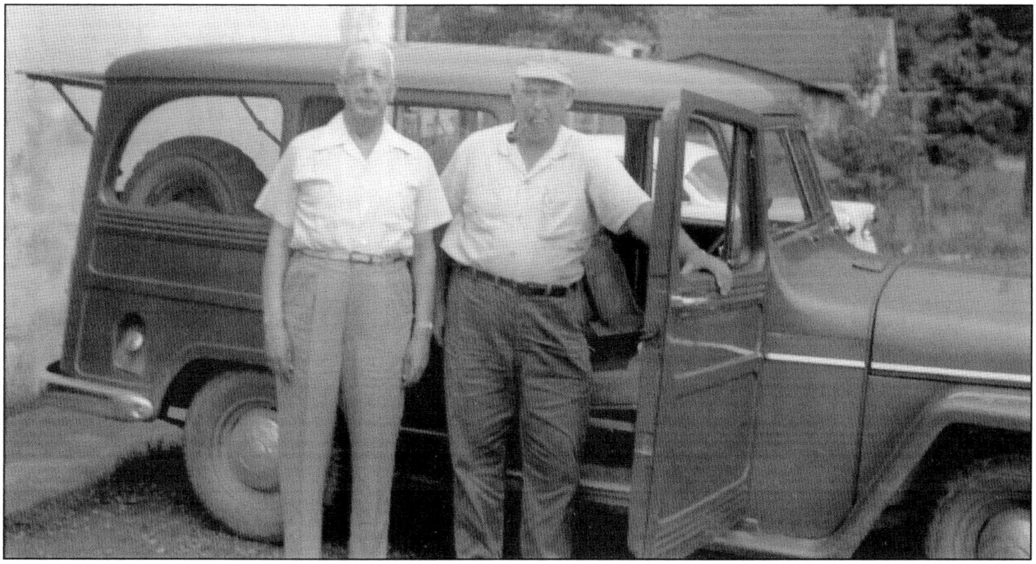

Rural delivery mail service to Swannanoa was established in 1909. The first mail carrier in Swannanoa was Paris Cecil Smith of High Point. On the 50th anniversary of his first mail delivery, Smith was invited to carry the mail for a ceremonial route. He remarked on the changes to Swannanoa since he had last been there. "Factories had sprung up where before there had only been swamp brush," he said. "Mud holes were now paved roads. What was once the Old Farm School was now Warren Wilson College." Despite the changes, many of the same residents still live along the route 50 years later, including Mary Bates, Mrs. Yancey Fortune, and Mrs. W.R. Patton. Seen here is one of the first home delivery postal workers, Hubert Patton (right, with pipe). (Courtesy of Brenda Parks Hughes.)

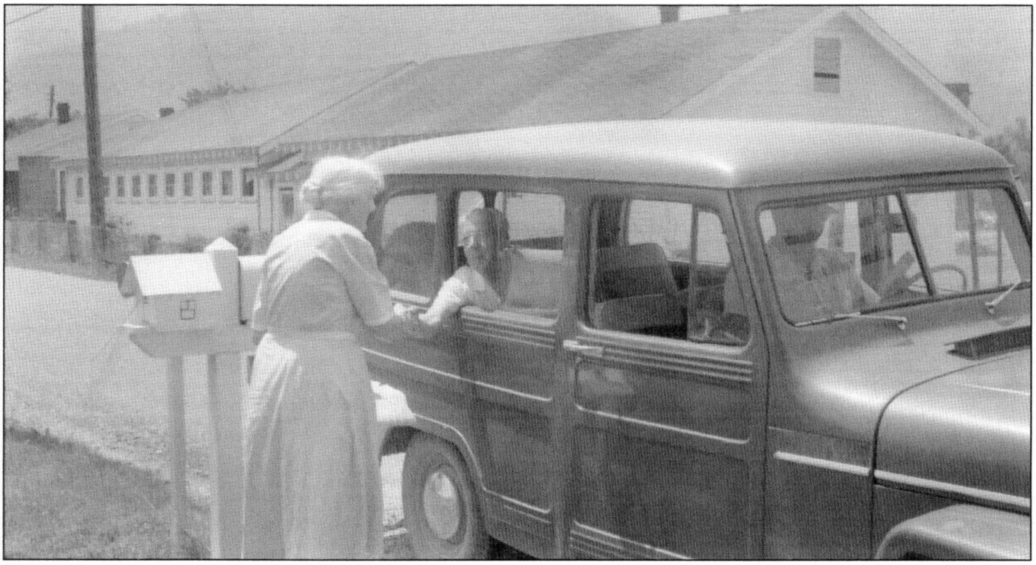

Minnie White collects her mail from home delivery postal worker Hubert Patton in 1959. In order to begin home delivery, all homes in the delivery area were assigned house numbers, and all residents were asked to display the numbers on their home regardless of whether they wanted home delivery. Anyone who did want the service had to install a proper mailbox. James H. Parks, the son of W.J. Parks, was postmaster of Swannanoa at the time. (Courtesy of Brenda Parks Hughes.)

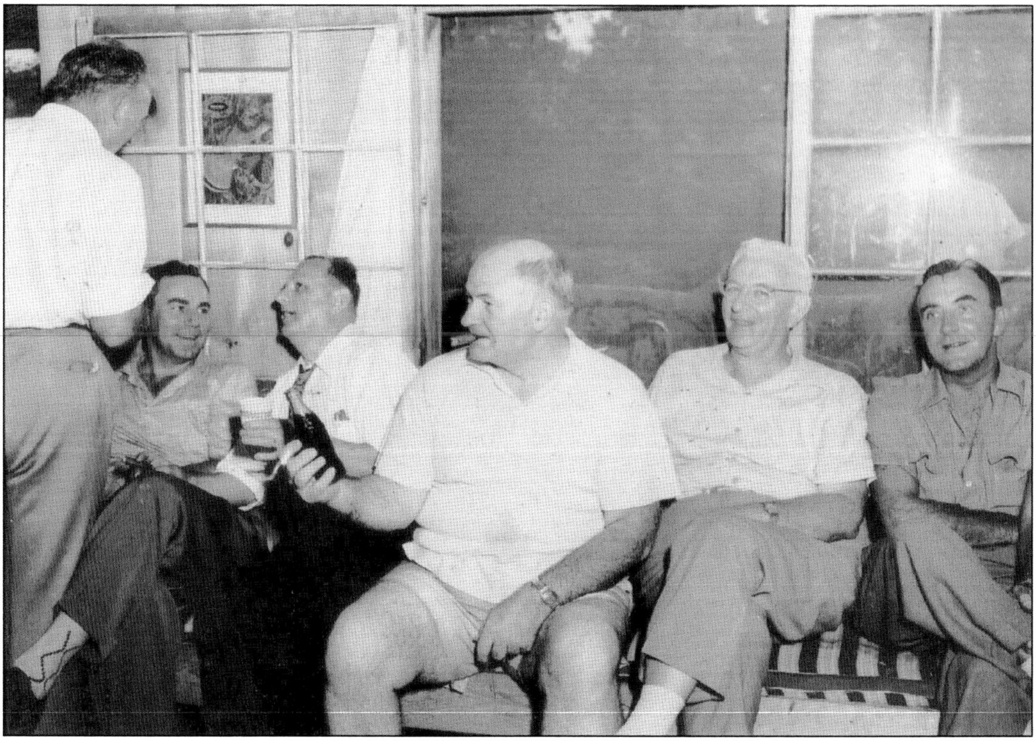

The Owen family provided more than housing, basic necessities, and infrastructure to their employees; they also provided recreational opportunities. The executives at Beacon and important visitors were no exception. In this photograph, Beacon executives relax at a lodge at the Grove Stone & Sand Company. Sydney Croy (center, with cigar), the paymaster for Beacon, is pictured here. (Courtesy of the Swannanoa Valley Museum.)

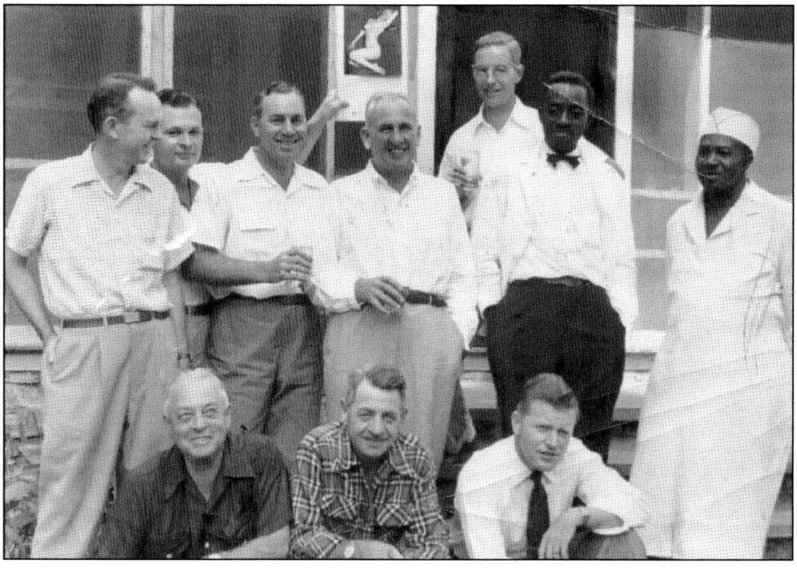

Weekends at the lodge in the Grove Stone quarry were generally reserved exclusively for the men of Beacon. Here, some of the lucky men invited to the lodge pose for a photograph with the cooking and serving staff and proudly display a pinup calendar of Marilyn Monroe. (Courtesy of the Swannanoa Valley Museum.)

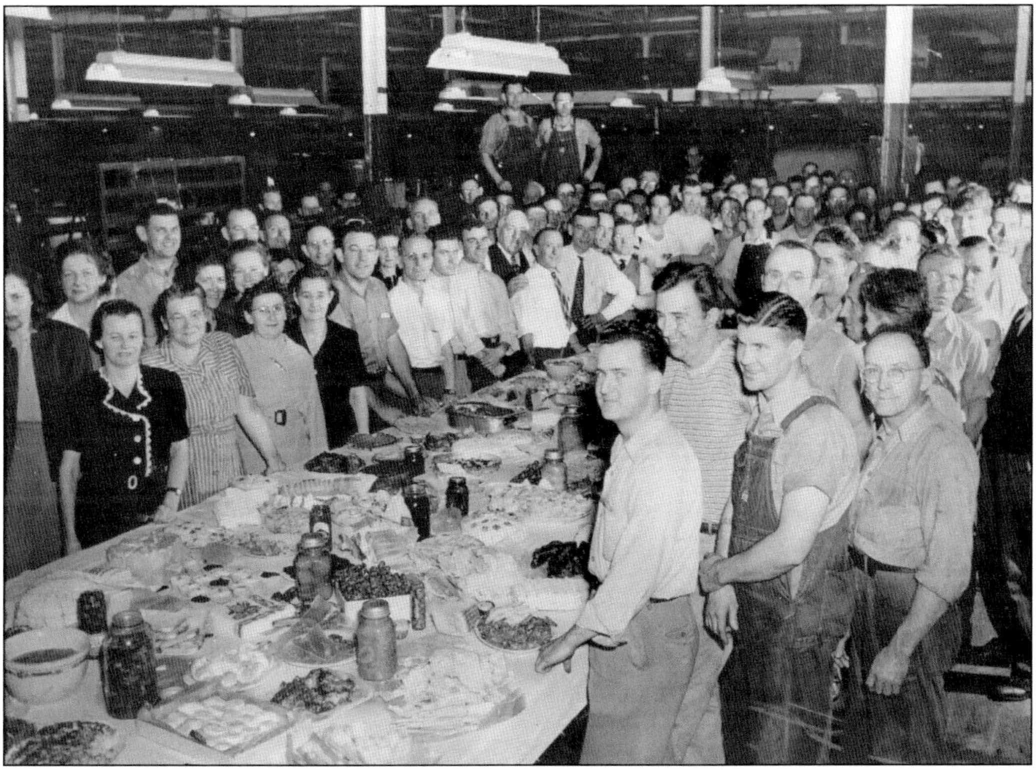

Every Christmas season, Beacon employees gathered for a company-wide potluck. A large tree was decorated inside the mill, carols were sung, and a photograph of all those in attendance was shot. Both of these photographs were taken at early-1940s company potlucks. (Both, courtesy of the Swannanoa Valley Museum.)

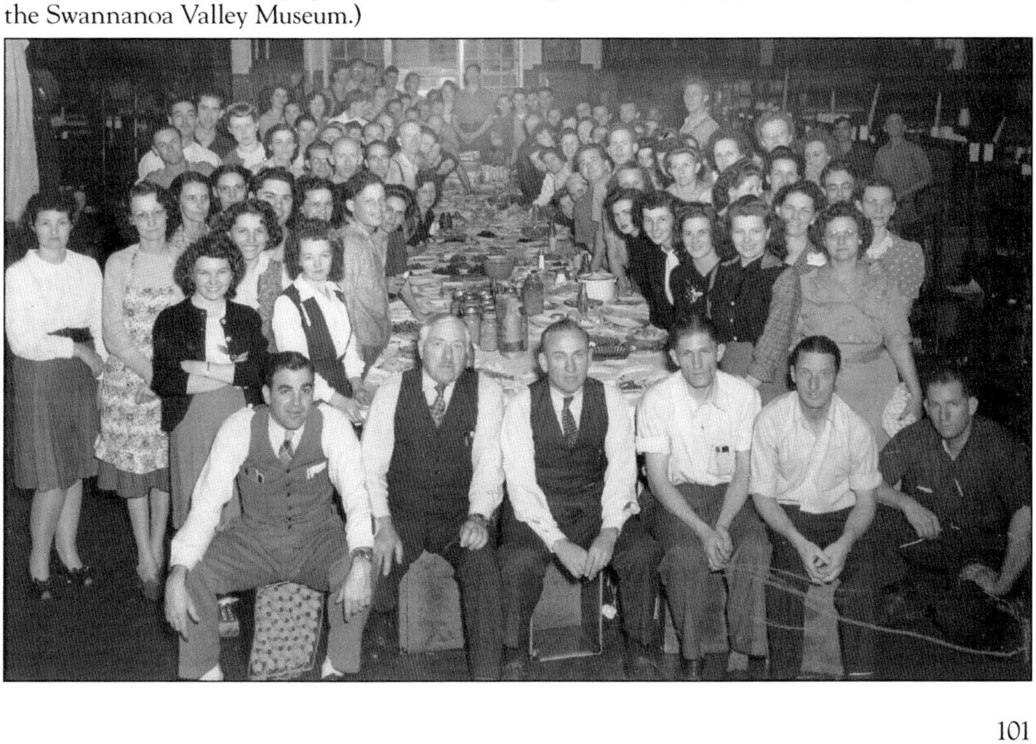

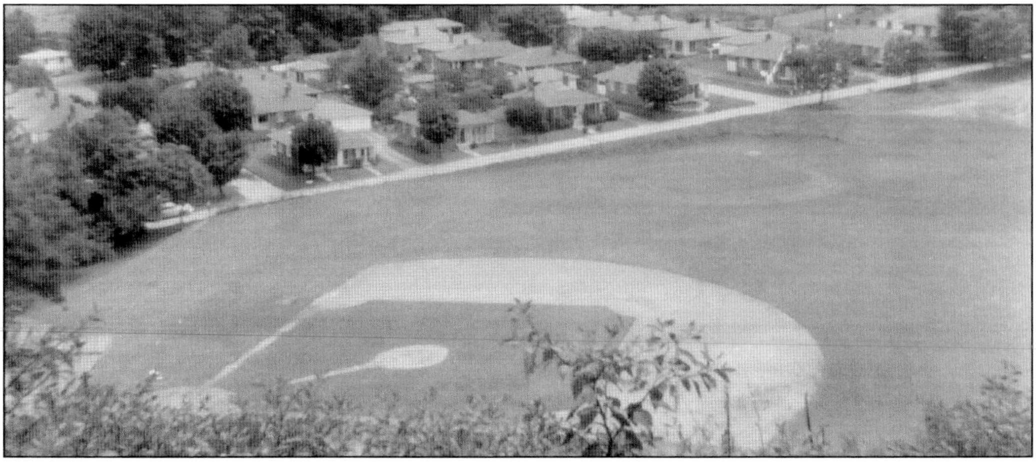

The Owen family often hired employees because they had qualifications outside of textile work. Fiddler Marcus Martin was supposedly hired because of his musical talents and his ability to entertain those living in the mill village. Other workers were chosen for employment because they were skilled baseball players. Nolen Baseball Field was built in the new village to provide recreational opportunities for the young men of the mill villages. The field was called Nolen Field until the mid-1950s, when the name was changed to Coman Field to honor Herb Coman, a former star football player at South Carolina and personnel manager for Beacon. This photograph shows Coman Field, the new village, and Dennis Street in 1961. (Courtesy of the Swannanoa Valley Museum.)

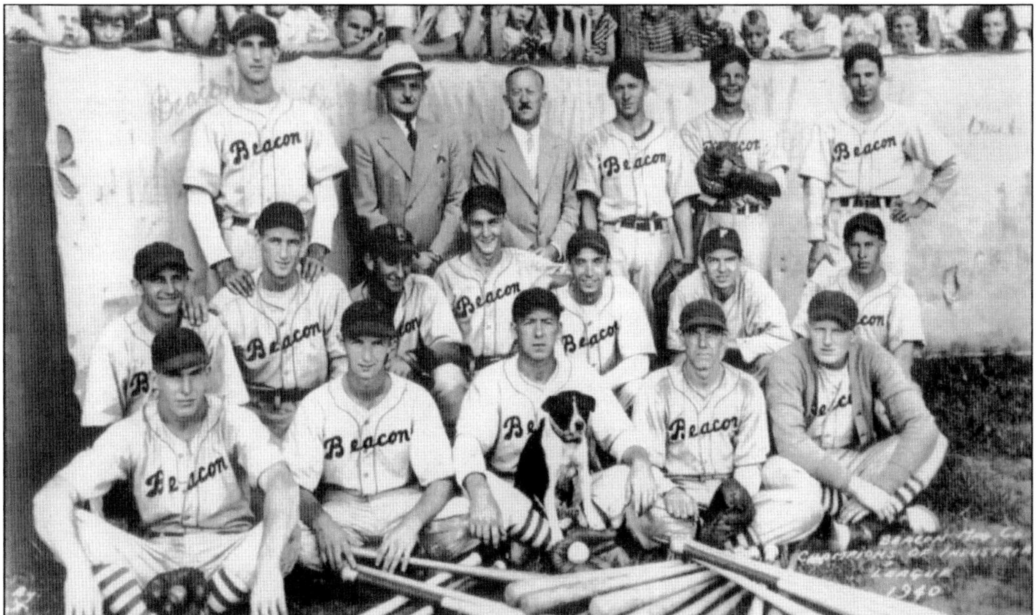

In 1940, the Beacon men's team won the Industrial League championship. The team includes, from left to right, (first row) Milton Ellis, Bassie Moore, Harley Fox, "Smokey" Henry Burrell, and Rex Byrant; (second row) Carl "Shorty" Poteat, Bill Horne, Wayne "Bozo" Martin, Mark Furgerson, Ray Nichols, Woodrow Patton, and Wade "Gob" Martin; (third row) Bill Barnwell, A.J. Magnant, Jack Shore, Pepper Martin, Charlie Talent, and Bill Rhymer. (Courtesy of the Swannanoa Valley Museum.)

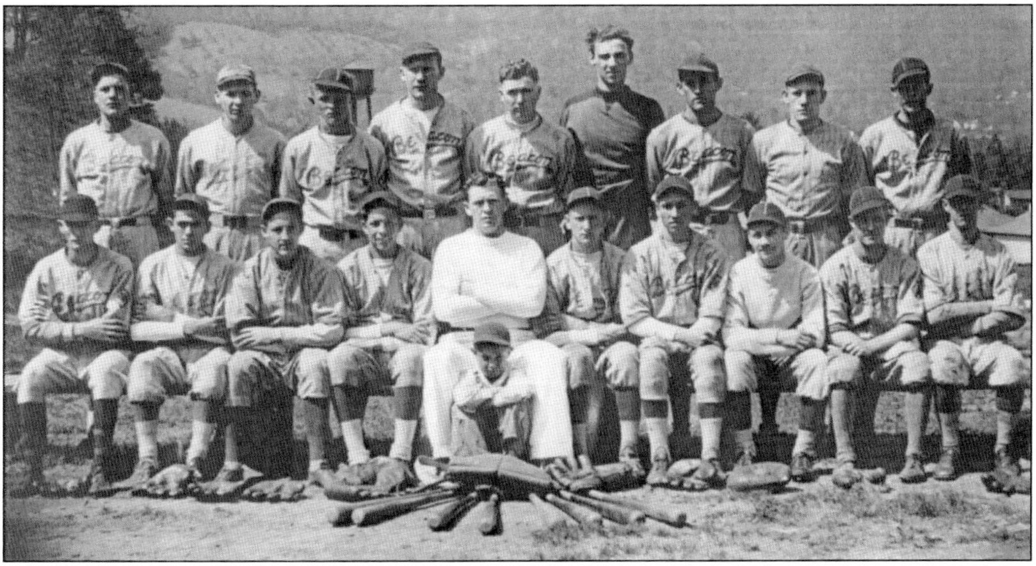

Beacon Manufacturing typically had a strong team, due to the preparation of players, beginning in Little League, as well as the company's policy of recruiting men to work at the mill because they were strong players. Playing for the Beacon Industrial League team was a great honor, and the men's team practiced almost every day after work. (Courtesy of the Swannanoa Valley Museum.)

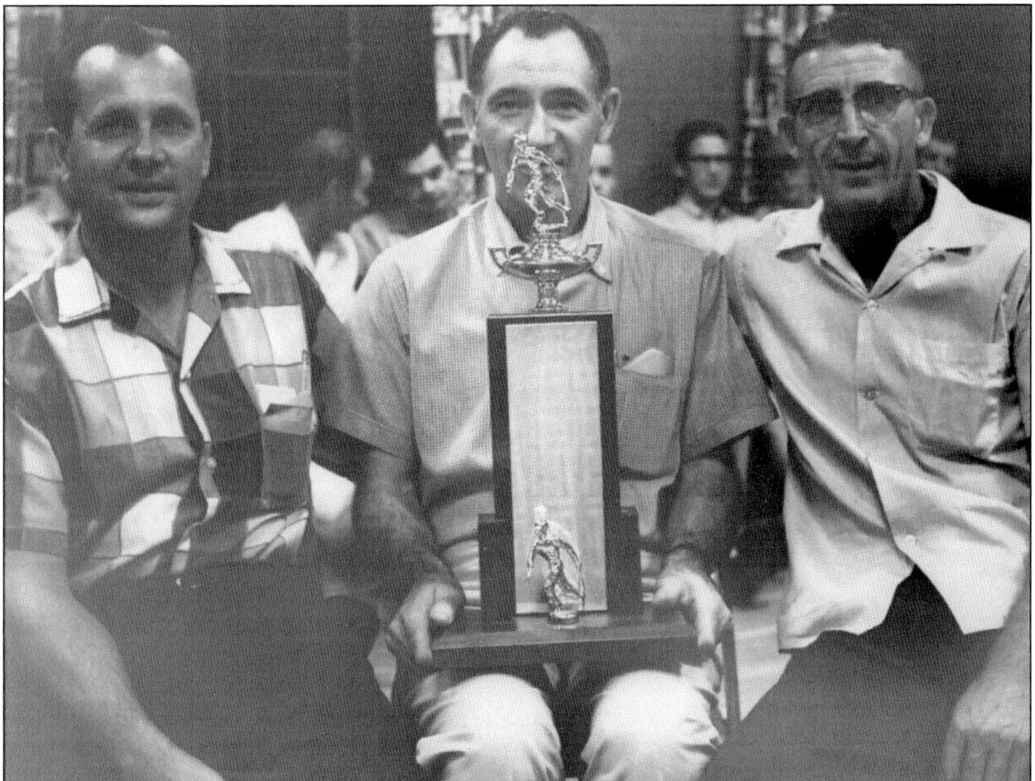

Seen here with their baseball championship trophy are, from left to right, Roy Franklin, Swinn Conner, and Tommy Suttles Sr. (Courtesy of the Swannanoa Valley Museum.)

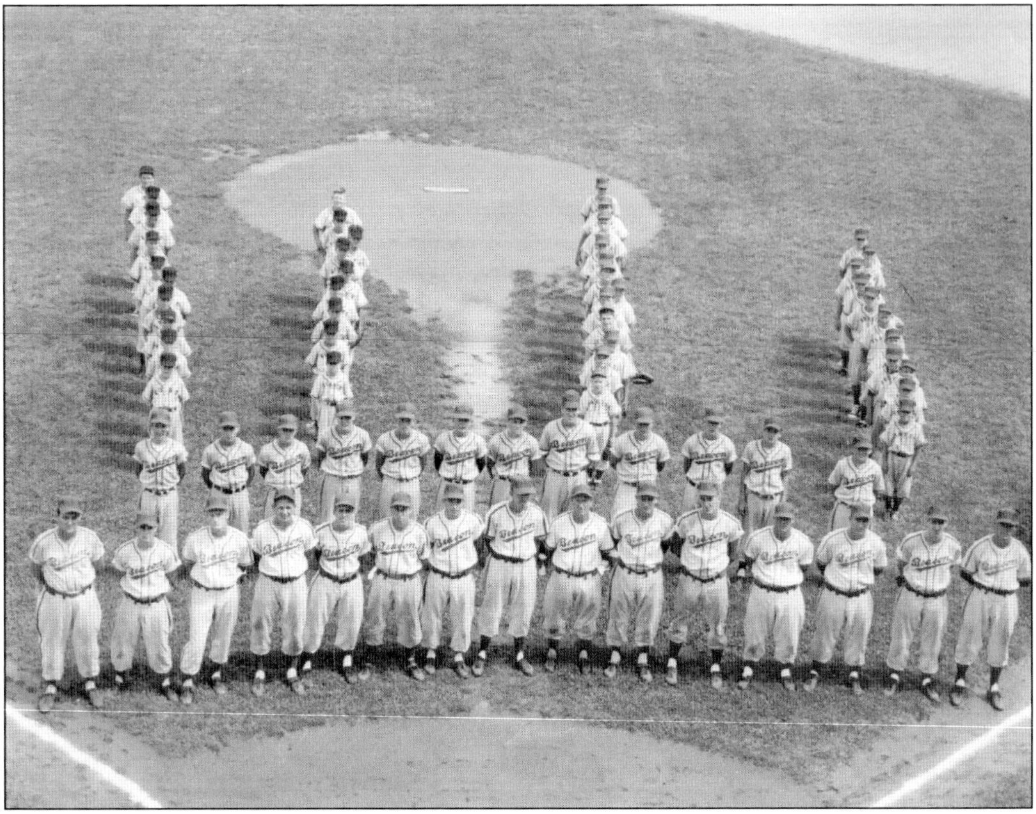

This overhead shot of Coman Field shows the three age levels of men and boys who played baseball for the Beacon teams. (Courtesy of the Swannanoa Valley Museum.)

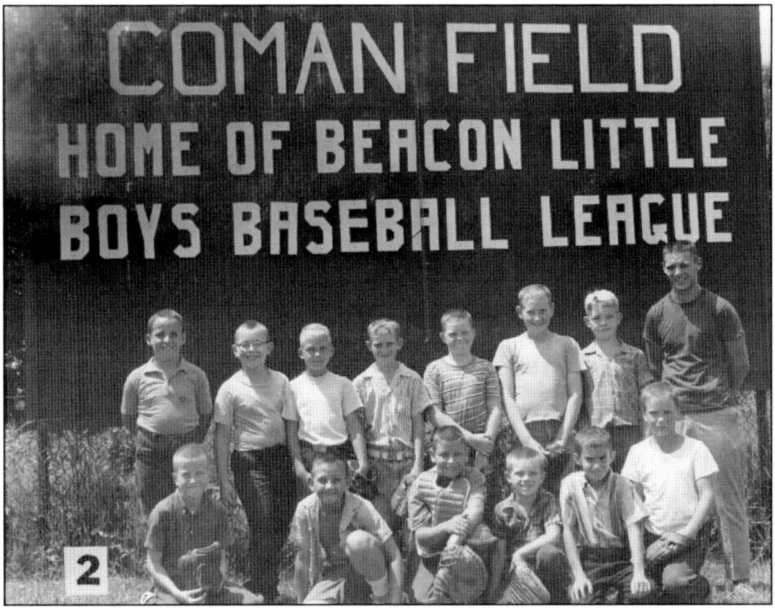

Preparing young boys to play baseball for a championship team took year-round practice. In this July 1963 image, Cecil Caldwell (second row, far right) manages a baseball clinic for pre–Little League boys at Coman Field. (Courtesy of the Swannanoa Valley Museum.)

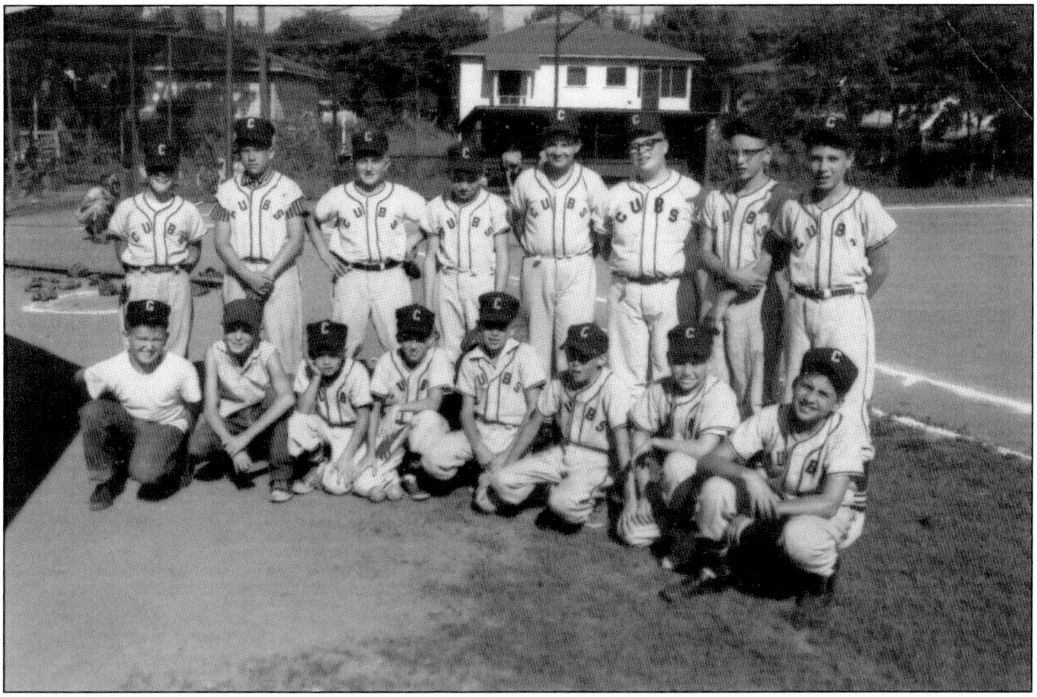

The 1960 Cubs Little League team poses for a team photographs before a game on Coman Field. The team was managed by Walter McGraw (not pictured). The new village is in the background. (Courtesy of the Swannanoa Valley Museum.)

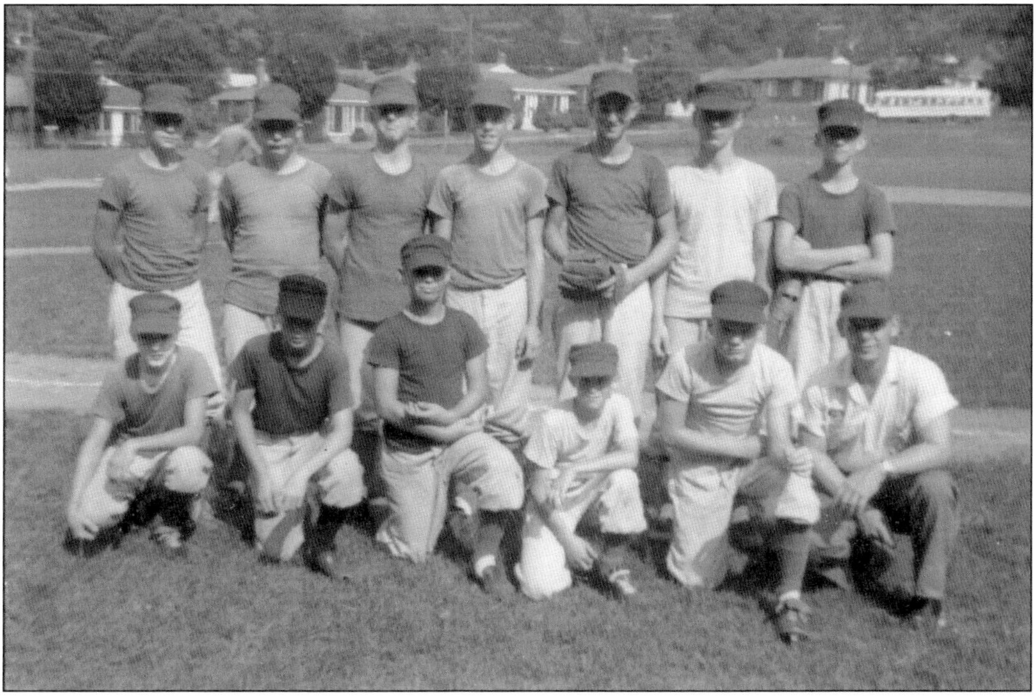

Some of the 1964 Beacon Little League team take a knee during an after school practice at Coman Field, beside the new village. (Courtesy of the Swannanoa Valley Museum.)

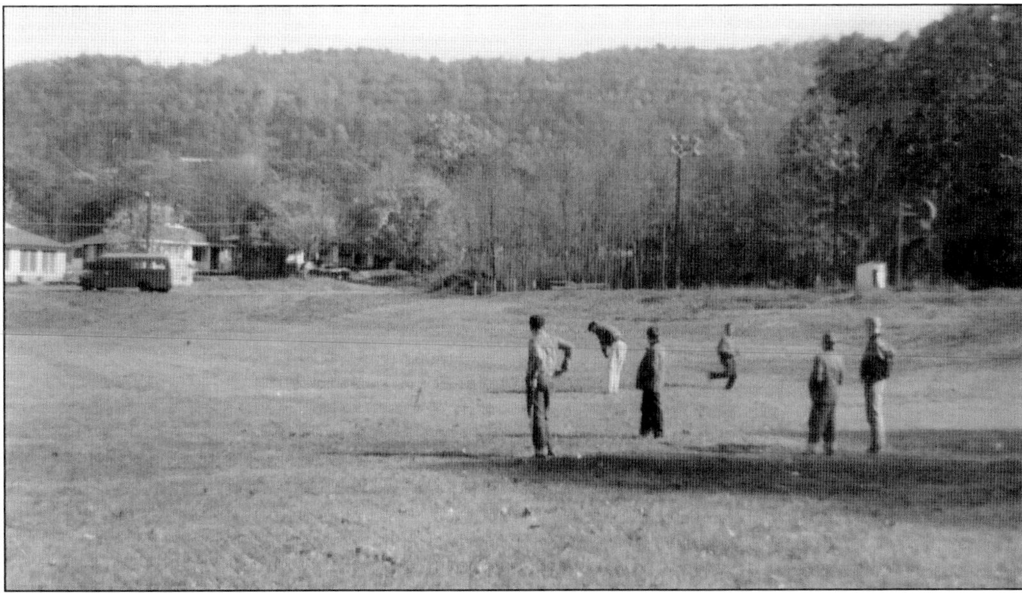

Though baseball was the most popular sport at Beacon, the Owen family provided the space for a variety of activities at Coman Field. Just past the outfield were a basketball court and a horseshoe pit. (Courtesy of the Swannanoa Valley Museum.)

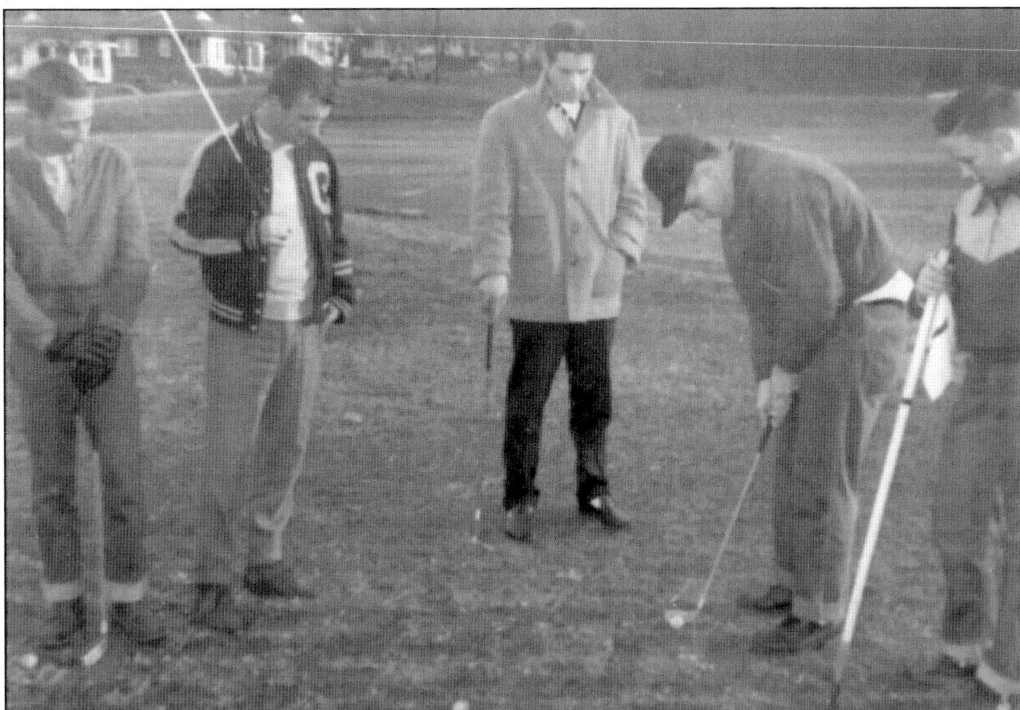

In the off-season, the baseball field was also used as a pitch-and-putt, nine-hole, par-three golf course. Athletic director Wade Martin gave trophies for holes-in-one. Seen here practicing their putting skills in 1961 are, from left to right, Ted Tipton, Millard Shook, Bill Bridges, Sam Wimberly, and unidentified. (Courtesy of the Swannanoa Valley Museum.)

Beside the basketball court was a croquet court. Here, Wayne Nichols taps the balls away from the wicket. (Courtesy of the Swannanoa Valley Museum.)

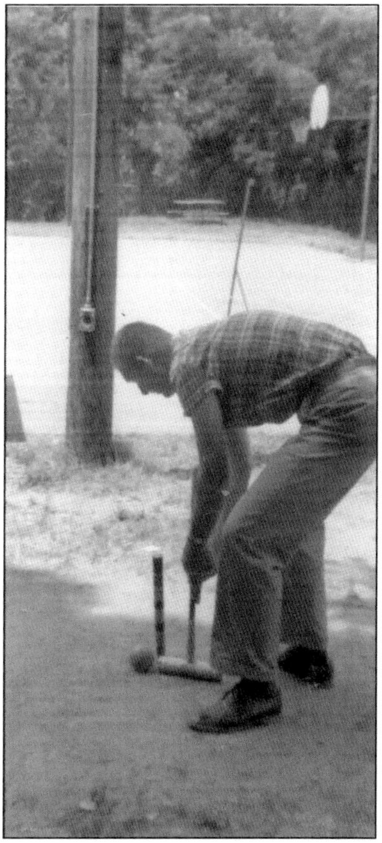

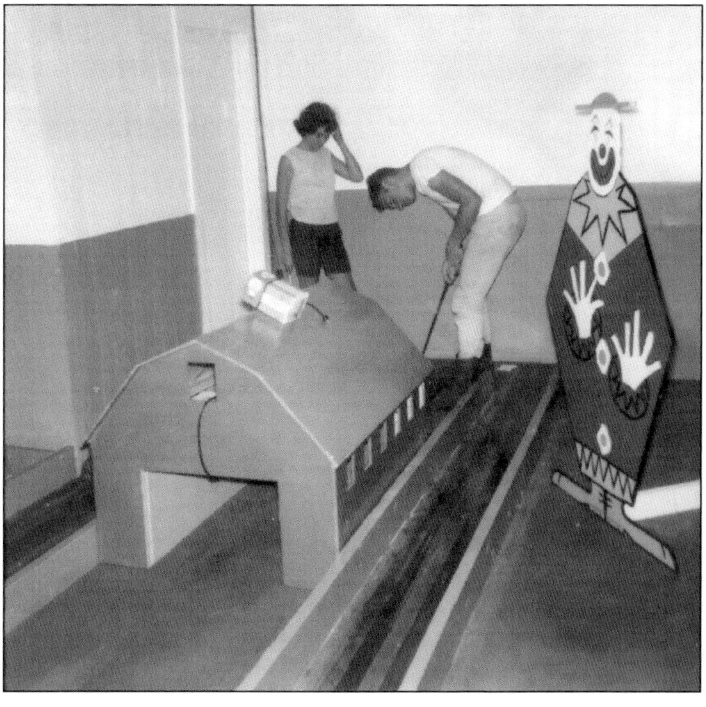

In 1965, the Buckner Building in Swannanoa was home to an indoor putt-putt course. (Courtesy of the Swannanoa Valley Museum.)

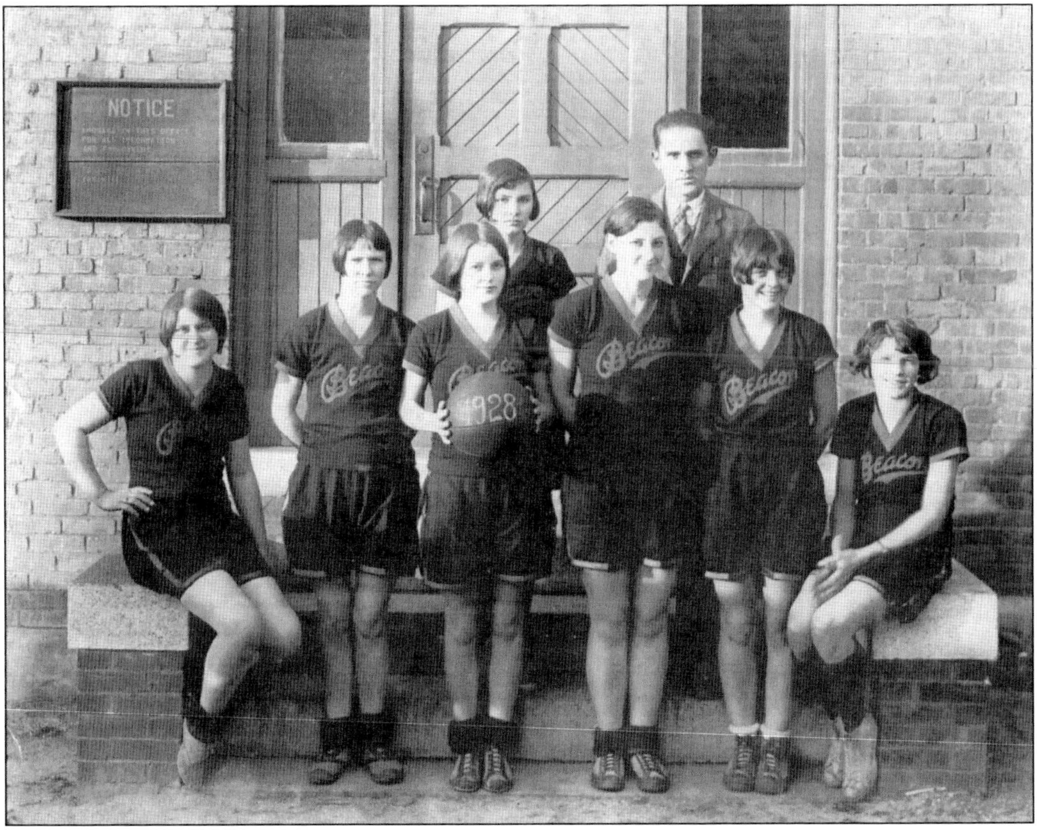

Though there were not many athletic activities provided for women, Beacon did sponsor a women's basketball team. Lillian King (second from left) is seen here with her teammates and coach on the 1928 team. (Courtesy of the Swannanoa Valley Museum.)

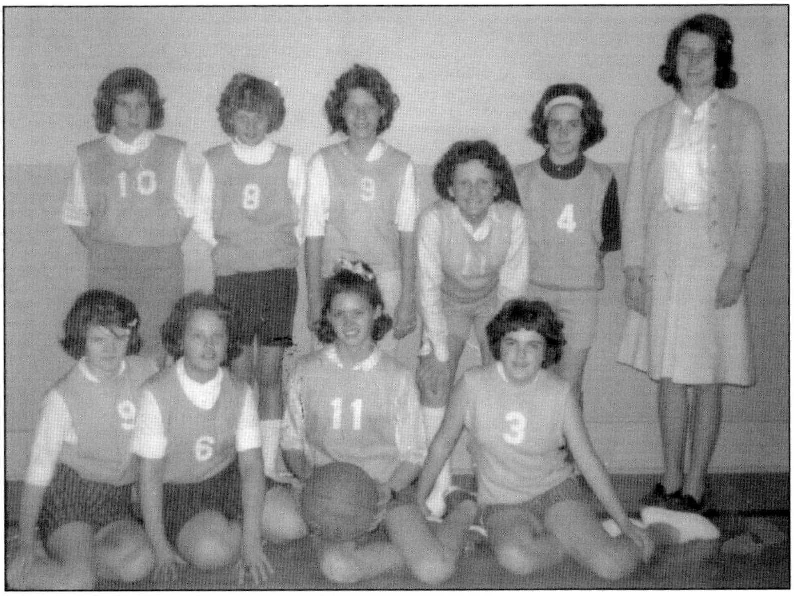

Beacon's basketball teams became more popular over the years. By 1964, the company had organized leagues for both boys and girls. Seen here in 1964 are the Ramblers, coached by Brenda Parks (standing, far right). (Courtesy of the Swannanoa Valley Museum.)

This photograph shows one of the boys' basketball teams, the Bushmen. (Courtesy of the Swannanoa Valley Museum.)

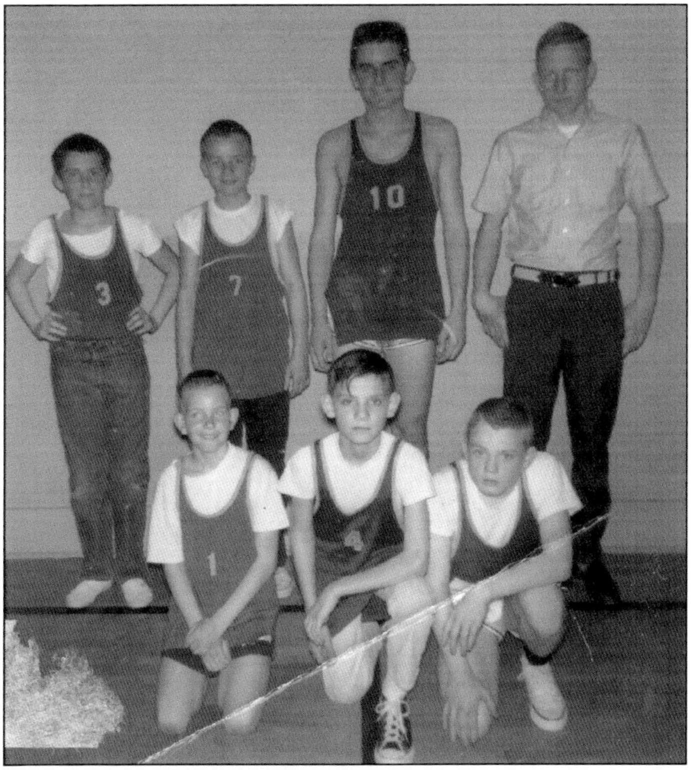

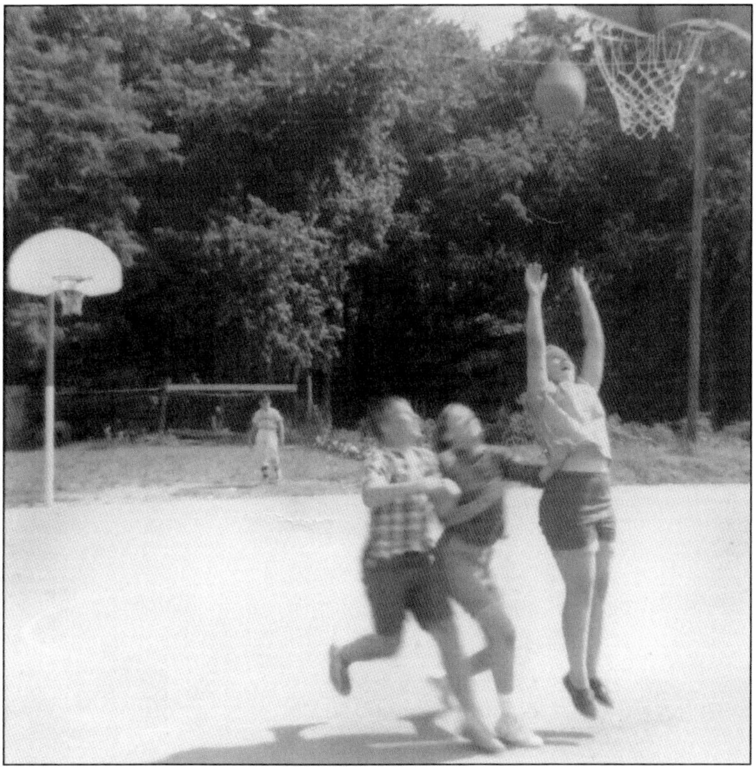

Pickup basketball games were common on the outdoor blacktop court in the new village. This photograph was taken in 1965. (Courtesy of the Swannanoa Valley Museum.)

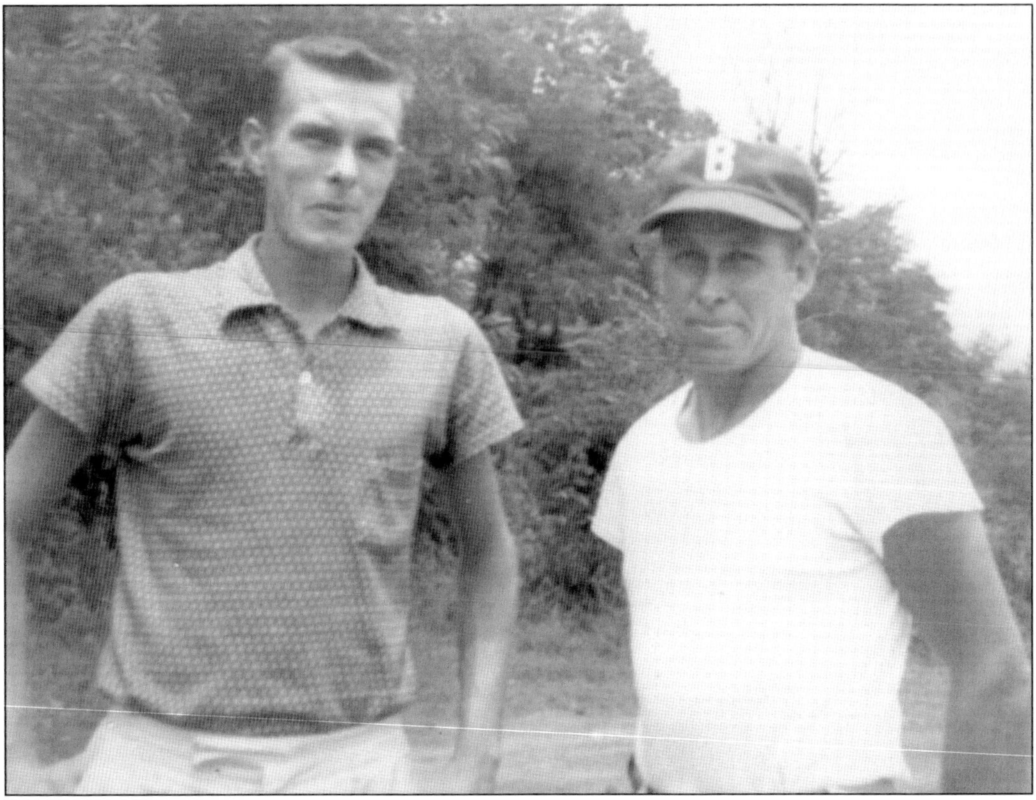

Important to the running of the leagues and the involvement of children and adults were the athletic directors, who managed the athletic activities. This 1960s photograph shows Buddy Farrell (left) standing with Beacon's athletic director Wade Martin. (Courtesy of the Swannanoa Valley Museum.)

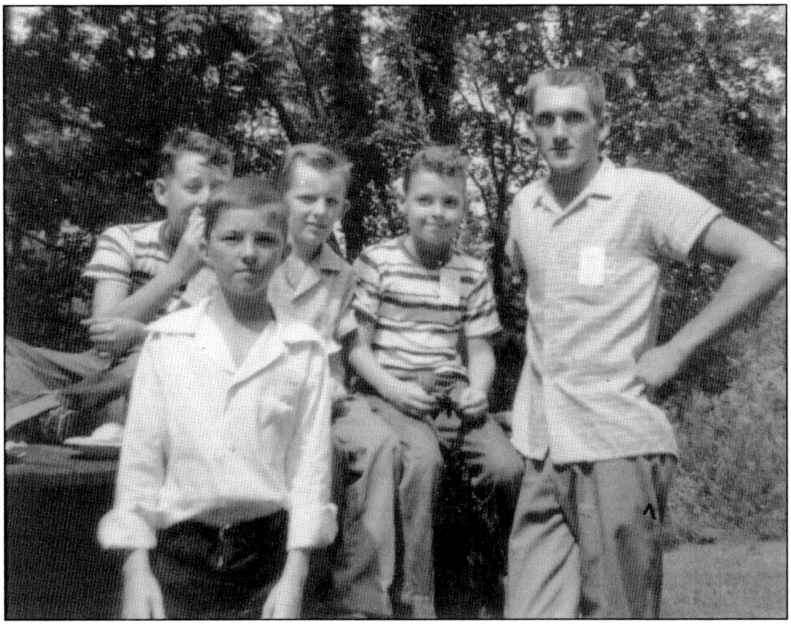

Buddy Farrell (far right) was a recreation student in 1960 and worked with many children in the community through the Beacon Recreation Program. (Courtesy of the Swannanoa Valley Museum.)

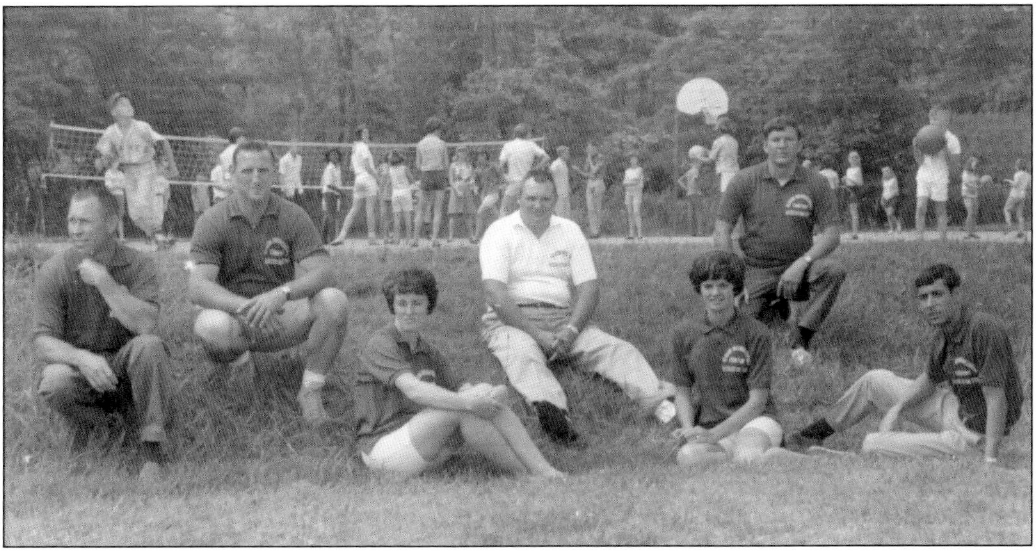

Beacon's 1967 summer recreation staff poses on the hill separating Coman Field from the basketball and volleyball courts. (Courtesy of the Swannanoa Valley Museum.)

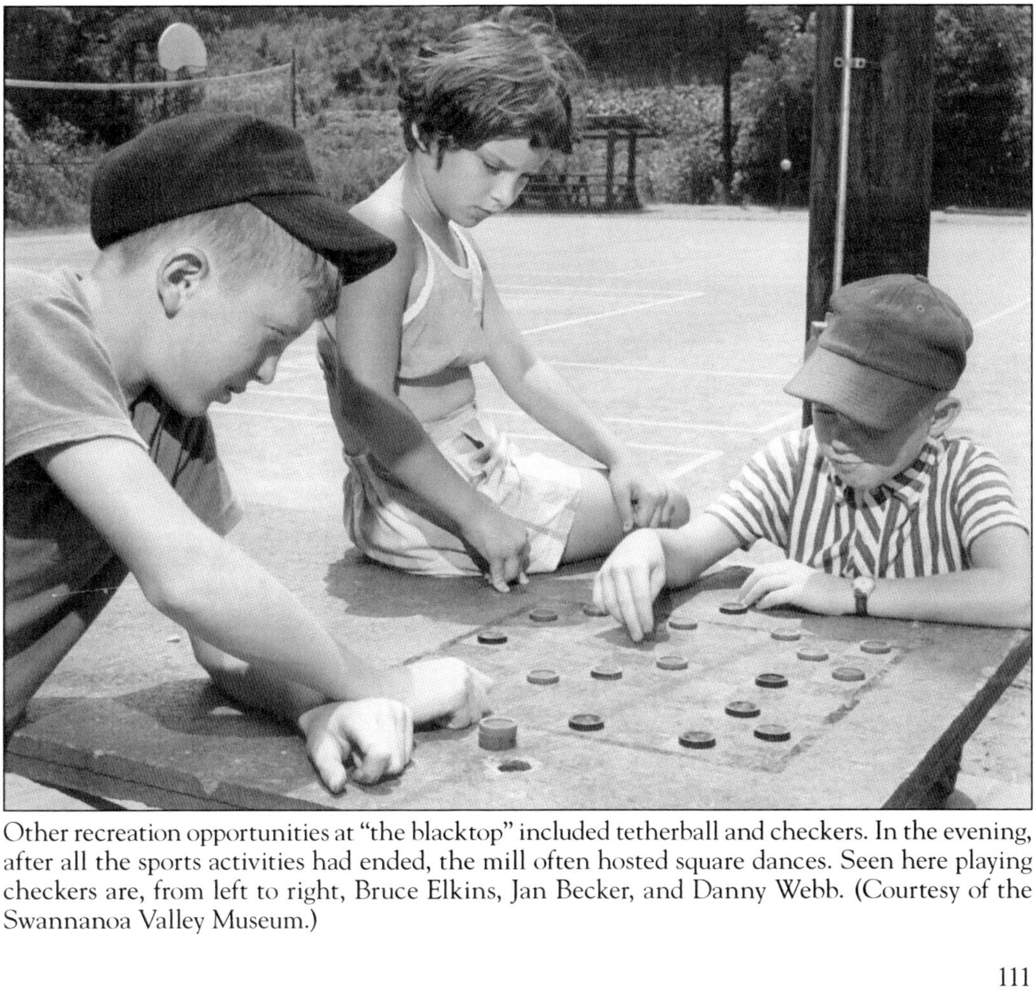

Other recreation opportunities at "the blacktop" included tetherball and checkers. In the evening, after all the sports activities had ended, the mill often hosted square dances. Seen here playing checkers are, from left to right, Bruce Elkins, Jan Becker, and Danny Webb. (Courtesy of the Swannanoa Valley Museum.)

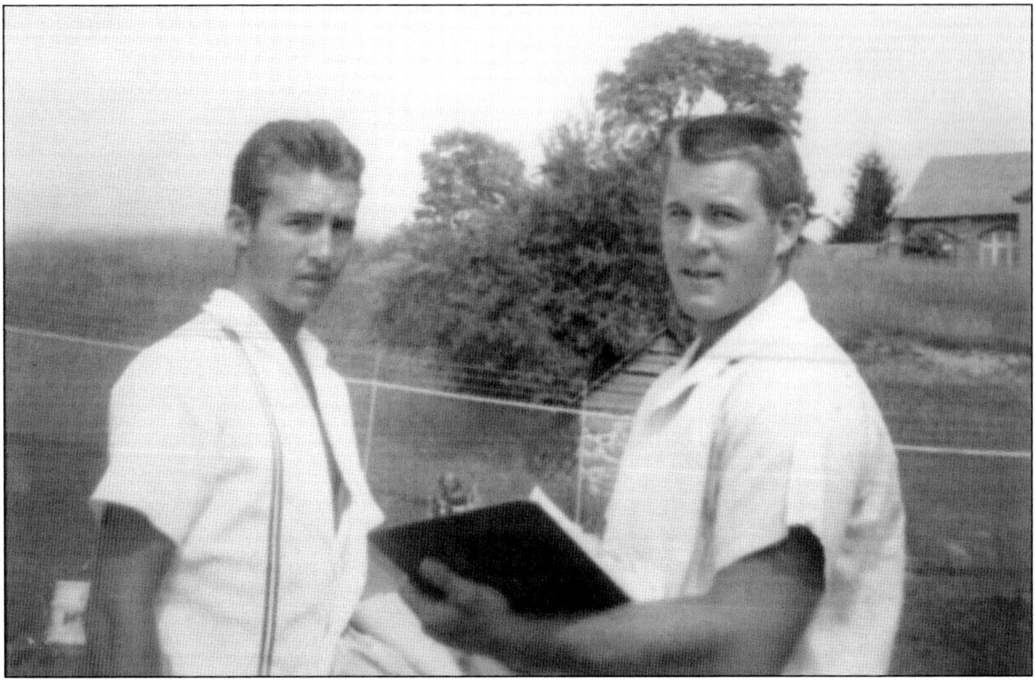

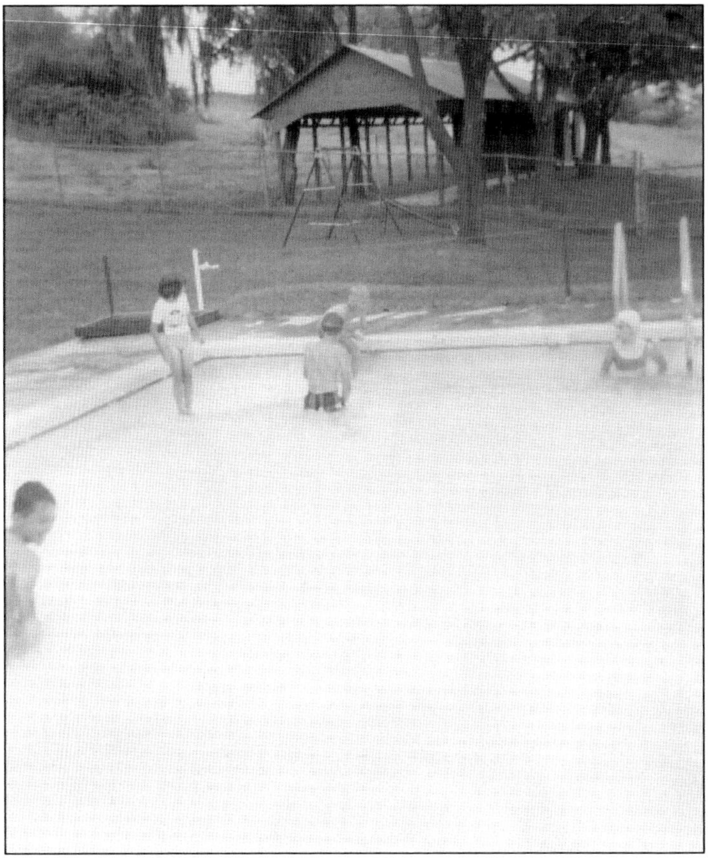

The community swimming pool was another popular place to be during Swannanoa's hot summers. Seen above are the pool's lifeguards in the summer of 1960, David Luckaddo (left) and Joe Robinson. At left, children cool off in the pool. (Both, courtesy of the Swannanoa Valley Museum.)

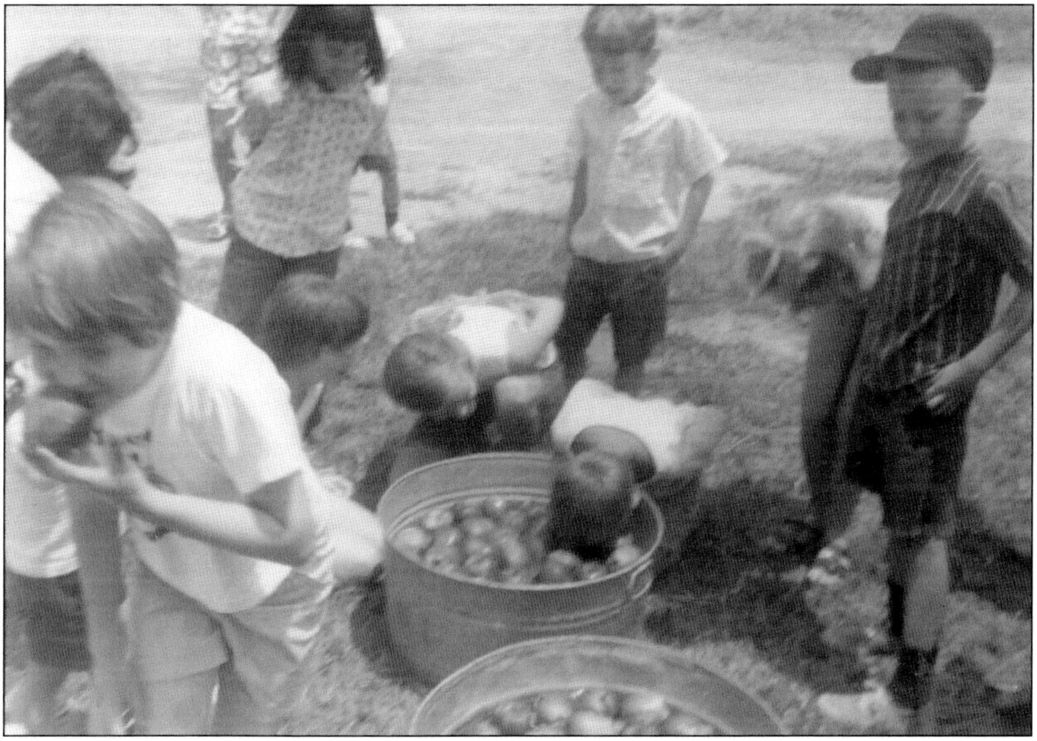

Bruce Martin bobs for apples with his friends during a special Beacon-sponsored recreational event. (Courtesy of the Swannanoa Valley Museum.)

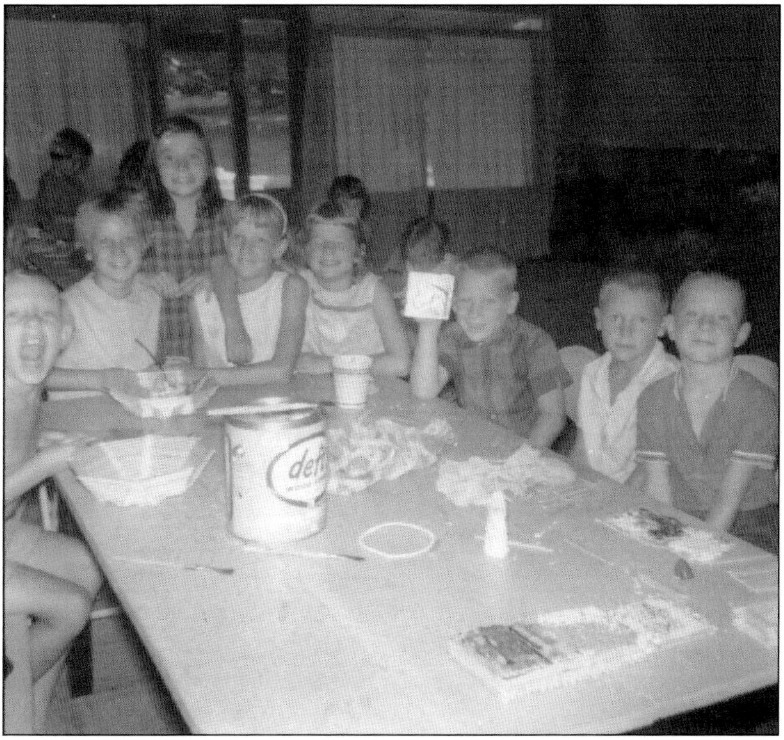

Summer arts and crafts programs were popular with children during their summers away from school. This 1964 program was set up by Beacon and led by North Carolina State University student Peggy Hollingsworth (not pictured). (Courtesy of the Swannanoa Valley Museum.)

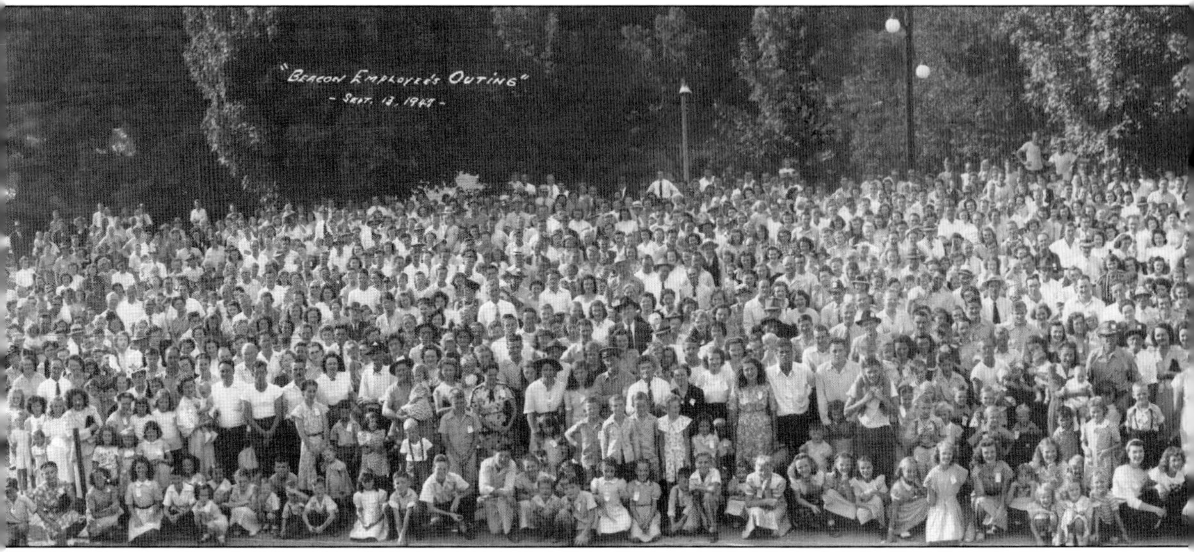

The Beacon community also shared Fourth of July picnics, regular outings, and baseball games on Sundays—activities that were all financed by the Owen family. This panoramic group photograph

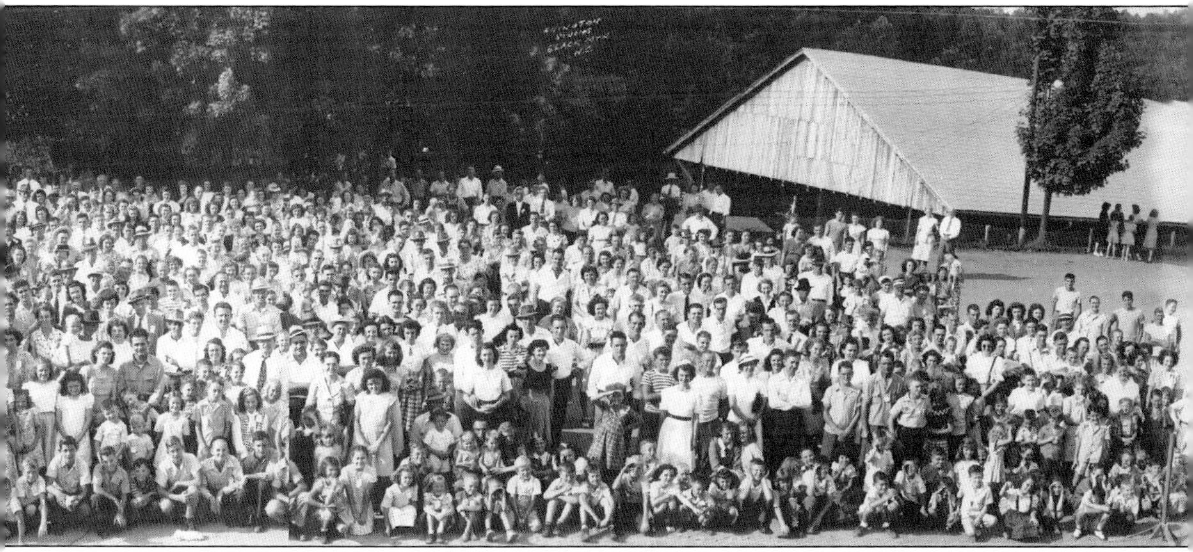

of a Beacon annual picnic for employees and their families at Asheville's Recreation Park was taken on September 13, 1947. (Courtesy of the Swannanoa Valley Museum.)

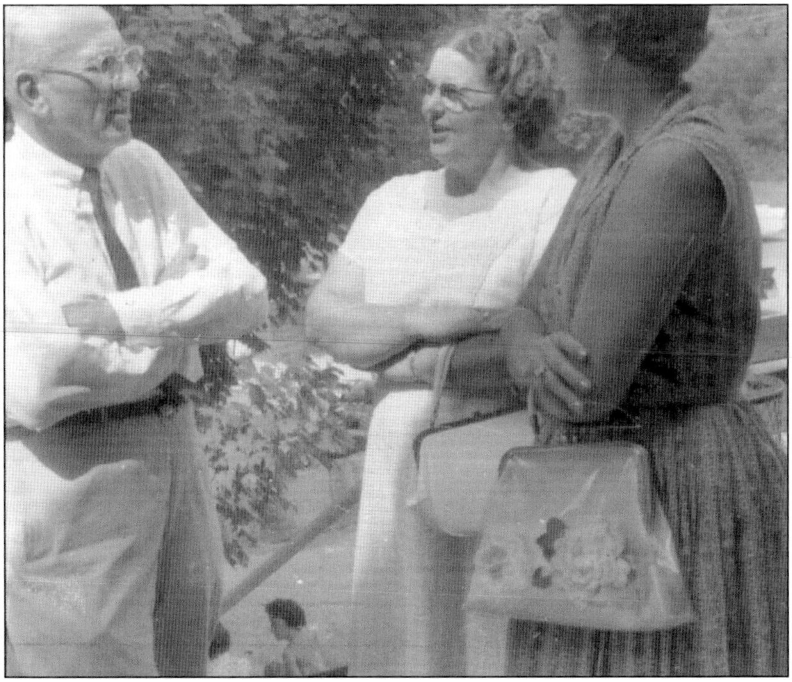

Charles D. Owen III spends time with two of his employees, Bulah Gilliam (center) and Linda Penley, at the mill's annual Fourth of July picnic at Asheville's Recreation Park. (Courtesy of the Swannanoa Valley Museum.)

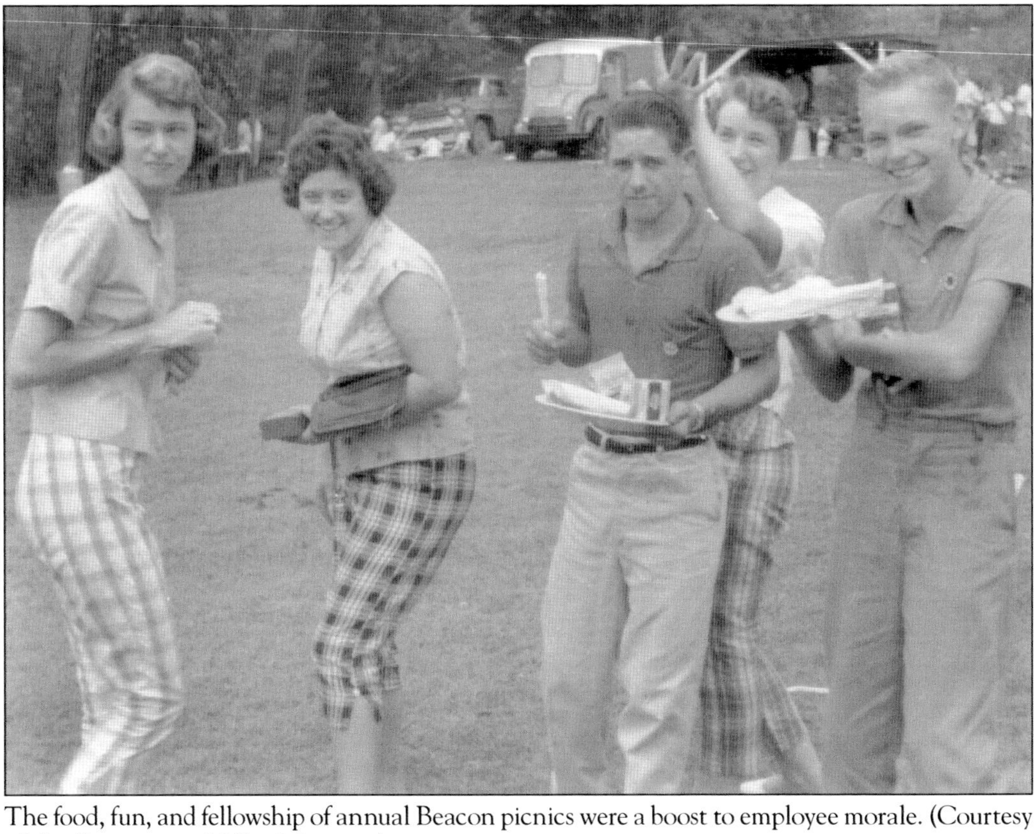

The food, fun, and fellowship of annual Beacon picnics were a boost to employee morale. (Courtesy of the Swannanoa Valley Museum.)

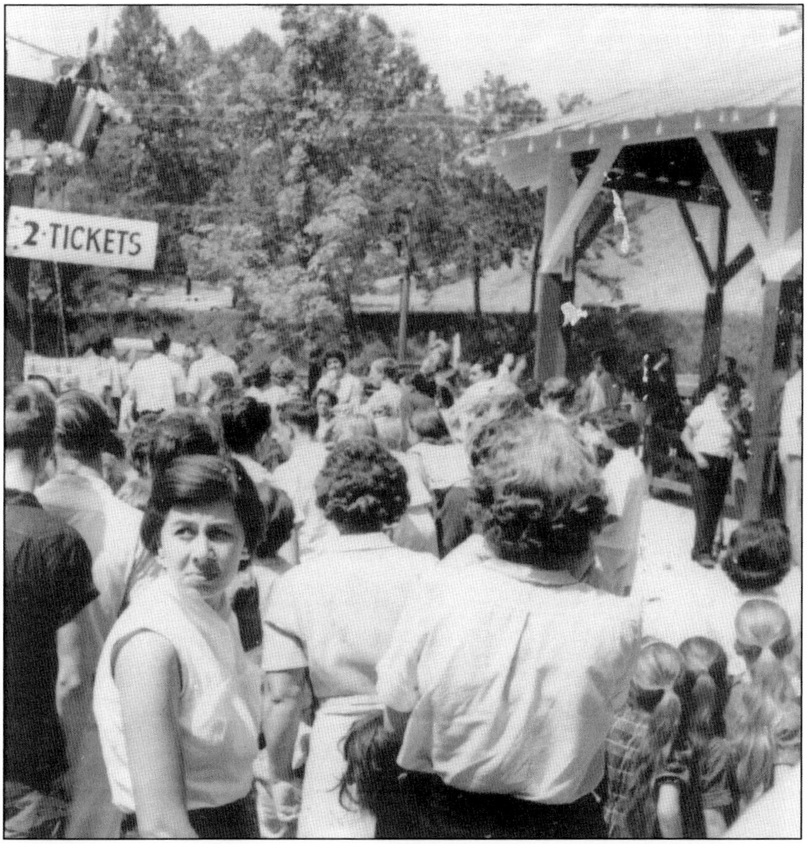

Because Beacon employees for the most part lived, worked, and spent their free time in the mill community, neighbors and employees of other businesses often felt like members of the family. In these images, Beacon employees and their families enjoy an annual Beacon outing to Asheville's Recreation Park. (Both, courtesy of the Swannanoa Valley Museum.)

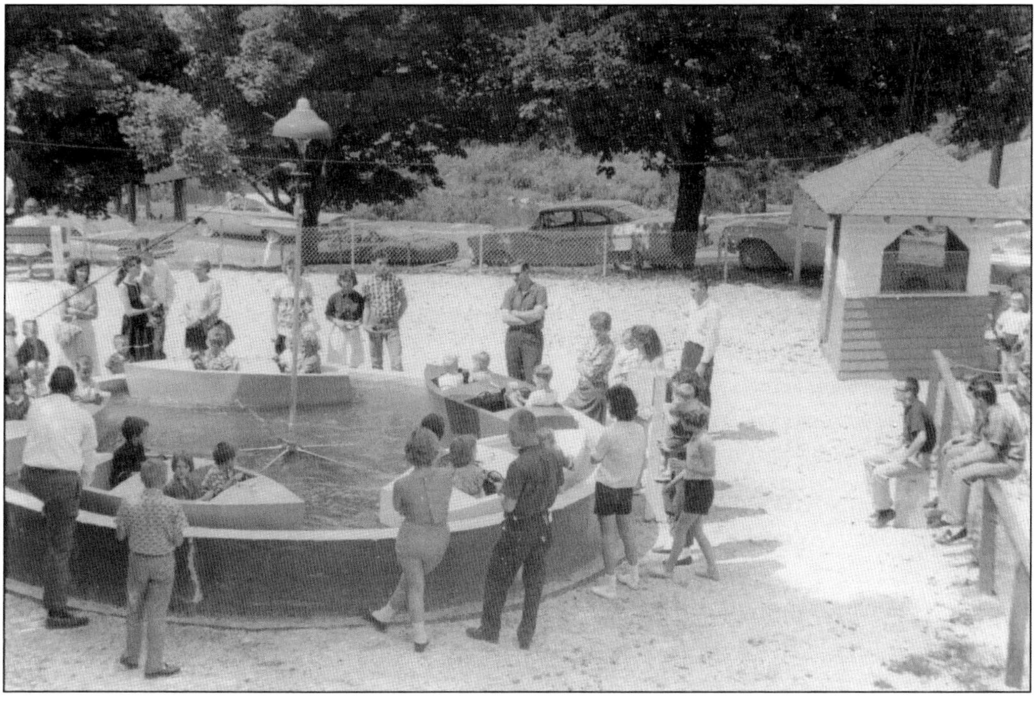

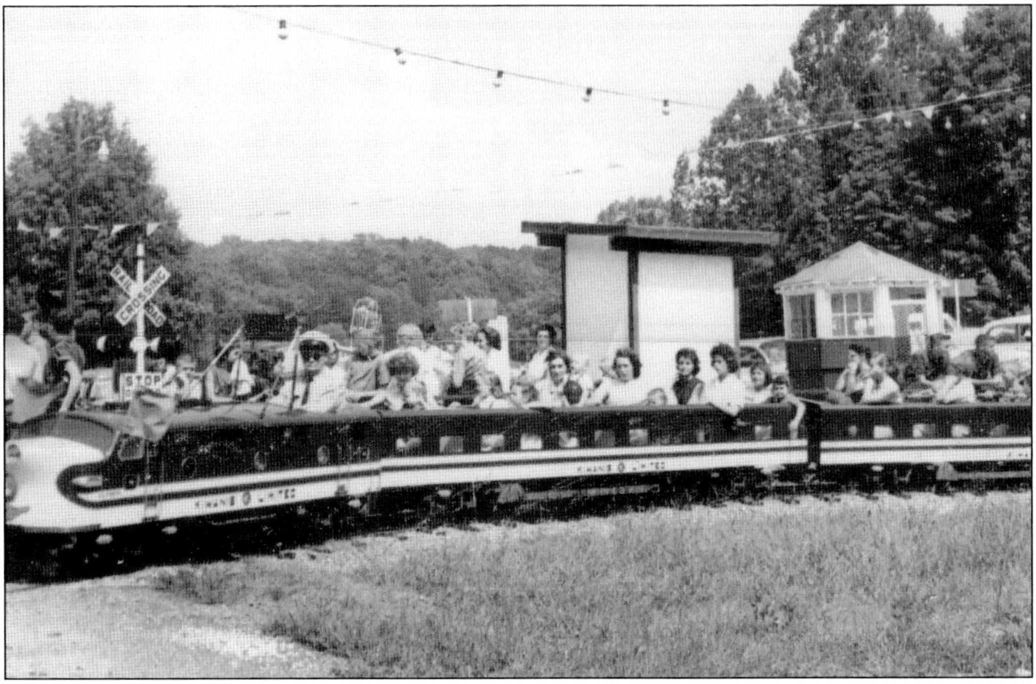

Beacon employees and their families ride the train and the roller coaster at Asheville's Recreation Park. All costs of the picnics were funded by the Owen family. (Both, courtesy of the Swannanoa Valley Museum.)

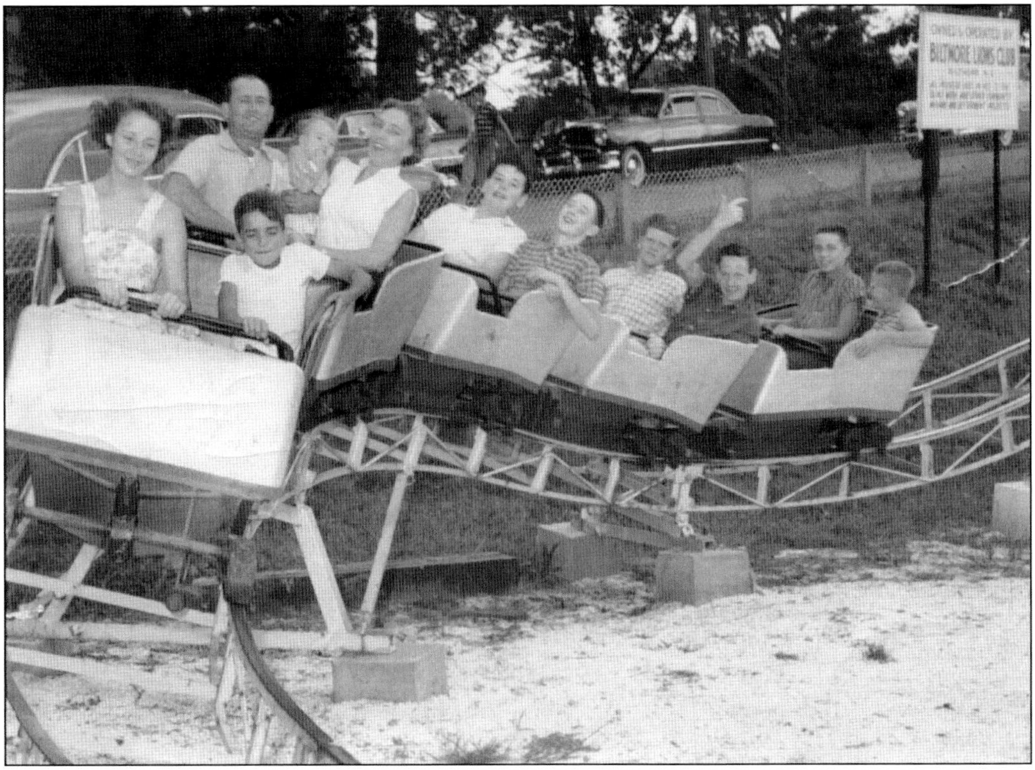

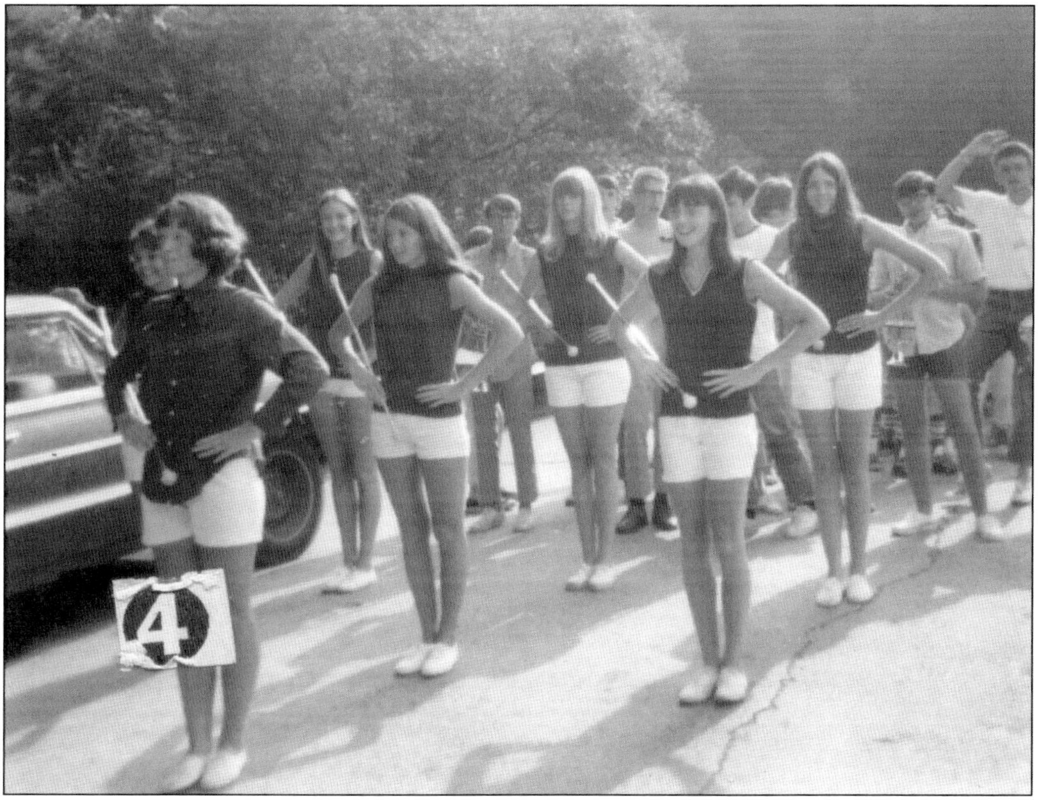

The Owens also provided the funds for several projects outside of the immediate Beacon community. When the high schools consolidated in the 1950s, the new high school that students from Swannanoa and Black Mountain began attending was named Charles D. Owen High School. The 1968 Owen High School flag bearers are seen above, and the Owen High School marching band is seen below in an annual parade held in downtown Black Mountain. (Both, courtesy of the Swannanoa Valley Museum.)

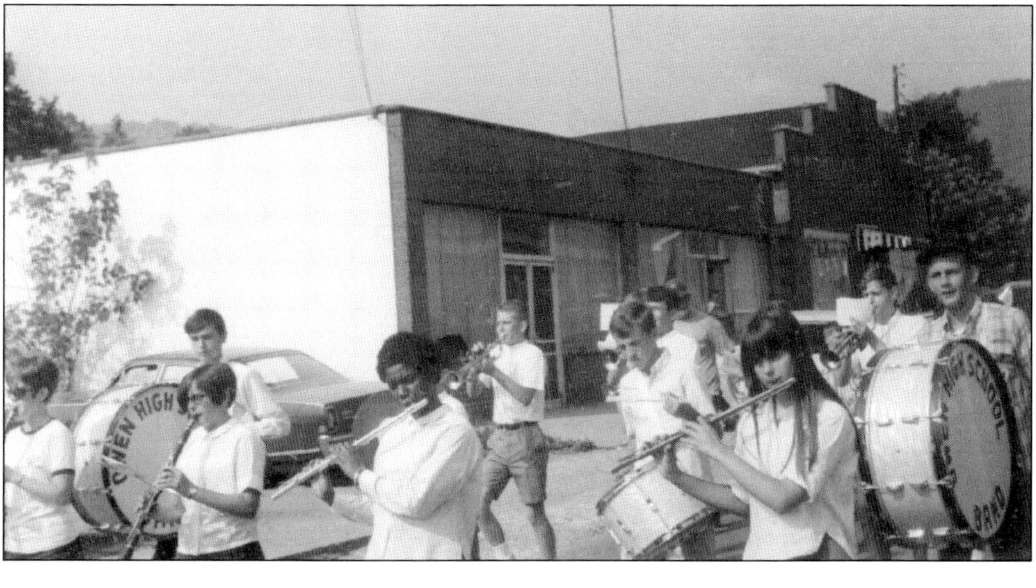

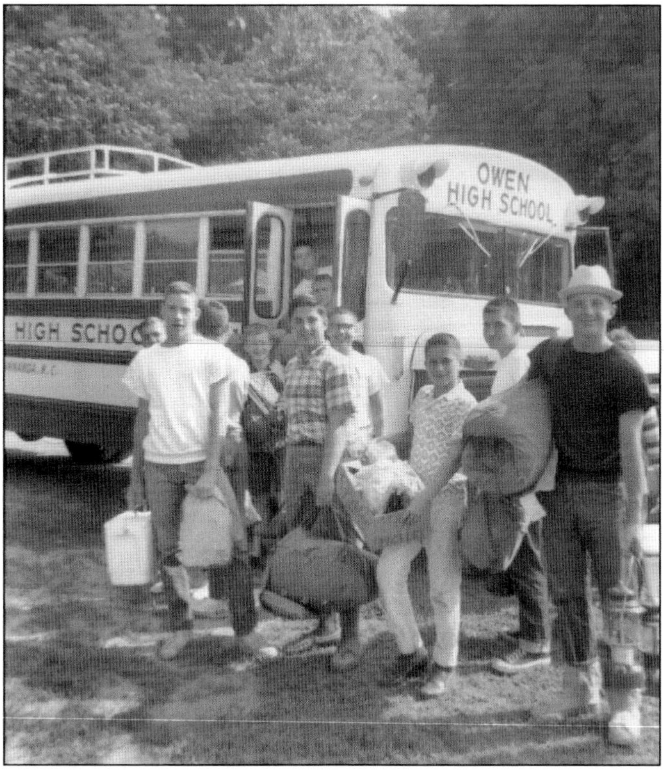

The Owen family also provided the money for the construction of a large lake, a baseball complex, and a park across the river from Beacon, behind their Owen Manufacturing plant, known as Owen Park. At left, Owen High School students prepare for an overnight camping trip near Mount Mitchell. Below, the new Owen Junior High School also sponsored a square dance team. (Both, courtesy of the Swannanoa Valley Museum.)

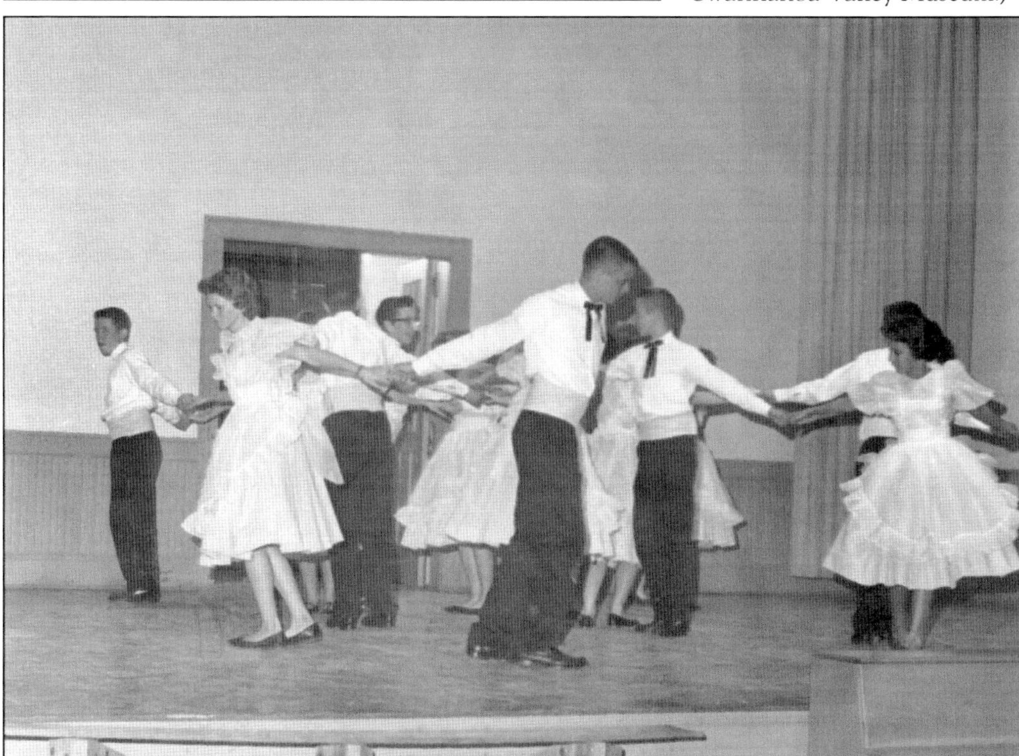

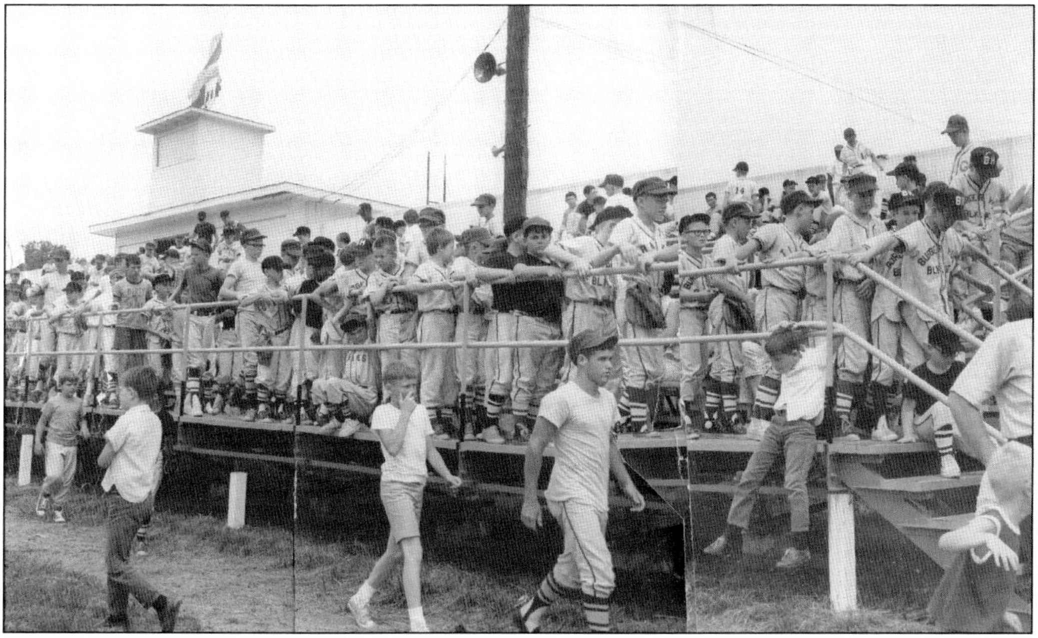

In 1964, half of all Beacon stock was purchased by National Distillers, and, by 1969, the Owen family had sold all of their stock to the company. It was during this time that the services provided to workers by the Owen family began to diminish. Recreation activities began to move outside of the mill community and to the public schools. In 1968, Owen High School sponsored a field day and picnic for the Swannanoa and Black Mountain communities at its football stadium (above). Below, a town-sponsored baseball team pulls hard in a tug-of-war on the same day. (Both, courtesy of the Swannanoa Valley Museum.)

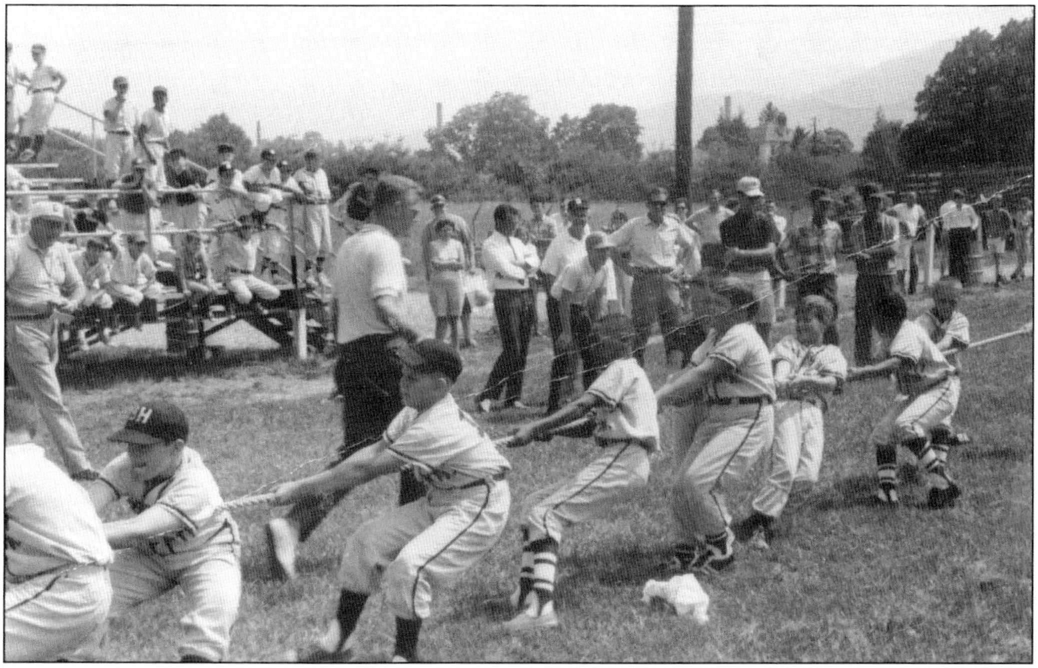

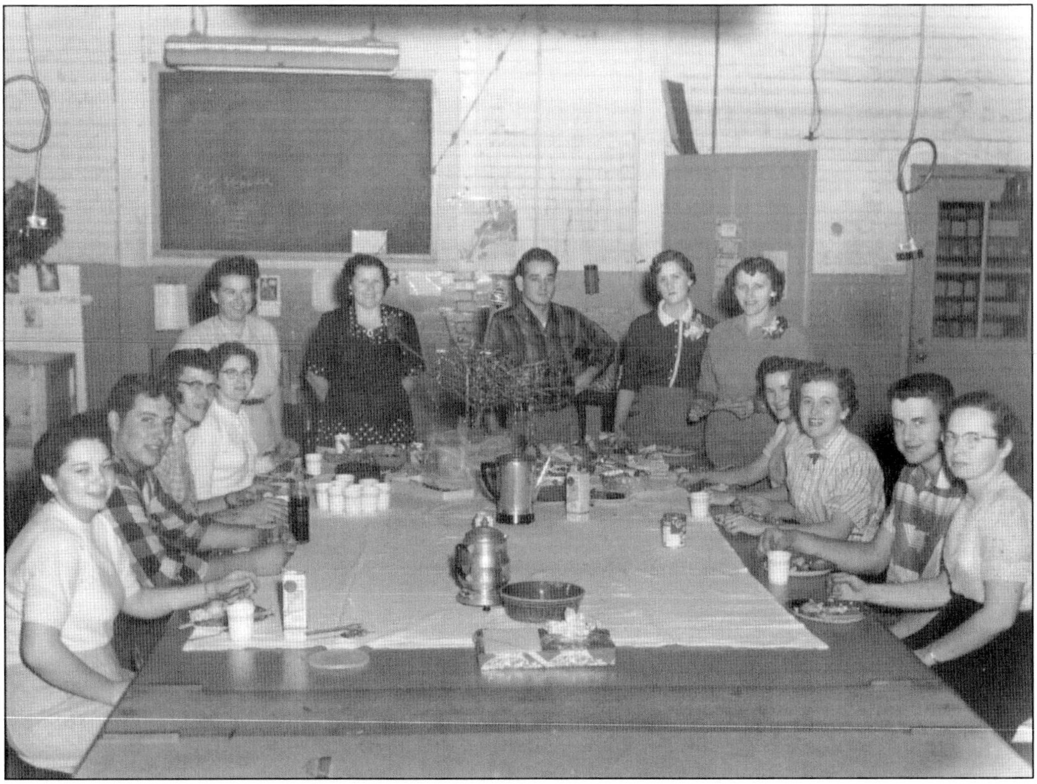

Despite the transfer of ownership, Beacon remained the main employer in Swannanoa. Above, having lunch in the Beacon break room in the late 1960s are, among others, Dallas Gragg (first man sitting on the left), ? Marlow (next to Gragg, in glasses), and Lib Whitaker (next to Marlow). The woman standing on the far right is Christine Smith White. Charles D. Owen III is seen below in 1967 with employees ? Campfield (left) and ? Oleton. (Above, courtesy of the Swannanoa Valley Museum, Bryant collection; below, courtesy of the Swannanoa Valley Museum.)

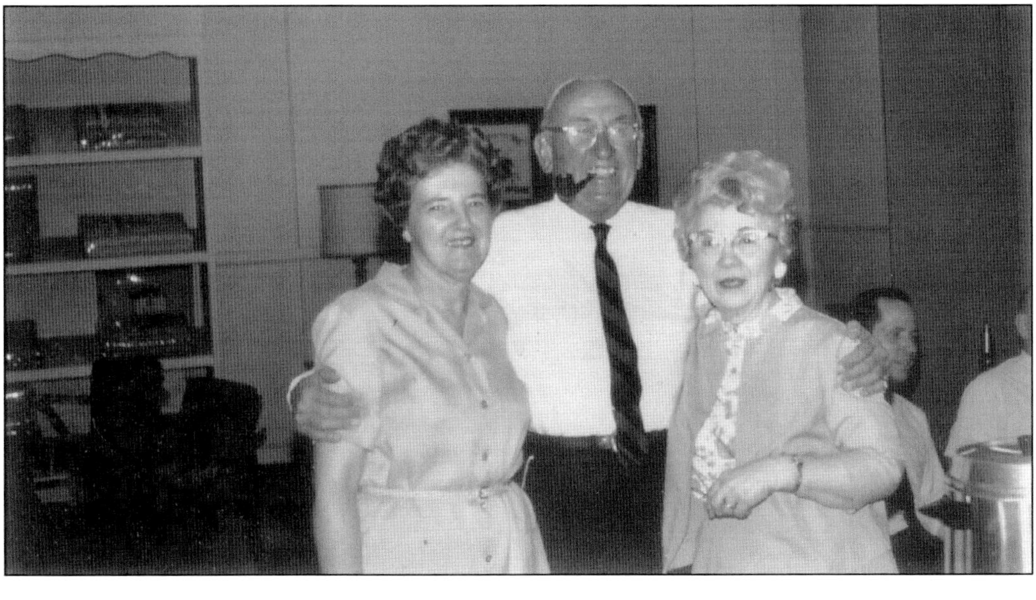

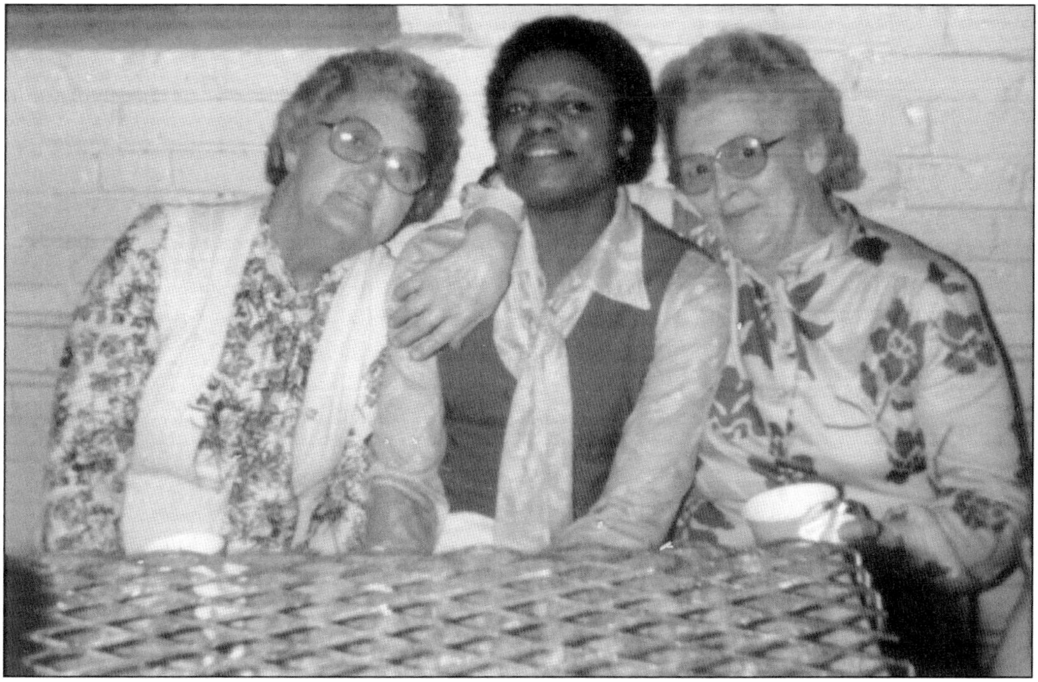

The Beacon plant changed hands several more times over the next couple of decades. In 1981, Cannon Mills purchased the complex. Then, in 1994, the mill was bought out by Pillowtex. Finally, in 2001, a group of private investors became the final owners of the Beacon Manufacturing Company. Even into the later part of the 20th century, the Beacon plant was still employing several hundred people, a few of whom are seen in these photographs. (Both, courtesy of the Swannanoa Valley Museum, Norton collection.)

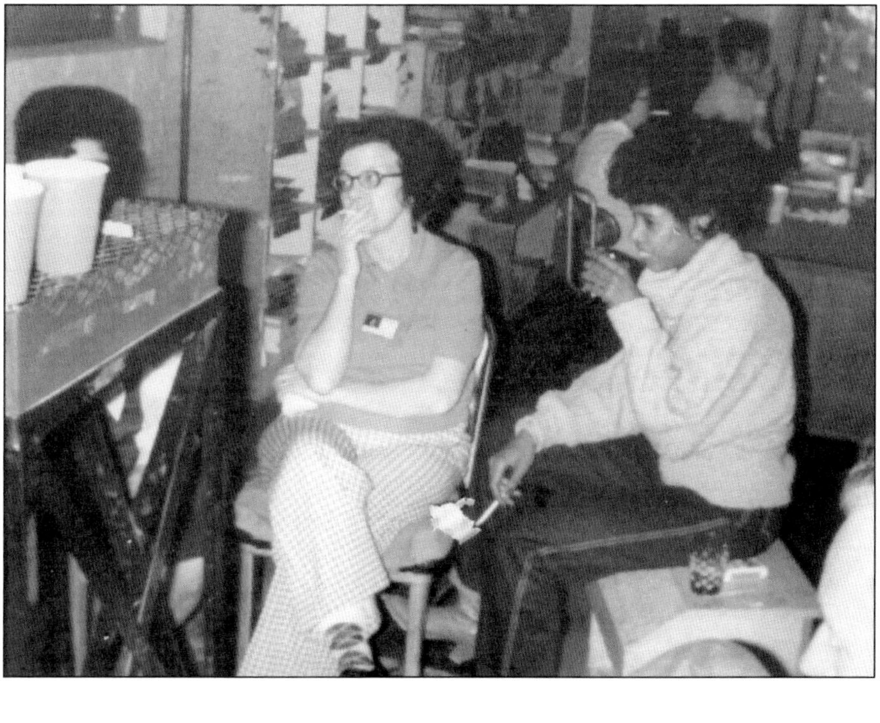

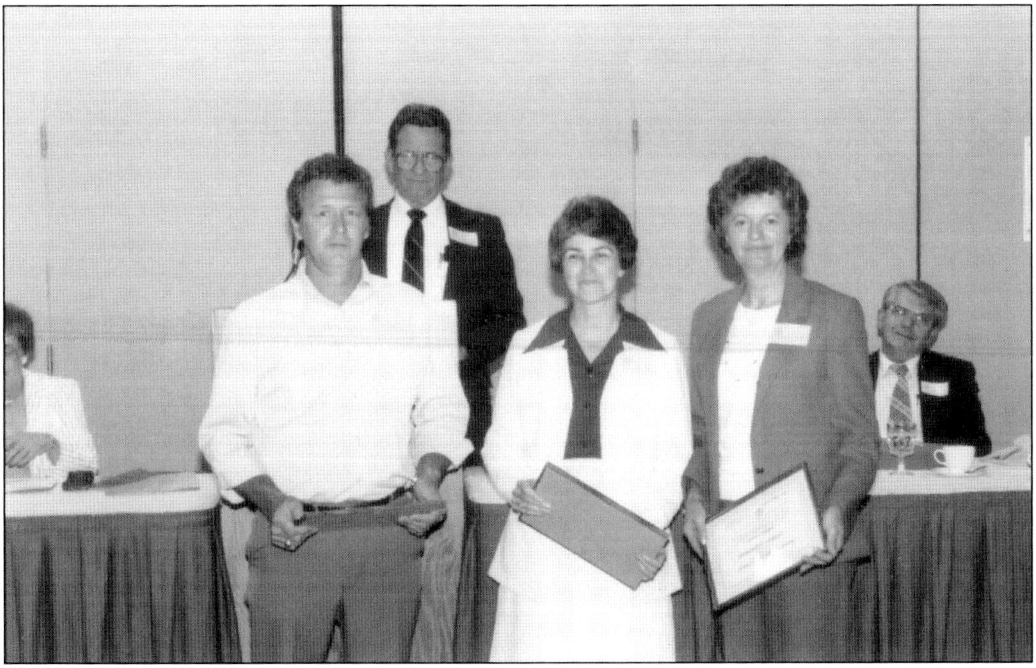

The Quarter Century Club was established to recognize Beacon employees with 25 years or more of service to the company. An annual dinner was held each year to honor this group. Seen above in 1985 are three new inductees into the club. Below, Kathleen Swann and Ruth Bailey enjoy the annual recognition dinner in 1990. By 1999, there were more than 300 employees in the Quarter Century Club, some with more than 40 years of service. (Both, courtesy of the Swannanoa Valley Museum.)

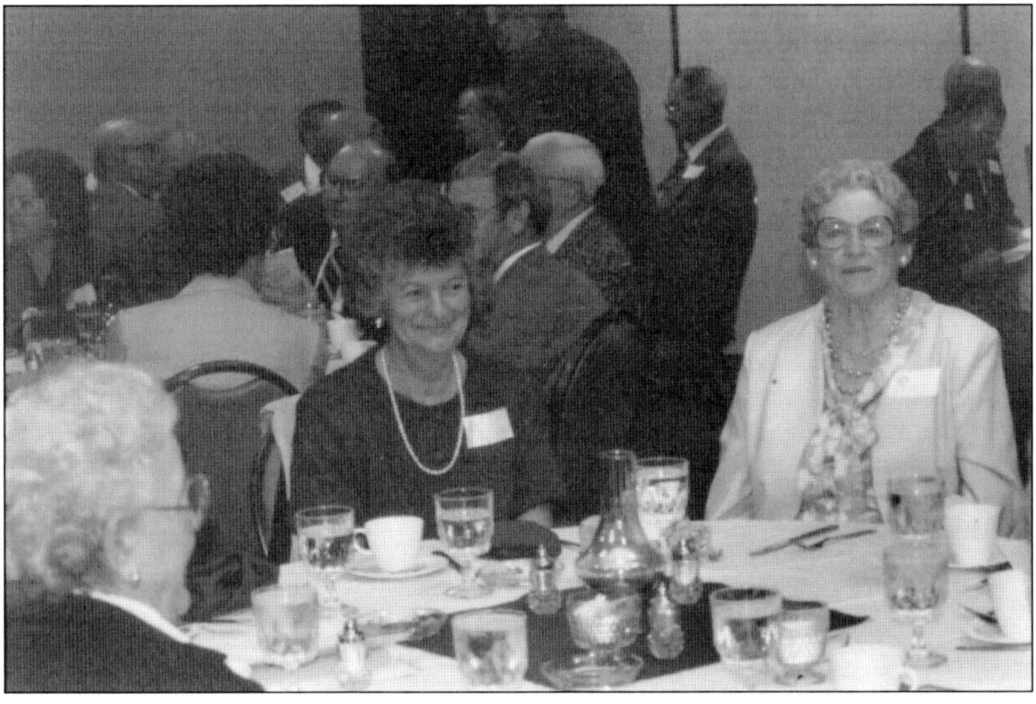

Eight

The End of an Era

Beacon Burns

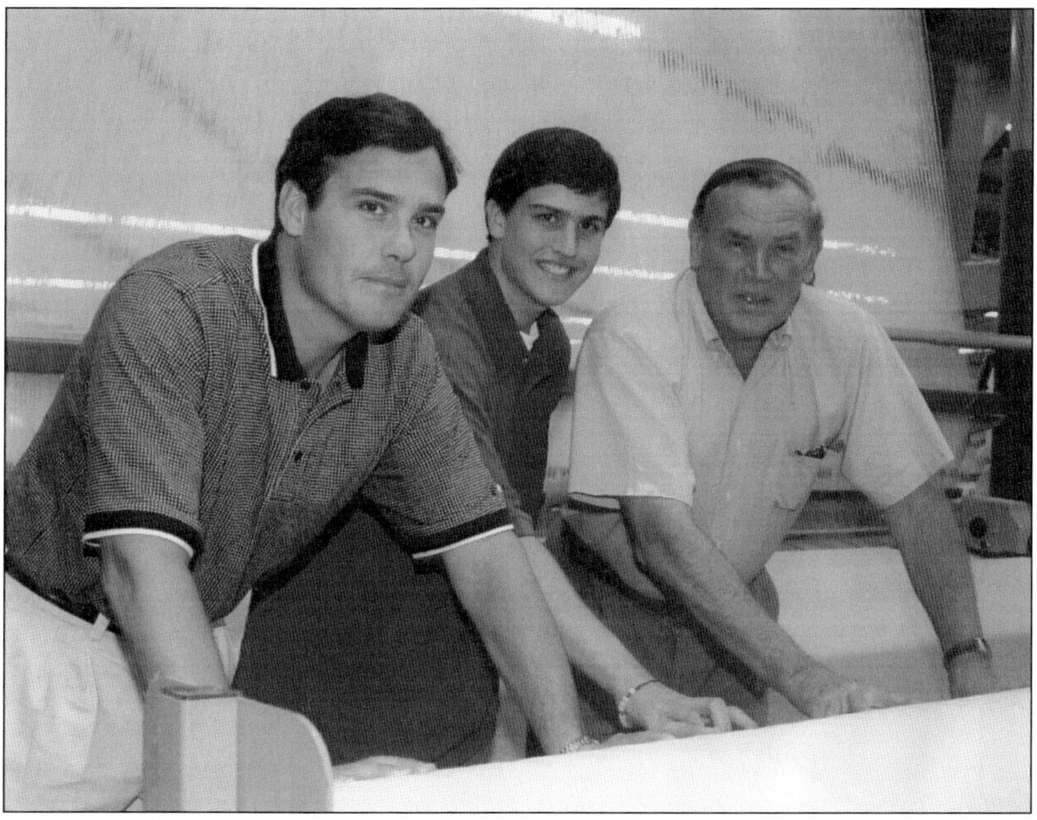

In 1972, Charles D. Owen IV built a new, modernized textile facility on Warren Wilson College Road, the only completely new textile facility built in America in more than 60 years, to compete with the Pillowtex plant at Beacon. The new facility employed 600 people, and its one-story building spanned one million square feet. Seen here are three generations of the Owen men: from left to right, Charles D. Owen IV, or "Young Charlie," his son "Little Charlie," and Charles D. Owen III, or "Old Charlie." (Courtesy of the Swannanoa Valley Museum.)

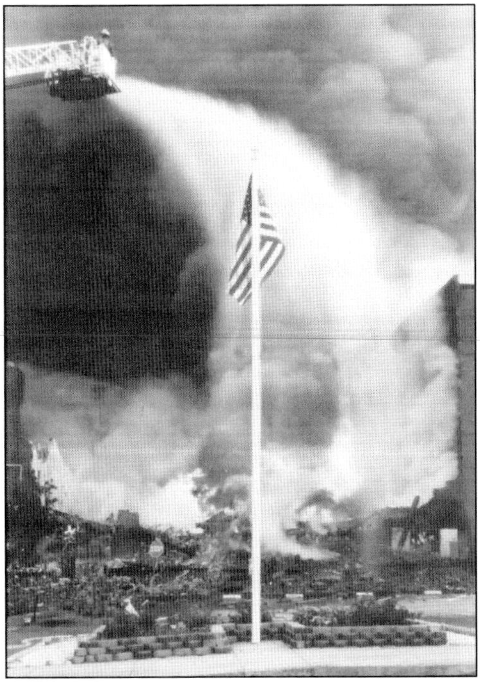

On April 15, 2002, the Beacon Manufacturing Company officially closed its Swannanoa plant, leaving the 300 remaining Beacon employees jobless. On September 4, 2003, an arsonist set the vacant plant ablaze. In a devastating fire that made national news, the Beacon Manufacturing Plant burned to the ground, ending Swannanoa's more than 75 years of blanket-making history. Former employees watched the mill burn, and many equated its destruction with the loss of a home. Firefighters are seen here attempting to extinguish the blaze. (Courtesy of the Swannanoa Valley Museum, Bill Alexander collection.)

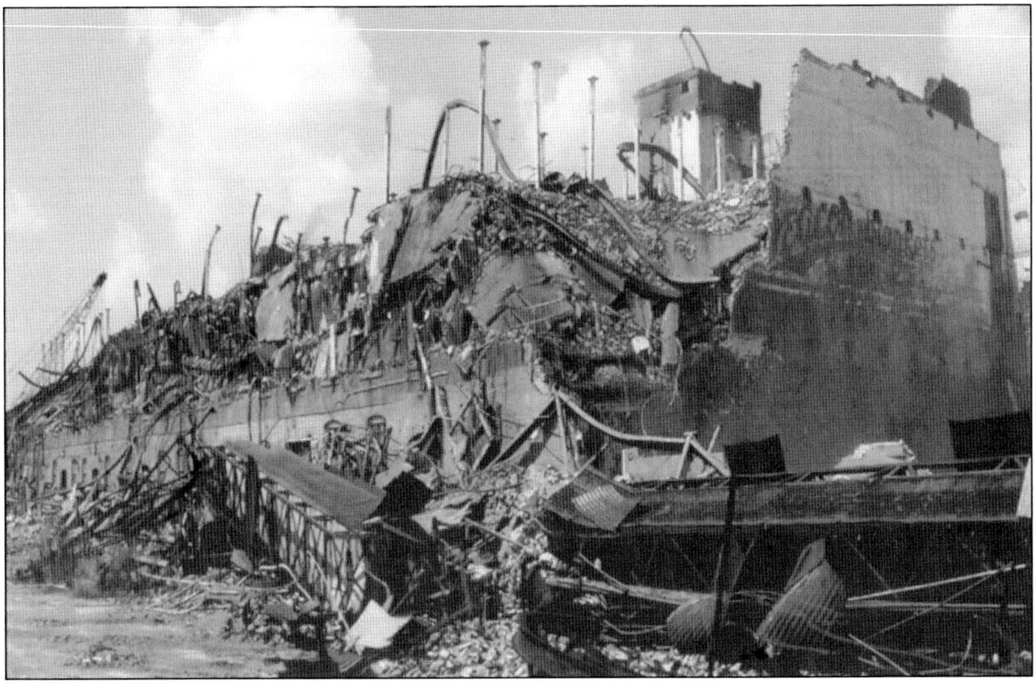

Soon after the fire, the ruins of Beacon were razed. Today, the 1,300-acre Beacon campus is only a vacant lot surrounded by a metal fence, but it is set to be redeveloped as a multiuse residential and commercial center. On August 31, 2012, the Charles D. Owen Manufacturing Company, the last remnant of the Owen blanket dynasty, permanently closed due to competition from foreign imports, and the final 53 workers employed by the Owen family lost their jobs. (Courtesy of the Swannanoa Valley Museum, Bill Alexander collection.)

About the Swannanoa Valley Museum

In 1989, a group of local citizens, many descended from the valley's original settlers, founded the Swannanoa Valley Museum. Their goal was to acknowledge and preserve the contributions of preceding generations and to create a collection that vividly depicts the history, culture, and character of the valley.

Today, the Swannanoa Valley Museum is recognized as the primary museum of general local history in Buncombe County and is an active member of Museums in Partnership and the American Association of State and Local History. The museum has twice been recognized by the Preservation Society of Asheville and Buncombe County with Griffin Awards for "extended efforts to preserve the history of the Swannanoa Valley" (1991) and for "external commercial restoration" (2009).

Inside the museum's historic building, designed in the 1920s by the supervising architect of the Biltmore Estate, Richard Sharp Smith, gallery exhibits include both artifacts and pictorial displays. Permanent exhibits show how the earning of a livelihood, transportation, construction, and social customs have evolved since the earliest times of human habitation. Each year, one or more special exhibits are mounted that highlight a local activity or give a local twist to a topic of regional or national interest. In the rear gallery, visitors can see many of the household items common in early mountain homes.

In addition to the gallery exhibits, the museum manages a large collection of original photographs and maintains a local library and vertical files to aid local history researchers. The museum's collection numbers over 5,000 objects. Among the museum's partners in bringing history to life are Montreat College, Warren Wilson College, the North Carolina Archives, the Asheville Water Department, and the Buncombe County school system.

The museum also offers a variety of programs off-site, including guided tours of historic homes, Grovemont, and the former campus of the famous Black Mountain College. The museum's Rim Hike Explorer Series covers some of the area's highest and most rugged terrain and was highlighted in *Our State* magazine. More information can be found on the museum's website, www.swannanoavalleymuseum.org.

Consistent with our mission to preserve history on a local level, this book was printed in South Carolina on American-made paper and manufactured entirely in the United States. Products carrying the accredited Forest Stewardship Council (FSC) label are printed on 100 percent FSC-certified paper.

MADE IN THE USA